Finished Jan. 1st, 1965

One may wonder why it was
published.

H. G. Brown

SCARLET LANCER

Also by James D. Lunt

CHARGE TO GLORY!

SCARLET LANCER

JAMES D. LUNT

HARCOURT, BRACE & WORLD, INC.   NEW YORK

To Muriel

"Nothing has ever been made until the soldier has made safe the field where the building shall be built; and the soldier is the scaffolding until it has been built, and the soldier gets no reward but honour."

—Eric Linklater

FOREWORD

The British Army officer of a hundred and fifty years ago
has not been having a very good press recently. There has
been a spate of Victoriana, and in book after book we have
been treated to a catalogue of imbecilities and incompetence,
on the part of either arrogant idiots like Lord Cardigan or
indecisive old gentlemen like Lord Raglan. This book is not
intended to refute these charges, since there is, unfortunately,
all too much evidence to prove that the British Army was in
the doldrums for the greater part of Queen Victoria's reign,
but it does attempt to show that there were plenty of ordinary regimental officers who retained their efficiency and
enthusiasm, despite the appalling frustrations to which they
were subjected. Moreover, it is important not to lose sight
of the fact that the nation gets the army it deserves, and in
times of apathy and neglect it has no right to expect the
soldier to rise above the circumstances in which his fellow-
citizens have placed him; that he has so often done so is a
tribute to the army's great tradition of service, and is no
credit to those who have denied him the means with which
to maintain his efficiency.

John Luard, who figures in this book as its central character, was an ordinary regimental officer, even though he began his career in the Royal Navy and found his main interest when not soldiering in art. He came from exactly the right background of the squirearchy, possessed independent means, and had sufficient influence and talent to assure himself a comfortable career outside the army. Despite all this he remained a soldier because he liked soldiering, fought throughout the Peninsular War, charged with his regiment at Waterloo, took part in a successful Indian campaign, and, as a staff officer, was a closely involved onlooker in one of the most disastrous episodes in the whole history of British arms in India. Throughout, he kept a diary, which he wrote in journal form toward the end of his long life, corresponded with his friends and his family, and has left behind him an interesting description of military life of the less flamboyant variety.

Like most army officers of his time, he served in several regiments, but perhaps the 16th Lancers, whose adjutant he was on the field of Waterloo, held the warmest place in his affections, and for this reason I have called this book *Scarlet Lancer*. The 16th Lancers was the only lancer regiment in the British Army to wear scarlet tunics, and the regimental nickname has ever since been "The Scarlets." Luard's great-great-grandson is serving with his old regiment today.

It is my hope that the reader will gain from these pages some idea of how an ordinary regimental officer lived during the first fifty years of the last century, how he enjoyed himself both on campaign and in camp, and how he employed his leisure. I hope also that it will show the important part that tradition has played in the story of the British Army, and how dependent that army always has been on those families who, from generation to generation, have sent their sons into the army to serve their country, certainly for no material reward as the world understands it, since the army is not a profession in which a man can expect to grow rich. However, in writing this book I have not set out to further any particular cause, to mount any special hobbyhorse of my own, or to sell any particular line of thought. I am of course aware of the fact that there are those today who believe that the army's traditional organization is a strait jacket which inhibits most desirable reforms, just as I am equally aware that there are those who honestly believe that the army will fall apart if such traditional organizations are tampered with. I seek to defend neither point of view, since I believe very strongly that if tradition is worth anything, it will survive of its own accord, and thereby be its own justification. Certainly the army, like any other organization in this fast-changing world, cannot afford to stand still and play the ostrich; this is what happened after Waterloo, and the Crimea was the dreadful result. But, equally, we should be foolish to ignore the value of tradition in military life, and I have no doubt that, as always, the real answer lies somewhere between the two extremes.

This book has been written in not always easy circumstances—partly in England, and partly in the steamy heat of Aden, not always within easy reach of sources, and sometimes during flights across the barren and roadless mountains of the Western Aden Protectorate on the way to or from some outlying garrison. If this somewhat unusual way of writing a book has done nothing else, it has taught me to appreciate the enormous difficulties with which Wellington had to contend when fighting his way across Spain, and the no less complex problems which confronted the generals during the campaign in Afghanistan from 1838 to 1842, when the advantages I have been able to derive from air transport were not even dreamt about. I hope it has made me slightly more charitable than I might otherwise have

ix

been when it comes to castigating the follies of our ancestors, who wrought so marvelously in so many ways, whose fortitude and sense of duty go far to redeem their many errors, and whose problems, although they were admittedly not bedeviled by the many imponderables that plague us today, ranked no less high in their estimation than our problems do in ours.

I am indebted to many people for their help in the writing of this book. I am most grateful to my wife and the other members of my family who have read the manuscript and helped with their criticism. Brigadier John Stephenson, of the Royal United Service Institution, has been of great assistance, as have the Librarian and Staff of the War Office Library, the Staff of the India Office Library, and the Librarian of the Royal Military Academy, Sandhurst. Lieutenant-Commander Peter Kemp, R.N., the Admiralty Archivist, has been kind enough to help me, and I am of course greatly in the debt of those authors and publishers who have so kindly allowed me to quote from previously published works. Last, but by no means least, I must thank Lieutenant-Colonel Peter Luard and Mrs. Norman Luard, without whom this book could certainly not have been written; they have been most patient and willing collaborators.

J. D. L.

Levy House,
Aden
March 1963

x

LIST OF ILLUSTRATIONS

(Unless otherwise stated, all these illustrations were drawn or painted by John Luard.)

Between pages 116 and 117

SCARLET LANCER

CHAPTER ONE

It was the late afternoon of Sunday, June 1, 1806, and the twelfth anniversary of Admiral Richard Howe's defeat of the French on the "Glorious First of June." The warships lying off Spithead had been dressed over-all in celebration of the victory, but that had been in the morning; now they lay rocking gently at their moorings, their crews drowsing away what remained of a day of summer sunshine. Nearly a year had passed since Trafalgar, Nelson lay in his grave in St. Paul's, and the navy he had served so well was reaping the reward of all his endeavors. Napoleon might be master of the Continent, with every sovereign in Europe trembling at his frown, but Britannia ruled the waves as never before in all England's history, and every French possession beyond the seas was ripe for the picking.

Among the ships assembled off Spithead was the eighty-gun H.M.S. *Foudroyant,* once Nelson's flagship in the Mediterranean and also for a short time the seat of a foreign government; the King of the Two Sicilies had taken refuge aboard her from the French in June 1799 and flew his royal standard at her main.

3

A watcher from the shore, leveling his glass at the great ships as they rode at anchor, would probably have remarked that only in the *Foudroyant* was there any sign of activity; whereas the rest of the fleet seemed to be taking their ease, the upper decks of the *Foudroyant* were crowded with sailors and marines. But the watcher would also have noticed, had his glass been good enough, that every ship's lookout was keeping a close watch on the shore. Clearly some important event was impending.

Suddenly from across the water came the shrill cry of bosuns' pipes. The sleeping ships came to life and soon every yardarm was manned and every quarterdeck echoed with the tramp of scarlet-coated marines. An admiral's barge put out from the shore and set course for the *Foudroyant;* Vice-Admiral Sir John Borlase Warren, Baronet and Knight of the Bath, was about to hoist his flag in her, before taking yet another naval squadron to sea with orders to seek out and destroy the elusive French.

Among those who manned ship to pay the Admiral the compliments that were his due was a young volunteer midshipman, John Luard. He had joined his ship, H.M.S. *Ramillies,* a leaky old seventy-four, only fifteen days previously and he was just sixteen. It was his first experience of the ceremony with which the Royal Navy greets an admiral about to hoist his flag at sea, and the memory of it remained with him for the rest of his long life; "nowhere else is pomp and circumstance rendered so splendidly as in the Royal Navy," he was to write in his journal sixty years later, and after a career which had included attendance at a great many ceremonial occasions. Of course, sixteen is an impressionable age, and admirals, where humble midshipmen are concerned, are very much a race apart. The British, moreover, were very conscious of their admirals at that particular period in their history; they, and the fleets which they

4

commanded, were all that stood between Napoleon and his dream of dominion of the world.

The navy that Luard had joined was very much a "closed shop," and it wielded an influence in the country that the army never has enjoyed. It was ruled by an oligarchy who believed profoundly in privilege and who therefore sought to officer the navy from those families which had provided Britain with her rulers and leaders for generations past. Most of the navy's officers came from families with sufficient influence to persuade a captain to enter their sons' names on his ship's books, and although the system depended largely on nepotism and resulted in flagrant anomalies, no one was much concerned by the fact. A young midshipman killed shortly after Trafalgar was only eleven; he had been reefing topsails in the foretop at the age of eight. Charles Boys, of the *Thetis,* endeared himself to the crew by his childish habit of sucking his thumb. He was taken away from school and sent to join Howe's flagship, the *Queen Charlotte,* in which he took part in the battle of the "Glorious First of June." He lost a leg in the battle, whereupon his parents sent him back to school with a wooden leg to continue his studies.

By 1800 an increasing number of young men were entering the navy by way of the naval academy at Portsmouth. The academy had been opened as far back as 1729, but neither Nelson nor any of the great admirals of his time passed through the academy. They were products of the system whereby individual captains, and not the Admiralty, chose the next generation of sea officers. It is therefore hardly surprising that the main concern of the naval hierarchy was to ensure that entry through the naval academy did not entail any lowering in the standard they deemed essential; only "the sons of noblemen and gentlemen" were considered fit to command His Majesty's ships, and every effort was

5

made to restrict entry to the academy to those who could lay claim to such distinguished parentage.

The Lords Commissioners of the Admiralty had no qualms over accepting John Luard; his father was a country gentleman who had never sullied his hands with trade or such other unsuitable activity. Peter Luard was of Huguenot descent, as was his wife, Louisa Dalbiac, and he had served for some years in the 4th Dragoons. It was during his military service that he met his wife, her two brothers also being officers in the 4th Dragoons, but after his marriage Peter Luard hung up his sword and settled down to the tranquil existence of a country squire. He moved from one country property to another, hunting, shooting, and fishing, and bringing into the world eight sons and one daughter, all of whom seem to have found him an affectionate and unexacting parent. He was heir to a large estate at Blyboro, in Lincolnshire, willed to him by an aunt, but he did not come into his inheritance until late in life. He died in 1830, having throughout his life been comfortably rather than well endowed with this world's goods.

John was Peter Luard's fourth son, born while the family were living in a house called the Priory near Abergavenny, in South Wales. That was in 1790, and John spent nine happy years in what seems to have been a quiet and unpretentious country home. It was there that he learned to ride, fish, and shoot, and his dislikes were confined to his mother's two sisters, who lived with them. "As boys," he wrote, "I think we were not very fond of our aunts. Susan was rather a flirt and she had a very red nose, which necessarily detracted from an otherwise agreeable countenance." The unfortunate woman appears to have been only too well aware of this blemish, for John Luard went on to say: "She consulted a medical man who gave her some ointment to paste on a pasteboard nose, which she put on at night. We

6

had seen her once or twice with this pasteboard nose on, and the noses themselves laying about in her room, tho' this nostrum for the red nose was a secret and when a nose was not in use it was generally locked up. Nonetheless we discovered that she wore a pasteboard nose and for this we rather despised her."

Poor Susan! Despite all her efforts, she never succeeded in overcoming her unfortunate defect, and died an old maid. Her sister, Harriet, was also disliked, "because she was delicate and dined sometimes on the brains of a hare or a rabbit. How curious are boys' dislikes! She fell downstairs one day and strained her leg so badly that she was obliged to walk with crutches; we disliked her the more for this!" Harriet, however, survived the dislike of her young nephews and eventually married the Physician-General in Ireland.

Neither the Luards nor the Dalbiacs came from seafaring stock, and it is therefore somewhat surprising that John Luard should have elected to make the navy his career. He explained the reasons for his choice in his journal.

"In 1799, when I was nine years old, my father took a house at Lyme Regis in Dorset. I was constantly on the beach, catching crabs, or climbing up the rigging of an old vessel, lying on the sands high and dry. All this gave me a taste for the sea, and a visit to Tor Bay to see a fleet of seven or eight sail of the line confirmed me in this feeling. We went on board the *Sans Pareil,* an 80 gun ship commanded I think by Lord Hugh Seymour, Admiral commanding the Fleet. I mixed with the midshipmen, jolly little fellows, and I thought them the finest fellows in the world, and the ship most magnificent, which she really was. That settled my fate—I resolved to be a midshipman."

Luard went on to say of this visit to the fleet that Torquay was then only a beach, "without a lodging house or shop in the place. Brixham was the nearest town—a nasty dirty fishing place, famous for its fishing cutters. I remember we had great difficulty getting beds and I was exceedingly tired after my visit to the *Sans Pareil,* and the smell of stinking fish was dreadful."

There is no mention of his father's reaction to this plan for entering the navy, but presumably he must have approved; as the father of several sons, and not being a wealthy man, Peter Luard was probably relieved by his son's decision. An officer's life in the Royal Navy was far less expensive than in the army, and there were better chances to distinguish oneself and win promotion. There was also the prospect of receiving a share in some really good "prize," such as the two Spanish ships loaded with Mexican treasure that were taken off Finisterre by four frigates; the value of the prizes amounted to more than £600,000, the four captains taking home £40,000 apiece, while even a midshipman received £791.

John Luard makes it plain, however, that he had little or no idea of what he was undertaking when he chose the navy as his profession. Boys of eleven and twelve can hardly be expected to bring much reasoning to bear on their choice of career, although the navy has always worked on the principle that it pays to "catch 'em young." Apart from the few months in Lyme Regis, the Luard family did not live by the sea, and John was sent to school at Worcester, about as far away from the sea as it is possible to be in England. This school was apparently not a success—"it was a black-guard place—enough!" was all John Luard had to say about it. But when he was twelve they moved nearer to London and took a house at Berkhamsted, where a naval officer was their neighbor. He was Francis Pickmore, a captain waiting for a ship, and he promised to enter John's name in his ship's books as soon as he was given one. This he sub-

8

sequently did, and John's entry into the Royal Navy was assured.

He entered the Royal Naval Academy on July 9, 1802, and four years later was appointed as a volunteer midshipman to H.M.S. *Ramillies,* Captain Francis Pickmore, Royal Navy, in command. While at the academy he was reported on as behaving in "a sober, decent and regular manner," and was even complimented on his conduct by Lord St. Vincent when that formidable naval martinet visited Portsmouth. It was at the academy that he first learned how to sketch, a pastime that was to become an absorbing interest in later years. Although the life was hard, it was no worse than in the schools of that period, and it was certainly no rougher than the life he could expect in the navy.

The Royal Navy of Nelson's time was a tough, self-sufficient, and remarkably arduous profession. It differed from the army in being well-regarded in public estimation, although there was little or no haste to join it, most people sharing Dr. Johnson's opinion that a man in a ship was worse than a man in a jail. Indeed, the navy's reputation was such that the only way it could recruit its crews was by means of the notorious press gangs. Life at sea was hideously uncomfortable, the discipline was draconian, and no concessions were made for the weakling. Ships remained at sea for months on end, sometimes even for years, their crews existing on a diet of foul water, maggoty pork, and weevilly biscuits. Flogging could be ordered for the slightest misdemeanor, and a captain was answerable for his conduct only to the Almighty and the Lords of the Admiralty—both sufficiently far removed to make instant redress unlikely. The seamen slept in hammocks with a standard allowance of space of fourteen inches, lived for much of the time in semidarkness between decks and in an atmosphere that

9

nauseated the not very squeamish stomachs of that time, and when they were not being suffocated by the heat in summer, they were frozen to the marrow in winter. It was an existence with little to commend it to the ordinary man.

Down on the orlop, the lowest of the decks, was the after cockpit, where John Luard messed and slept with the other midshipmen in the *Ramillies*. The orlop was below the water line and therefore the safest place when the ship was in action. In the after cockpit the ship's surgeon bandaged bloody limbs and amputated others, sawing away on the midshipmen's sea chests and mess tables, the orlop deck being painted red as some disguise for the bloodstains. It is scarcely surprising that young men nurtured in such a demanding and harsh tradition should have grown up to be something of a breed apart. Their roots may have lain deep in the English countryside, in pleasant manor houses or in dignified rectories set among well-trimmed yew hedges, but their life at sea was scarcely less isolated than in a monastery, and almost as austere. Below them were the heaving decks, and all around, the constant creaking and groaning of the timbers. The ship was never silent, even when at anchor, and privacy was harder to come by than in a prison. At any moment they must be prepared to rush from the fetid depths below and go swarming up the leaping shrouds, setting the sails as the ship plunged and tossed like a soul tormented, and struggling desperately for a foothold as the wind clutched and tore at them. The men they commanded were often the sweepings of seaport slums—convicts who had chosen to expiate their crimes at sea instead of being transported to Botany Bay, or unhappy landlubbers swept up by the press gangs. The entire navy code of discipline was designed to ensure that an efficient crew could be fashioned from such unpromising material, and it took no heed

10

of the poltroon or the incompetent.[1] It was a service that men grew either to love or to loathe. There were no half-tones about it—everything was black or white. And yet it set a stamp on a man which remained with him until he died, whether he willed it or not. Until the end of his life John Luard bore the imprint of his early years in the Royal Navy, although he was to write many years later, "I did not much care for the life of a sailor."

It is not difficult to find a reason for this. Luard was a quiet and rather studious boy who found it hard to adjust himself to the crowded conditions and the constant horse-play which were features of a midshipman's life at sea. Bully-ing was rampant, and the food usually unspeakable, often uneatable. "We live on beef which has been ten or eleven years in the cask," wrote one of his contemporaries, "and on biscuit which makes your throat cold in eating it owing to the maggots, which are very cold when you eat them, like calfs-foot jelly or blomange, being very fat indeed! We drink water the colour of the bark of a pear tree with plenty of little maggots and weevils in it, and wine, which is exactly like bullock's blood and saw-dust mixed together."[2] Mod-ern dieticians would hardly approve of such a diet for grow-ing boys, and yet they seem to have thrived on it. They even held weevil races on the mess tables and gambled away their pay on the results. The poor light down on the orlop was more a reason for complaint than was the food, and also

---

[1] The Royal Navy took no chances with its crews. Weapons were issued only when the seamen were being exercised in their use; for the rest of the time they were locked up under marine guard. The marines were quartered between the seamen and the officers, so that they would be at hand in the event of mutiny, and when the ship was in port, a marine sentry was mounted on a special platform by the bowsprit, called the "marine's walk," as a discouragement for any sailor who might be contemplating desertion.

[2] Randolph Pears, *Young Sea Dogs*, London, 1960, p. 65.

the stench, which in warm weather was almost insupportable, and was caused by the livestock kept on the orlop deck, where there were pigsties and fowl runs and sometimes as many as a dozen bullocks tethered up to their hocks in manure.

The year John Luard joined the navy was a year of mixed fortune for England. At sea she ruled supreme, her warships chasing the French around the oceans, boarding and seizing all vessels engaged in trade with the Continent, and earning for her sea captains the reputation of being a proud and stiff-necked breed. But on land it was a different story: Napoleon had triumphed at Austerlitz and Jena, and Hapsburg and Hohenzollern had capitulated to the parvenu from Corsica. "Roll up that map," Prime Minister William Pitt had said after Austerlitz, as Winston Churchill might equally well have said after Dunkirk, for Europe, then as later, was lost for a time to tyranny. Only the seas remained free, and the keys to that freedom were the ships of the Royal Navy. They held the trade of the world in forfeit, and in the long run Napoleon would be strangled.

The news that Admiral Warren was taking a squadron to sea aroused great excitement in the after cockpit of the *Ramillies,* every midshipman yearning to smell powder and prove himself a second Nelson, and speculation was rife when Captain Pickmore called for his boat's crew and pulled across to the *Foudroyant* to wait upon the Admiral. On his return all hands were beat to quarters and Pickmore informed his ship's company that they were to sail for the West Indies to intercept a French squadron that had managed to slip through the blockade. Three days later the *Ramillies* weighed anchor and made sail, in company with the *Foudroyant, Namur,* and *Courageous.*

It was disappointing, after setting out with such high hopes, to have to record in one's journal: "Arrived at Barbados after sixteen days' passage without sighting the French." True, the *Ramillies* gave chase to a suspicious sail, but it turned out to be an American privateer, which soon showed a clean pair of heels to the slow and lumbering old *Ramillies*. The absence of any action seems to have early disenchanted young Luard with a life on the rolling waves, and he noted in his journal that "life at sea has a tedium all its own."

The *Ramillies* was then sent north to Halifax, where she remained for several months, cruising off the North American coast in search of American blockade-runners. She was old, leaky, and a poor sailer, but as happiness went in those days, she was a happy ship, and Pickmore was a popular captain. Luard's log records comparatively few punishments, but the following is a typical example:

"14th July, 1807. Punished Wm Dawson with 12 lashes for disobedience, Edward Nichols with 30 for mutinous expressions, Wm Jones with 18 for drunkenness, and Andrew Wilkinson with 18 for desertion."

There is a similar kind of entry every two months in Luard's log, but in other ships the discipline was fiercer and the lash was used more frequently. H.M.S. *Jason* was at Halifax with the *Ramillies,* and Luard records that on September 29, 1807, ten of her seamen were condemned to death for mutiny. "The cause of the mutiny was the severity of Captain Cochrane," wrote Luard. The Captain of the *Jason* was one of the finest seamen in the navy, but notoriously hard to serve.

Men like Thomas Cochrane rose rapidly to the rank of captain, as much on account of the influence possessed by their families as by their professional ability. But some measure of ability they had to have, for without it they could not secure the co-operation of the long-service sailors who formed the backbone of every ship's crew. A coward or an

13

"old woman" was unlikely to go very far in the Royal Navy; he would be found out sooner or later—by the elements, if not by the enemy. Besides, the sea was a merciless tutor, and the living conditions would soon break a boy of weak character. Nevertheless, an officer had to possess "interest," as well as character and the ability to master his profession, if he was to be a post-captain by twenty, as Nelson was when appointed to command H.M.S. *Hinchinbroke*. It would be as well, too, if he kept clear of any matrimonial entanglement, or else he might fall foul of some old sea dog like Sir John Jervis, Earl St. Vincent, who believed that "when an officer marries he is damned for the service." The old Admiral felt so strongly about wives and naval officers not mixing that he wrote to one offender:

Sir, You having thought fit to take to yourself a wife, are to look for no further attentions from;

Your humble servant,

John Jervis.[3]

Not that John Luard, beating backward and forward from the southern tip of Newfoundland to Latitude 42°, had any ideas of marriage. There were few enough opportunities to meet a girl when month followed month at sea, and in any case the need among the young for female companionship seems to have been far less felt in Luard's time than is the case today. When in port, the sailors used to bring women on board, drink themselves drunk with raw spirits, and dance jigs around the guns while the fiddlers sawed away like men possessed. Down on the orlop, however, the midshipmen were denied such privileges, although the older ones used to hold the rest enthralled as they retailed their

[3] E. S. Turner, *Gallant Gentlemen: A Portrait of the British Officer, 1600-1956*, London, 1956, p. 99.

amorous exploits in the noisome dockland alleys. John Luard did not attempt to emulate his seniors' experiences, and he went ashore only three times during the long stay of the *Ramillies* at Halifax. There were few amenities in the town and there was plenty to keep him occupied on board. "No one sees more of the world than a midshipman in the Royal Navy," he wrote home at this time, adding, "and yet at the same time knows so little about it." One cannot help feeling that he might perhaps have made better use of his opportunities.

On October 5, 1807, the *Ramillies* sailed from Halifax for the West Indies. Denmark, as a result of a secret clause in the Treaty of Tilsit, had entered the lists against England, and Sir Arthur Wellesley, fresh from his triumphs in India, had sailed with his division to invest Copenhagen. Meanwhile, the Danish possessions in the West Indies—Saint Thomas, Saint John, and Santa Cruz—were at the mercy of the Royal Navy, and an expeditionary force was hastily formed to capture them from the Danes. Rear-Admiral Cochrane was to command the ships, and Major-General Thomas Bowyer the troops.

The *Ramillies,* on her way to Carlisle Bay in Barbados, where she was to embark troops, ran aground on Needham's Point while working into the bay. "At 5.30 grounded upon Needham's Point," recorded Luard in his log. "Got a hawser out to H.M.S. *Camilla* and hove upon it. At 8 she wore round and got out all the boats and spars to lighten her. She struck repeatedly hard. Ship's company run fore and aft with shot to lighten her.[4] Got an anchor out. At 11.30 she got off."

[4] The maneuver described by Luard was intended to shift the weight of the ship rapidly from bow to stern, or from port to starboard, in an attempt to rock the ship off the obstruction that was holding her. In order to increase the normal weight of the crew, each man was made to carry a cannon ball.

Although no great damage had been done, there was much concern in the *Ramillies* lest the Admiral should decide to leave her behind for repairs. Her captain therefore resolved to demonstrate the martial ardor of his crew by landing them every morning at dawn and marching them around all day, "to fit us all for cut and thrust with the enemy." These unusual military exercises were much approved by John Luard, but his enthusiasm was not shared by his shipmates; "there was much grumbling by the seamen and two of them threw their muskets into the sea." Whatever their feelings, the captain's plan had the desired result and the *Ramillies* was ordered to embark the soldiers.

These came from the 70th Foot, at that time garrisoned in Saint Kitts. They were a regiment with good cause to know the unhealthiness of islands that have since become a holidaymaker's paradise. They had landed at English Harbour in Antigua on New Year's Day, 1804, with a strength of twenty-seven officers and 440 rank and file fit for duty; by the end of that year they had buried twelve officers and 152 soldiers, and many others had died while being invalided to Canada or England. One of their officers, a Colonel Leach, had this to say of their dreadful experience:

"In the month of July we were suddenly visited with an attack of yellow fever, that eternal curse and scourge of Europeans, which in a few days filled the hospitals to such an extent as has perhaps never been exceeded in any regiment, and but rarely equalled. Between the months of June and October we buried two-thirds of the officers who came out with the regiment from England, six of whom were captains. The ravages occasioned by this infernal pestilence amongst the soldiers, their wives and children bore a full proportion to that of the officers, and . . . by the end of 1804 the regiment was a perfect skeleton, and could with great difficulty furnish men to perform the regimental

16

duties." Leach went on to say that, "Owing to the great number of deaths in the garrison, the Governor, General Dunlop, ordered that all funeral ceremonies be discontinued, and that the coffins of officers should be carried to the grave without band or drums and without a firing party. The general ordered that these instructions should apply if necessary to his own funeral. The order was obeyed to the letter, and both he and his brigade-major, who died within a few days of each other, were taken to their graves in a light wagon, attended by a few of our officers and soldiers who were able to do their duty, and by a small party of artillerymen." [5]

Leach himself survived an attack of the dreaded fever, attributing his cure to the quarts of boiling Madeira that he drank at frequent intervals during the course of his illness.

His account of the sufferings of his regiment is doubtless somewhat exaggerated, but there can be no doubt that the 70th Foot, after three years in the West Indies, were not in very good shape. Their appearance certainly did not impress John Luard: ". . . the soldiers lacked spirit, possibly due to the climate and the time they had spent in the West Indies." On December 8, 1807, eighty of them trudged up the gangway of the *Ramillies* and then scrambled awkwardly down the rope ladders to the lower decks. There they made themselves as comfortable as they could manage in an overcrowded ship, which was hot, stinking, and dark. Those of them who had done duty in the hulks thought the barefooted sailors, with their matted hair and uncouth jargon, little different from convicts, while the sailors roared with laughter when the clumsy redcoats tripped over the lashings, fell down the rope ladders, and banged their powdered heads against the low decks.

[5] H. W. Pearse, *History of the East Surrey Regiment,* London, 1916, p. 298.

On December 21 the fleet sighted Saint Thomas, and the drums beat to quarters. Flat-bottomed boats, which had been taken aboard at Saint Kitts, were hoisted out, and the *Ramillies* cleared for action. "I took my party down the ship's side," wrote Luard, "and we waited in the boat for orders to cast off. The soldiers were slow and very clumsy." Eventually all was ready, but at that moment a lookout spotted a white flag fluttering over the citadel and reported that a vessel flying a flag of truce was making her way out from the shore. "You can imagine how disappointed we were," said Luard, and the sailors probably gave vent to their feelings by taking it out of the soldiers. Spirits were so low that not even the sight of a captain of the 70th Foot missing his footing and falling into the sea could raise more than a feeble cheer. "We were all thoroughly disgusted" was how John Luard described his feelings as he watched Captain Francis Pickmore going ashore with General Maitland to settle the terms of surrender. The following day Saint Thomas passed into the hands of King George III, and Santa Cruz and Saint John followed a few days later.[6] Not a shot had had to be fired, or a single soldier or sailor landed. It was an impressive demonstration of the virtues of sea power for any young midshipman to witness, but Luard was not impressed. "It was not for this that I joined the navy" was his summing up of the whole affair.

The Admiral was pleased, however, and so was the General, since admirals and generals are not on the whole so bloodthirsty as midshipmen and subalterns. The bloodless occupation of the three islands would be duly noted at the Admiralty and the Horse Guards and would be chalked up to their credit. There was no such consolation for John Luard, and "it was shortly after we returned to St Kitts that

[6] The islands were returned to Denmark after the peace and were sold by the Danes to the United States in 1917.

I formed the resolution to leave the navy. The service held out little attraction for me and the prospect of action against the French seemed remote." The life of action he had expected to find in the navy appeared to Luard to have ended with Nelson's death off Trafalgar; henceforward, or so it seemed, there would only be days and weeks and months of blockading the enemy coasts, in fair weather and foul, with only the merest chance of falling in with a Frenchman. For months the *Ramillies* had been doing just that, beating up and down the trade winds, either on lonely patrol or ensuring "the safe and timely arrival" of a convoy of merchantmen. John Luard's log, which he kept meticulously throughout his time at sea, is a record of receipt of stores ("10 bullocks from the shore"), of punishments ("punished John Lawrence with 24 lashes"), of deaths ("departed this life Thos. Harkett committed his body to the deep"), and of such incidents as the one logged on November 5, 1807: "fired a salute in commemoration of the Gunpowder Treason." and as day followed monotonous day, John Luard's decision to leave the navy became firmer in his mind, although there is nowhere any suggestion that he discussed the matter with his captain or confided in any of his fellow-midshipmen. Perhaps he feared lest he be overpersuaded to stay, or perhaps he wished first to consult his father.

Indeed, the mechanics of leaving the navy at that time were not easy. Midshipmen did not hold commissions, nor do they do so today, but Luard would face a charge of desertion if he left without being officially discharged. He could get his discharge as a result of wounds or a court-martial verdict, or he could just "disappear" and hope not to be recognized and brought back on a desertion charge. It is clear that a young man in Luard's position was unlikely to take such an extreme course, and one must assume either that his father was able to pull sufficient strings to obtain

19

his son's discharge or, more likely, that he had not yet been officially rated midshipman, which did not normally happen until a "volunteer" had completed three years' service. While still a "volunteer," he could leave on the grounds of incompatibility.

He had been just sixteen when the *Ramillies* weighed anchor at Spithead and sailed for Barbados; he was a few months short of nineteen when he saw the Lizard again through the driving mists of an October day. The *Ramillies* dropped anchor in the Downs, and her crew were paid off. Luard was appointed to the *Thetis,* a forty-four-gun frigate lying at Sheerness, in Kent, but he never joined her.

"On the 6th November I obtained leave of absence for a week. On the 7th I left Sheerness for Northampton. To the former I never returned, having a few days after my arrival at the latter obtained my discharge from the Royal Navy." So ends the last entry in Luard's log.

His service in the navy had been short and had ended abruptly; almost, it would seem, on impulse. Now he was about to try his hand as a soldier and find that trade more to his liking.

CHAPTER TWO

Nowhere in John Luard's journal is there any suggestion
that his desire to leave the navy met with parental opposition, and the matter is dismissed in one short sentence:
". . . soon after I left the navy my father purchased me a
cornetcy in the 4th Dragoons." There must have been some
discussion, however, since in those days a subaltern's commission in the cavalry cost £800, and John Luard's uniform
and saddlery cost a further £500. This contrasted forcibly
with the navy, where a midshipman's uniform cost very
little—possibly not more than £4 by today's values—and
there was no question of having to purchase an officer's
commission. Nevertheless, John Luard must have won any
argument that there may have been, because on May 25,
1809, the London *Gazette* contained the announcement that
he had been granted the King's commission.

Family connection dictated his choice of regiment. His
father had served with the 4th Dragoons until 1789, and his
elder brother, George, was already a subaltern in the regiment. Two of his mother's brothers were also 4th Dragoons:
Charles Dalbiac was second-in-command to the Colonel,

Lord Edward Somerset, and George Dalbiac commanded a squadron. There was therefore no particular probem in finding him a place in the regiment, providing his father was prepared to purchase his commission, since there was virtually no other way of becoming an officer in those days in the cavalry. Nor, under normal conditions, would there have been any delay in his joining the regiment; recruit training was regarded as a comparatively simple affair, there being no requirement for the elaborate training organizations with which we became so familiar during the era of National Service, and commanding officers were left to get along with training their newly joined officers and recruits as they thought fit. However, the 4th Dragoons were overseas in Portugal, and it was conceded by the Horse Guards that regiments on active service had better things to do than lick their raw material into shape. Consequently, depots had been formed in England to train recruits for those regiments which were overseas, and John Luard was ordered to report to Shoreham, in Sussex, where one of the cavalry depots was situated.

What kind of an army did Luard join in 1809, and how did it differ from the service he had just quitted? To begin with, it lacked the standing in the country of the Royal Navy, the British traditionally distrusting the concept of a standing army, partly on account of the legacy of Cromwell and his major-generals, and partly because the "lobsters," as the scarlet-coated soldiers were called, were so often used to deal with civil unrest. There was virtually no police force, and during the Gordon Riots in 1780 it had required all the Guards regiments, plus several cavalry, to restore order in the looted and burning city of London. In the course of this unpleasant affair, the 3rd and 4th Dragoons between them killed 101 people, which, although doubtless both necessary and salutary, was hardly calculated to endear their profession to their fellow-citizens.

The army moreover lacked the victorious tradition of the navy, and, apart from a few like Dr. Johnson, most people failed to see anything glamorous in a soldier's career. There was no soldier as popular in public estimation as Nelson, and even Wellington at the height of his fame failed to stir the same emotions in the hearts of his countrymen; he was certainly respected, but it is doubtful if he was ever really loved. Army officers were more conspicuous for their aristocratic hauteur than for their skill in the field, and the fact that a long purse meant quick promotion deterred the majority of Englishmen from aspiring to the King's commission. In any case, the prospect of long years of exile in some fever-haunted West Indian island, or the tedium of garrison duty in the backwaters of Connemara or Kerry, was enough to dissuade most young men from joining the army—not to mention the stiff and awkward drill, the pipe clay and the polishing, the poor pay, and a disciplinary code that was as savage as the navy's and equally brutalizing. All these things, some true and some absurdly magnified, brought the army into disrepute. It was not a popular service.

As in the navy, the majority of army officers came from the landowning class, and in those days of large families the pattern frequently worked out as the eldest son inheriting the estate, the cleverest son entering the church or the law, and the remaining sons divided between the army and the navy, with the former slightly predominating. There were some families which traditionally provided officers for the army, just as there were families like the Cochranes and Seymours who gravitated naturally to the navy; but whereas in the navy a measure of professional ability, coupled with more than one's fair share of luck, might overcome a lack of family influence, in the army an officer without private means might have to wait years and years for promotion.

Without such financial backing, a man, however brave and competent, might wait for years before he was promoted captain. Wellington, for example, bought his way through five regiments and ended as colonel of the 33rd Foot at the age of twenty-four; whereas Robert Blakeney, who served throughout the Peninsular War with the 28th and 36th Foot, being wounded in the process and several times commended for bravery, so lacked money and influence that he was still carrying out the same duties in 1828 as he had done as a subaltern twenty-three years before. In the intervening years he had risen only to captain and was unlikely to become a major until he was fifty-four. John Luard, whose career was nothing like so meteoric as Wellington's, or as depressingly slow as Blakeney's, reached the rank of lieutenant-colonel by the age of forty-eight. Yet before one dismisses the system of promotion by purchase as iniquitous, which it undoubtedly was, it is well to remember that it was this system which facilitated the careers of military geniuses like Wolfe and Wellington, even though it may have broken the hearts of many poor but devoted officers.

It is hard for us to understand why men continued to serve under such conditions, and particularly when they saw younger and often less-competent officers being promoted over their heads. The mere thought drove Sir Henry Havelock to distraction thirty years later, and led Blakeney to memorialize the commander in chief on three separate occasions without receiving his due. The answer, of course, lies in the intense pride of regiment which gripped a man from the outset of his service and which never relaxed its grip until he died. Nor was this *esprit de corps* confined only to the more fashionable regiments, or to the more

24

aristocratic and wealthy officers, as the following example will suffice to show. In 1783 the second battalion of the 73rd Highlanders (Lord MacLeod's) returned home after a long and arduous tour of duty at Gibraltar. No sooner had they arrived in Stirling than they were told that the battalion was to be disbanded. The choice before them was either retirement or joining the first battalion of the regiment, which was in India. If they chose the latter, they would have to sail almost immediately, pay their own passages, and almost certainly leave their families behind. Every single officer volunteered to go, and so did most of the men; it would have been unthinkable to leave the regiment, the more especially since it was on active service.

The soldiers shared with their officers this passionate devotion to their regiments, perhaps even more strongly, since for many of them the regiment was their only home. Wellington referred to them as "scum" and said that most of them enlisted only for drink. It was a sweeping statement, such as Wellington was inclined to make on occasion, but it contained more than a grain of truth. Men had to be tough to survive in Britain in those days, not only in the army but in everyday life as well. The British soldier was typical of his background—rough, usually illiterate, on occasion brutal, and more often than not licentious. He lived in a world where only the fittest could hope to survive, where sanitation was crude, cholera killed as many as did tuberculosis, and venereal disease was commonplace. And yet, for all this crudeness and coarseness, there was also a shrewd, uncompromising skill, largely instinctive, difficult to analyze, but masterly when seen in action. It was this that made the British soldier, when properly led, one of the most formidable fighting men in the world, but on the reverse side of the coin it made him one of the most difficult to handle under normal peacetime conditions. Pride of regiment, skill at arms, and a supreme contempt for the enemy were the articles of faith of the British soldier, and it was this army that John Luard had joined, and it was these men he would shortly have to lead.

The depot at Shoreham, where John Luard joined the army in the early summer of 1809, was not a very inspiring place. "I wish they would send me over to Portugal," he wrote to his father at this time, fretting as all young officers do lest the war should be over before he could get to it. The training consisted mainly of long periods in the riding school, much of it wasted on John Luard, who had ridden horses ever since he was nine, although doubtless essential for the yokels who had never ridden anything except a plow horse before they took the King's shilling. There was drill as well, of course, and a certain amount of bookwork—mostly field sketching, which came easily to John after his early training in the navy. In fact, it was his early naval training that made Shoreham seem so irksome; after three years at sea he was much more mature than his contemporaries at Shoreham and therefore more inclined to be critical of the inadequate training facilities. His commanding officer was an elderly major—"doddery and very passionate"—who had served with John's father in the 4th Dragoons and who was long past his prime. In every war retired officers are recalled to train the soldiers which a parsimonious government refuses to maintain in peace, but in 1809 there was no need to recall officers to active duty. There were quite enough serving, unfit and almost senile, who could not be taken on campaign and who were therefore left to staff the training depots. This Major, whose name does not appear in Luard's journal, was one such. He wandered around the squads, slapping his thigh with his whip, and apparently saying nothing but "Damn! Damn! Damn!"

There was no proper organization for training young officers. When commissions were bought, young men joined their regiments with little or no idea of their professional duties. George Bell, who joined the army two years after John Luard, was still at school when his commission in the 34th Foot was gazetted on March 11, 1811, whereupon he jumped up, shook hands with his schoolmates, said good-by to his headmaster, and "bolted out of the house, no one seeming to know what it was all about until I was clear away, and sent back a newspaper with the Gazette, which fully explained my retreat from thraldom." [1] The experiences of Captain Gronow in the Guards were no different; he had scarcely learned his left from his right when he was expected to command a platoon in action, and, not surprisingly, found the whole affair somewhat alarming. It was all part of the upbringing of a nation and a class which regarded leadership as its birthright.

Even this early in his career, John Luard had no use for the "amateur" officer who regarded soldiering as just an excuse to wear a dashing uniform and become a society fop. "There are those here who care little for their exercises," he wrote, "but who spend their time travelling backwards and forwards to London." There were plenty of young men of this type serving in the army at this period, although, to be fair, most of them were in the militia or the yeomanry. One exception was the notorious Beau Brummel, who served for a time as a cornet in the 10th Hussars (then, the 10th Light Dragoons). He attended parades so seldom in that socially elite corps that he could only recognize his

---

[1] George Bell, *Rough Notes by an Old Soldier,* London, 1867, p. 1.

place in the ranks by a blue-nosed old trooper in the front rank. When, on one occasion, the trooper was drafted to another troop, Brummel, arriving late on parade, scanned the ranks and finally found his landmark and placed himself opposite him. Thereupon the colonel rode up and rebuked Brummel for being in the wrong troop. "No, no, I know better than that," protested the indignant Brummel. "A pretty thing indeed if I did not know my own troop!" He may or may not have been a typical cavalry officer, but there were many like him, who joined the army more for the social cachet than for any desire to smell powder. Some of them proved themselves good soldiers when it came to active service, while others resigned as soon as their regiments were ordered out of the country. Cornet Brummel resigned on even slenderer grounds. He learned that his regiment was about to be moved from Brighton and sought out his friend and patron the Prince Regent to explain his resignation. "I really could not go with them," he said. "Think, your Royal Highness—Manchester!"

Nothing of this kind applied to John Luard. Small, wiry, and fit, he had joined the navy because he sought an active life, and, not having found it, had transferred to the army. He chafed at every minute that kept him at Shoreham tramping around the barracks in respectful conversation with his father's old comrade or undergoing the tedium of elementary squad drill; it was even less exciting than wallowing through the Caribbean in the lumbering old *Ramillies*. "I found this period in my life very dull," he wrote later in that vein of understatement so typical of the Victorians. There was nothing dashing about the life of a dragoon as lived at Shoreham.

Dragoons had not always been a particularly colorful branch of the cavalry. Back in 1685, when the 4th Dragoons were first raised by the Honorable John Berkeley as "The Princess Anne of Denmark's Regiment of Horse," the cavalry was divided basically into regiments of horse and dragoons. The horse were employed mainly for shock action against the infantry, whereas the dragoons were really a form of mounted infantry, using their horses to close with the enemy but thereafter taking to their feet and using their carbines, or muskets. "What troops or squadrons in the world can beat our dragoons?" asked Colonel Hawley in 1720. "What are Horse for, then, especially Horse Guards, a useless expense to the nation, a clog to our King as to numbers and the use of troops?" The gallant Colonel, who commanded the 4th Dragoons until promoted under the peculiar arrangements of those days to command an infantry regiment, and who was to acquire an unenviable reputation for brutality after the Second Jacobite Rebellion in 1745, was voicing the antipathy that then existed between the two branches of the cavalry. The regiments of horse tended to despise the dragoon as a mere mounted infantryman, while the dragoon in his turn regarded the soldier of horse as a "Fop, with their curled locks and Holland stockings to keep their white thread ones clean under their boots." [2]

The distinction between horse and dragoons soon became blurred in the British Army, although in 1755 the Duke of Cumberland saw fit to remind the "whole Corps of Dragoons" that "they are still Dragoons and not Horse, that they are to March and attack on foot, if there is occasion when dismounted. Therefore the men's boots are not to be encumbered with great spur-leathers and chains, to hinder them from getting over a hedge, ditch or works, when they are ordered to attack, and whenever they are ordered on

[2] David Scott Daniell, *4th Hussar,* Aldershot, 1959, p. 38.

such service, they are to sling their swords over their shoulders." Yet, then as now, individual colonels saw fit to interpret the regulations according to their own inclinations, and dragoon regiments gradually became indistinguishable from the rest of the cavalry, except for a tendency to recruit bigger men and mount them on heavier horses. By the time John Luard joined the army, there was really little difference between the heavy and light cavalry, although this was not the case elsewhere. "You must," wrote Napoleon to his War Minister, Louis A. Berthier, in 1803, "consider Cuirassiers, Dragoons and Hussars as forming three different arms, and never put up to me transfers from one arm to the other"; and, again, to Joachim Murat, "I am sorry to see your light cavalry and dragoons are intermingled—they are two different arms." [3]

Napoleon's earnest professionalism would have meant very little to the average British cavalry officer of that period: all he wanted was the chance to charge the enemy, and be damned to theory. The 4th Dragoons had spent the past sixty years scattered in small detachments all over England and Scotland, acting more as a mounted police force than anything else, and collecting together at rare intervals for the glittering reviews which in those days passed for military exercises. Since the colonel drew so much money for every man under his command, the ranks were seldom filled; dead men's names remained on the muster rolls for years after they had been buried, and their pay was solemnly drawn and pocketed by the colonel, the paymaster receiving his share for keeping his mouth shut. Men grew older and older in the service, one dragoon owning to sixty-

[3] An interesting hangover of this controversy is the argument that has long persisted in the Royal Armoured Corps as to the advisability, or otherwise, of making armored (tank) regiments switch over with armored-car regiments from time to time.

30

five, although his comrades averred he was over eighty. The days were filled by grooming the horses in the mornings and by snoozing around the inn tables in the evenings, with patrols along the highroads fetlock-deep in mire and enlivened by occasional forays against the highwaymen. If this was the life of the trooper, the officer did even less: balls and visiting, hunting, shooting, and fishing, and long absences from duty while the body recuperated its strength at the more fashionable watering places. One gallant subaltern was five years with his regiment without once venturing near it, and when at last he did so, his colonel had to inquire his name. Small wonder then that active service was so eagerly sought after as a break in such ossifying tedium.

But if field training was neglected for police work and formal reviews, and if the majority of officers were more at home at balls and assemblies than on parade, there was one subject that occupied the attention of generals and colonels above all else. "The army attaches a lot more importance to drill and to uniforms than we did in the Royal Navy," wrote John Luard when giving his father his first impressions of military life. "Here at Shoreham we spend a great deal more time on our dress than in learning about our weapons."

Regulations of the most searching nature laid down the exact length of a coat, the particular color of lace, and even the width of shoe buckles. The good officer was the one who could pick out at a glance the slightest deviation from dress regulations, and, since uniforms were designed more for show than for serviceability, and because the conservative-minded soldier was slow to adapt his costume to the changing dictates of fashion, the 4th Dragoons took the field in 1809 not greatly different in appearance from their predecessors who had invaded Spain in 1707 under the command of the Earl of Peterborough.

31

John Luard's uniform in the navy cost virtually nothing. Most after cockpits had one or two decent coats owned communally, which were worn when necessary, such as for going ashore, but any old clothes served while on board. The midshipman's uniform consisted of a plain blue coat with stand-up collar and buttons on the sleeves, white waistcoat, white breeches, black shoes, and tricorn hat. A dirk was rarely worn at that time. But as a cornet of dragoons, Luard was required to provide himself with a wardrobe as out-of-date as it was elaborate. A heavy cocked hat provided little protection from the weather and hardly any shade from the sun, bore heavily on the temples, and was the cause of endless headaches. The scarlet jacket was short and tight-waisted, faced with green collar and cuffs and with thick cloth epaulettes to turn aside sword cuts. Thick white breeches came up to the waist, and there were heavy jack-boots reaching above the thighs. It was not the kind of costume that allowed a man to leap nimbly into the saddle, and when dismounted the dragoon was little more agile than a trussed fowl. The swords were straight, long, and heavy, used more for pointing than for cutting, and were suspended from the waist belt by slings. In the case of officers, they were kept in place by embroidered sabretaches. This article of equipment fulfilled various functions, and John Luard used his to carry his sketching materials. The ordinary dragoon carried a haversack in place of a sabretache, and a canteen marked with the initials of the regiment and the letter of his troop; he also carried a musket and bayonet, soon to be discarded as an outmoded relic of the days when the dragoon was expected to fight on foot. The trumpeters were Negroes, dressed in oriental magnificence, with turbans, plumes, and jackets so padded that they looked like pouter pigeons.

It would have been hard to devise a costume less suited

to the rigors of war, when battles do not necessarily take place while the sun is shining and when the cavalry's most important role is outpost duty in all weathers. Nor did it take into account the climatic extremes in countries like Spain and Portugal, where long, hot, and dusty summers are followed by wet autumns and bitterly cold winters. The cavalryman's most sensible article of dress was his long red cloak, which kept him warm at night when the infantry-man was shivering without his blankets.

John Luard was to find, however, that the army was in advance of the navy in one particular aspect. Most of the sailors in the *Ramillies* had worn their hair long, gathered together tightly at the back of the head and tied into a pig-tail, or queue. The same had long been true in the army, but an order in 1796 laid down that queues were not to exceed ten inches in length, which was later reduced to nine inches. In 1808 queues were finally abolished in the army, but not without a good deal of opposition from the diehards, whose views on the martial value of long hair must have derived from Samson. The army as a whole welcomed the abolition of an unhygienic and uncomfortable hair style which had paid more attention to the length of the queue than to the cleanliness of the hair; one old fusilier in Antigua employed a mulatto boy to pick over his head every Sunday morning.

As he bumped around the riding school at Shoreham, his clumsy jackboots cutting into his thighs, John Luard must have had the gravest doubts about the utility of his costume, since he was to write in his journal years later, and after he had written a book on military uniforms which he illustrated himself, "the dragoons' uniform of that time was not very handsome and quite unsuited to campaign-ing." Fortunately, the rigors of active service have usually had a moderating influence on the more ridiculous military

33

fashions, as he was to find when he joined his regiment, the more so since Wellington was a commander who seldom concerned himself with the sit of a button or the color of a jacket, being content with clean and serviceable weapons, boots in good repair, and greatcoats that were reasonably waterproof. The pipe clay and gold lace that absorbed the attention of lesser men meant little to Wellington, although his own appearance was always so neat and immaculate that his officers nicknamed him "The Beau." It is true that he disliked eccentricities in dress, having on one occasion to admonish officers of the Grenadier Guards for carrying umbrellas in action. "Lord Wellington does not approve of the use of umbrellas during the enemy's firing," was the message delivered to Colonel Tynling of the Grenadiers, and a few days later the unfortunate Colonel was admonished by Wellington in person. "The Guards may in uniform, when on duty at St James's, carry them if they please; but in the field it is not only ridiculous but unmilitary."[4]

John Luard was also critical of the quality of horseflesh that was collected at Shoreham to provide remounts for the regiments overseas. "Dragoon regiments have for many years been provided with a heavy breed of horse," he wrote, "but those at Shoreham had little breeding and nothing to commend them except their size." The fashion went back to the days when dragoons were invariably bigger men than the rest of the cavalry and carried heavier equipment; consequently it became necessary to provide them with something approaching cart horses if they were to be able to get across country. This kind of animal soon lost condition when forage was poor and had much less stamina than lighter breeds, nor did they stand up well to the hardship of being transported overseas. Of the 740 horses which sailed

[4] *Reminiscences & Recollections of Captain Gronow,* London, 1900, Vol. II, p. 11.

from England with the 4th Dragoons, no fewer than ten died in the course of the passage to Lisbon. Arrived off the Tagus, the horses were slung overboard and left to make their own way ashore, no small physical strain after being cooped up in the stifling holds of the ships for more than nine days. While at sea, they were packed so tightly that they could barely move from side to side, and many of them strained muscles and tendons from the corkscrew motion of the ship. Those which lost their footing in the holds were left to thrash around until either they were exhausted or someone could get close enough to put them out of their agony.

At last the longed-for release from Shoreham was received. John Luard was just about to set off home for Christmas when the order arrived for him to join his regiment in Portugal. "Even the disappointment at not being able to bid farewell to my father and mother could not overcome my delight at the prospect ahead," he wrote, and on Christmas Eve he set off with a party of recruits for Plymouth, marching via Guildford. There they took over a draft of heavy black horses from the 3rd Dragoons which were to prove a sad liability in the months ahead. The 3rd had been mounted according to dragoon custom on black horses, but it had been decided that they were too heavy to make good cavalry chargers. The discarded black horses were therefore to be shipped to Portugal, although why they should be better on active service than on peacetime duties was never explained to the curious John Luard.

The party crossed Dartmoor in a blinding snowstorm, losing a horse and two dragoons from exposure, and sailed from Plymouth on January 24, 1811; it had taken them a month to march from Guildford. The weather was vile, the ship rolled like a pig, and even as hardened a sailor as

35

John Luard was violently seasick. The food was bad, "there was no mess for the officers," and the horses suffered terribly from cold and the motion of the ship. The passage to Lisbon took twenty days and remained in Luard's memory as the worst voyage he ever undertook; he never thought if it in later years without a shudder. But they reached Lisbon at last, the horses were slung overboard, and the soldiers were marched away through the stinking streets to the transit camp at Belém.

After more than twelve months of waiting, John Luard had arrived at the seat of the war, and he would not set foot in England again until the Union Jack had been planted on the parapets of Toulouse and Napoleon was an exile on Elba.

CHAPTER THREE

Lisbon, even as John Luard first saw it from the heaving decks of a transport and through the driving rain of a winter's day, was a very handsome city. Its magnificent port was a forest of masts and spars, while the seven-mile-wide Tagus provided an anchorage for ships of every size and description. Offshore lay a score or more British ships of the line, newly returned from bombarding the French; stubby little schooners and barkentines were tied up along the quays, their skippers waxing rich on the contraband trade; and far out in midstream a brace of privateers tugged at their cables, looking, with their rake-helly lines, like a leash of falcons waiting on before they stooped on their quarry.

The city was built on steep-sided hills, so that the narrow streets climbed upward from the port, flanked throughout most of their length by fortress-like monasteries and palaces of startling dilapidation. Seen from the Tagus, the city lay sprawled across its hills, a picture of white and yellow, with a background of distant mountains, hazy and blue and crested with snow. Lisbon looked not only beautiful but also strangely romantic, and it was a thousand pities that only a few minutes ashore could shatter this splendid illusion. The streets, so picturesque when seen from seaward, were little more than open sewers, and at any moment an upper window might open and a shower of kitchen garbage or worse would come tumbling down on the heads of the passers-by. Scavenging dogs flitted furtively through the dingy alleys, and every open space was piled high with rubbish and manure, often surmounted by the carcass of a dog or donkey which had been thrown thereon to rot. And over everywhere hung the all-pervading stench of Portugal's capital city, a compound of garlic, decaying fish, and human ordure, amid which the citizens went about their business with little apparent concern and in a state of perpetual clamor and seeming disorder.

"What an ignorant, superstitious, priest-ridden, dirty, lousy set of poor devils are the Portuguese," wrote Private Wheeler. "Without seeing them it is impossible to conceive there exists a people in Europe so debased. The filthiest pig sty is a palace to the filthy houses in this dirty stinking city, all the dirt made in the house is thrown in the streets, where it remains baking for months until a storm of rain washes it away. The streets are crowded with half starved dogs, fat priests and lousy people." The outraged Wheeler went on to say that "in the middle of the day the sunny sides of the streets swarms with men and women picking the vermin from their bodies, and it is no uncommon sight to see two respectable dressed persons meet and do a friendly office for each other by picking a few crawlers from each others persons." [1]

For all its drawbacks, John Luard found his first view of Lisbon "one of the pleasantest I can ever recall; I should

[1] William Wheeler, *Letters, 1809-1828,* edited by B. H. Liddell Hart, London, 1951, Cambridge, Mass., 1952, p. 49.

have welcomed any where after that passage across the bay."
At the quayside to greet him was quite a family party—his
brother George, who had obtained leave from the front,
and also his uncle George Dalbiac. Charles Dalbiac had
been laid low with fever, but his wife, Susan, came to welcome John. She had come hurrying out from England to
nurse her husband through a fever he had contracted the
previous summer in the steaming valley of the Guadiana.
By so doing, Susan had braved the disapproval of the commander in chief, who expressed himself often and forcibly
about the propriety of officers' wives accompanying their
husbands on a campaign, but this had little effect on Susan,
who was no respecter of persons. Indeed, she found campaigning so much to her taste that she stayed on in Portugal
after her husband had recovered, and acquired quite a name
for herself by the time the war ended.

There was much to talk about. George Luard and John
had not seen each other since John went to sea five years
before, and in the interval George had been fighting for
more than a year and was an old campaigner. There were
a dozen skirmishes and battles to be fought over again for
the benefit of the newly joined Cornet, such as Talavera,
fought in the blazing heat of a July day in 1809, when the
French under Claude Victor were fought to such a standstill
that they lacked the heart to renew the action next day:
". . . had they done so," wrote Charles Dalbiac to his
mother, "I doubt if Lord Wellington could have stopped
them. We were all done up and there were no fresh troops
nearer than Lisbon." Talavera had been followed by weeks
of marching and countermarching through the stony Estre-
maduran valleys, from Ciudad Rodrigo in the north to
beyond Badajoz in the south, weary work for the cavalry,
advancing one week and retreating the next, and all the
time watching the superior numbers of the enemy for any

sign of a resumed offensive. "We soon learnt to sleep in the day or night," wrote Lieutenant William Tomkinson of the 16th Light Dragoons. "We never undressed and at night all the horses were bridled up, the men sleeping at their heads, and the officers of each troop close to their horses." [2] Supplies were short, the valleys full of fever, and the villages poor and infested with vermin.

All this and more had to be told once the family party had repaired to Lisbon's best inn to await the unloading of John's baggage. The dining room was thronged with officers from almost every regiment in the British Army, for Lisbon had been the main British base in the peninsula ever since the first redcoats marched into the city in the autumn of 1808. There were green-jacketed riflemen from the 95th, and British officers serving with the Portuguese Army in varying shades of green and dark blue; but the predominant color was scarlet, faded by wind and sun and rain until it was nearer pink, patched and sewn and shabby, so that John Luard's bright coat stood out among the rest like a palm tree in the desert. Regiments arrived in Lisbon from England gorgeously attired in scarlet and gold, their facings gosling green, buff, yellow, and most of the other colors in the spectrum, but it required only a few weeks of campaigning for all this splendid uniform to become weathered and faded. The Royal Dragoons, for example, had not received an issue of hats for three years, and their general appearance was described as follows:

"An old pair of yarn stockings with an old rusty spur at heel, an old pair of shag breeches; the hat was superlative, no old dustman in London ever wore so filthy or so dusty an apology for a hat, not a vestige of its former shape was to be seen. It was not considered safe to give out to the men

[2] William Tomkinson, *Diary of a Cavalry Officer*, London, 1895, p. 30.

all their new appointments at once. Staff officers in that case would not have known the old Royals again!" [3]

"The army when I joined it was withdrawn behind the lines of Torres Vedras," wrote Luard, "where it had been since the autumn of the previous year." During the long retreat from the Spanish frontier, the 4th Dragoons had been with the rear guard. They had admired the steadiness of the British and Portuguese infantry at Bussaco the previous September and had passed the winter on outpost duties, harrying the French foraging parties and cutting out the occasional straggler. All this had to be recounted by George to his admiring younger brother, as well as advice on the kit he would require at the front, how to make love to the black-eyed Portuguese girls, and how to avoid offending the extremely touchy religious susceptibilities of the locals—a matter on which Wellington held the strongest of views. As for the regiment, he must avoid falling foul of Lord Edward Somerset, commanding officer of the 4th Dragoons and a man who suffered fools badly, while both Majors Ainslie and Leighton could be crotchety at times. But he was lucky to be a 4th Dragoon; it was the best regiment in the army, and his troop commander, Captain James Hugonin, was the best soldier in the regiment. [4]

Portugal was an enemy-occupied country, and Lisbon was a city under siege. Wellington had withdrawn his heavily outnumbered army from the frontier during August of 1810, and had taken up a position behind the fortified lines of Torres Vedras in October; these lines had taken nearly a year to construct, and they stretched across the isthmus on which Lisbon stands, one end of the fortifications resting

[3] C. T. Atkinson, *History of the Royal Dragoons,* Glasgow, 1934, p. 267.
[4] The Hugonins had followed each other, father and son, in the 4th Dragoons since 1747; among them they totaled the remarkable figure of 132 years' service.

41

on the River Tagus and the other on the Atlantic coast. The country beyond had been devastated to such an extent that there was scarcely enough food for a battalion, let alone for the 70,000 men that Marshal André Masséna had been marching so triumphantly across Portugal in pursuit of the retreating British. Secure in the knowledge that his communications with England—and therefore his supplies— were assured by the Royal Navy, Wellington settled down behind his fortifications to wait patiently until starvation and the bitter Portuguese winter forced Masséna to retreat.

Although the admiral commanding the British fleet in the Tagus did not share Wellington's optimism, refusing to take up residence ashore for fear he should have to decamp and leave his possessions behind, the French were very nearly at the end of their tether by the time John Luard joined the 4th Dragoons in the outpost line. "March 3rd. Sunday. I joined my Troop at Alemqer quartered in a convent," he wrote. "The inside was totally gutted by the French, who had lately occupied it. I rode to see my brother George who was on picket. Dined with Captain Onslow." The next day's entry reads: "March 4th. Rode to a Quinta (country house), about five miles, to an inspection of the black remount horses I brought out. 21 of them were cast as unfit for service." Those which remained soon succumbed to the poor forage and unaccustomed climate.

John Luard had joined his regiment at the right moment. Throughout the past five months, the 4th Dragoons had been taking it in turn with the 3rd Dragoon Guards to watch Wellington's right flank, and their task, although important, had been dull and uninteresting, while for most of the time the weather had been unspeakable. Within a few hours of joining his troop, John rode forward with another subaltern, Charles Madden, to have his first sight of the enemy. "I could see with my naked eye," wrote Madden, "the different picquets of the enemy on the other side of the water, and could plainly trace all their breast works and encampments round the hill of Santarem. When my troop went to the river to water they could easily converse with the French dragoons watering on the other side, and could plainly see each picquet in front of us relieving their vedettes. I could see the soldiers in the windows of the town with my glass and those standing around fires in the town." [5]

Madden makes war sound a positively gentlemanly affair, but in reality the French were starving and growing rapidly demoralized. Luard was soon to discover that there was another side to war than just gazing at the enemy across a broad river, exchanging pleasantries, and admiring each other's horses. In the early hours of March 5, Masséna gave up his attempt to starve out the British, and under cover of the early-morning mist long columns of dispirited French soldiers began the weary trudge back into Spain. Over 70,000 of them had entered Portugal the previous October, but only 44,000 set out on the return march; the balance had died from hunger and exposure in front of Torres Vedras. As they withdrew the French exacted a terrible revenge from the Portuguese peasants who had scorched their fields on the orders of Wellington. Houses were leveled to the ground, bridges were destroyed, and at Alçabaca the French even removed the embalmed bodies of the kings and queens of Portugal which had been interred there. Like a swarm of locusts, devouring, devastating, and destroying, the French straggled back toward Spain through valleys drenched with rain and across mountain passes still deep in snow. They bayoneted men, women, and children, horrifying the British by their bestialities, and John Luard came across "two Portuguese scalped and yet living." Tomkinson

[5] *4th Hussar*, p. 94.

43

could not bring himself to repeat the cruelty done to a peasant girl who was picked up dying by Assistant-Surgeon Evans, and it was widely rumored that the French were even shooting their own sick. Yet, as always, atrocities provoked equally hideous reprisals. As the demoralized French soldiers plundered, raped, and killed, the desperate Portuguese villagers retaliated by torturing every straggler and wounded man who fell into their clutches. The advancing British found Frenchmen lying in pools of blood, their genital organs severed and stuffed into their mouths, and Luard records at least one instance of an enemy soldier being buried alive. No quarter was asked, or given, and the wake of the retreating French was strewn with horror.

At first Wellington followed cautiously, but on March 12, 1811, John Luard had his first brush with the enemy, outside the town of Pombal. The British had come up with Masséna's rear guard the night before, and the 95th (the Rifles) had headed the Light Division [6] in a dashing attack on the citadel.

"At daybreak the enemy had left their position," wrote Luard. "We marched, the Light Infantry in front who came up with the enemy and began skirmishing. At 12 o'clock our Brigade was halted to allow more infantry to go to the front. . . . We soon heard sharp musketry fire and artillery firing; at half-past one our Brigade moved on and formed on a hill near Redhina in front of the enemy's artillery. The 3rd Dragoon Guards on our right, 14th and 16th Light Dragoons in our front. A sharp fire of artillery was drawn upon us. We lost three horses, one next to me was killed, and a sergeant lost his leg. On showing ourselves on the advance the enemy's artillery withdrew, and we advanced to the

[6] The Light Division owed its origin to the Light Brigade trained by Sir John Moore at Shorncliffe in 1802; it rapidly became the *corps d'élite* of the Peninsular army.

44

summit of the hill. . . . At 5 the enemy retired leaving about 400 killed, wounded and made prisoners. Our loss was trifling."

This matter-of-fact account was written several years later, by which time Pombal was but one of many battles in which John Luard had taken part; it is doubtful if he regarded it quite so casually at the time. There is no occasion in a soldier's life that can ever compare with his first experience of actual battle. The swish of bullets, the thunder of the guns, the smoke that drifts across the front and obscures everything from view—all these combine to create a feeling of such all-embracing danger that it seems virtually impossible for any living being to survive. That battle will remain in his memory until the end of his days, as will the moment of horror when for the first time the soldier standing beside him fell to the ground in a welter of blood, torn flesh, and screaming pain.

Another 4th Dragoon has left a record of the fight outside Pombal, which gives an interesting picture of how the battlefield must have looked to those taking part in the battle.

"We moved on in slow time as our lines were at too great a distance to commence fire, except with artillery. We had only two horses killed and a sergeant's leg broke. A finer sight was scarce ever witnessed than the formation and motion of our Army on the plain; there was not a shrub or object to break the sight, and the whole could be seen at one view. The day was very clear, and the sight of the lines with the Colours of each regiment flying, was grand in the extreme. On the close approach of our first line, the French began to fall back, when an immense firing commenced which continued for about an hour; after which a sharp skirmishing continued until night, about 4 p.m. We marched to our camp ground; the night was fine. We took three officers and about one hundred men. The ground in many places was covered with dead bodies." [7]

It is hard to visualize such a battlefield scene today, when man has succeeded in putting a girdle around the earth through space and when most battles take place with the opposing armies so far apart that hand-to-hand combat has become a comparative rarity. But in Wellington's time, and for many years afterward, battles were fought within the space of only a few square miles. Men did hold their fire until they literally could see the whites of their enemies' eyes, and it was perfectly possible to watch the enemy artillerymen as they rammed home the shot, applied the match to the touchhole, and then stood clear as the shot came belching forth through the flame and smoke. It took well-disciplined troops to remain steady in such circumstances. Wellington, whenever he fought on ground of his own choosing, used to draw up his troops on the reverse slope behind a crest, his object being to conceal his position from the enemy and to expose his men as little as possible to the enemy fire. Then, as the long columns of French infantry came tramping forward, the drums and fifes beating the step and the colors fluttering in the breeze, the British infantry would double forward in one long line, halt on the crest, fire one or more controlled volleys at almost point-blank range, and then charge home with the bayonet as the French reeled under the shock. Why the latter persisted in marching forward in close column is hard to understand. It had been the traditional assault formation of the French armies ever since the Revolution, and it had the advantage of being easy to control when the soldiers were mainly conscripts. But when employed against soldiers as well trained

[7] *4th Hussar*, p. 96.

in their weapons as were the British infantry, it was virtually suicidal.

Brown Bess, the muzzle-loading musket with which Wellington's infantry were equipped, was smooth-bored; it had not changed in essentials since the time it was introduced into the British Army during the reign of Charles II. It could kill at a range of 500 yards, but was so inaccurate at that distance that a hit would be mere chance; for this reason the soldiers were trained to hold their fire until a hundred yards or less. Loading was complicated, and involved pouring powder down the muzzle, followed by the ball and a wad, and then ramming the contents home with a long ramrod. Powder was sprinkled into the firing pan, which was ignited by a flint, and this in turn fired the charge in the barrel. Well-trained troops might be able to accomplish this operation twice in a minute, but they would be forced to stop from time to time to clear the accumulated deposit of gunpowder from the interior of the barrel; flints had to be changed every thirty shots. The gunpowder was coarse, and this meant that barrels had to be washed clean at frequent intervals. The French musket required cleaning even more often than the British, and at Marengo, where water was unobtainable, the French were reduced to urinating down their musket barrels to remove the saltpeter deposit. A heavy rainstorm could render the musket useless, because the powder got damp and would not explode. The most that can be said for this weighty and inefficient weapon is that it discharged a bullet heavy enough to stop a charging rhinoceros dead in its tracks; a volley, delivered at short range, and by well-disciplined troops, could wreak as much damage as a machine gun, and inflict appalling wounds.

Ensign George Bell of the 34th Foot was very critical of Brown Bess, complaining that many a soldier lost his life while going through the lengthy process of reloading; however, he consoled himself with the thought that the French were no better off. It was only when it came to the bayonet that he felt really uplifted, "and when the word was delivered, 'Prepare to charge,' the very hills echoed back the mighty cheer of thousands with overwhelming terror, for the charge was irresistible." [8]

The same was true of the cavalry, of course. Every officer and trooper itched for the moment when he would be let loose on the enemy, to cut and thrust with the heavy cavalry swords. The lance had yet to be introduced into the British Army, although Napoleon's regiments of Polish lancers had already distinguished themselves in Spain (at Somosierra in 1808), and a cavalry charge depended as much on the sheer weight of galloping horses as it did on cold steel. Indeed, if the infantry stood firm and met the cavalry with regular volleys, they were unlikely to suffer much damage from them. Wellington was always complaining that his cavalry were far too dashing and nothing like steady enough. It was a common complaint throughout the Napoleonic Wars, and was commented upon by French General R. J. I. Exelmans after Waterloo. "Your horses are the finest in the world," he said, "and your men ride better than any Continental soldiers; with such material the English cavalry ought to have done more than has ever been accomplished by them on the field of battle. The great deficiency is in your officers . . . the British cavalry officer seems to be impressed by the conviction that he can dash or ride after everything; as if the art of war were precisely the same as that of fox-hunting." [9]

Shortly after the skirmish outside Pombal, John Luard took part in his first cavalry charge, that most exhilarating

[8] *Rough Notes,* p. 86.
[9] *Reminiscences & Recollections of Captain Gronow,* p. 79.

and exciting experience of all the experiences in a soldier's life. He wrote:

"March 25th. Marched at 8 o'clock. When within 2 miles of Campo Major we formed in columns of half squadrons and ordered to trot. Passed Campo Major leaving it a quarter mile to our right. Some skirmishing in our front. Continued to trot for a league, then formed line, the 3rd Dragoon Guards on our right, the 13th Light Dragoons and Portuguese cavalry on our left. Continued to advance at a swinging trot until the 3rd Dragoon Guards had outflanked the enemy on the right, when we halted in front of the enemy, about 500 yards from them, ready to charge. The 13th Dragoons charged on the left, went through and took some artillery and pushed on to Badajoz. We were not allowed to support the 13th Light Dragoons. Our artillery came up and opened fire on the enemy, but were stopped by Marshal Beresford who came on the ground. The enemy consisting of two cavalry and two infantry regiments were allowed to retire by the road to Badajoz when they might all have been made prisoners. . . . It was altogether a mismanaged affair by Beresford."

It is interesting to learn from this account that in cavalry encounters in the peninsula, the initial action took place at the trot, and that it was only in the actual charge that horses were spurred into the gallop. It is also of interest that the opposing forces should have closed to as little as 500 yards before the charge took place, but presumably this was essential if the ranks were not to be disorganized. William Carr Beresford, who comes in for criticism elsewhere in Luard's journal, being variously described as "choleric," "a bad judge of ground," and "unduly cautious when in face of the enemy," was nevertheless an extremely good trainer of men. It was Beresford whom Wellington appointed to pull the Portuguese Army together—his rank of

49

marshal was of Portuguese and not British origin—and he succeeded so well that by the end of the campaign there was little to choose between the battle-hardened Portuguese units and the British.

Meanwhile, the French withdrawal continued, Wellington pressing them relentlessly but unable to bring them to general action. "Each day we expected them to turn and fight," wrote Luard, "but all we encountered were their rearguards who made off as soon as we appeared over the horizon." By the end of May 1811, the last French soldier on Portuguese soil was either dead or a prisoner, and in England people awaited the news of an advance into Spain. But so long as the two frontier fortresses of Ciudad Rodrigo and Badajoz remained in French hands, Wellington dared not advance; if he did so, he would be in danger of exposing his communications with Lisbon to French counterattack. The frontier fortresses would have to be taken, and in the absence of an adequate siege train this promised to be a lengthy business and expensive in soldiers' lives. Nevertheless, the attempt had to be made, and the cavalry were employed during the long and hot summer of 1811 on their traditional task of watch and ward, while the commander in chief laboriously gathered together the artillery and engineers required to reduce the fortresses.

The work was hard, and the weather made it even harder. The sirocco blew as if from the gates of hell, parching throats, cracking lips and skin, and coating everything with dust. The only shelter from the sun was the horse blankets rigged up on branches to provide some form of shade, and when this could not be done, men lay panting in the shade of their horses' bellies. There was fever, too, in the low-lying valleys of the Tagus and Guadiana, and John Luard succumbed to an attack. However, the ubiquitous Aunt Susan had made her way through the mountains in the wake of the army, wheedling her way past the Provost Marshal and standing no truck from lesser mortals, and she took charge of the ailing Cornet. "A dose of salts, an emetic, and the kindness of Colonel Dalbiac and Aunt Susan" soon had him on his feet again, and he was back to the monotony of the patrol line.

By now he regarded himself as a hardened campaigner and was writing home for "some moleskin breeches for they are more likely to withstand the horrid climate of this abominable Portugal." The heavy jackboots and close-fitting breeches of the dragoons had long been thrown aside for trousers that strapped under the foot, while the sun had bleached his scarlet tunic until it was almost the color of his hair. This had been bleached white, and his complexion was so tanned that he wrote, "I look exactly like a Portuguese." Days in the saddle had made him wiry and supple, and he was a naturally good horseman, "although not so good alas, as my brother George." When he was not on outpost duties, he was coursing his greyhounds with his brother subalterns, poaching partridges and deer, courting the *señoritas,* wining, dining, and holding balls in improbable places like convents, for Wellington's was a high-spirited army, and the cavalry set the pace for gaiety. For weeks on end he slept out in all weathers, wrapped only in a cloak, shivering from cold or fever, and aching from long hours on foot or in the saddle. Tents were used during the later stages of the campaign, but for the first four years both officers and men were either lucky enough to find shelter in a peasant's flea-ridden cabin or they slept out under the stars. In later years many Peninsular veterans were martyrs to rheumatism, but not John Luard; he attributed his immunity to his invariable practice of changing his shirt and underwear at every opportunity, and by drinking sufficient mulled claret "to keep the circulation going."

The officers had to be tough, for the men they commanded were astonishingly so. One artilleryman had both legs and an arm amputated without any form of anesthetic and was found the following morning, propped up on the only elbow he had left, smoking his pipe. There is a similar story concerning a soldier in the 1st Royal Dragoons who, "while undergoing the amputation of an arm below the elbow, held the injured limb with the other hand without betraying the slightest emotion, save occasionally helping out his pain by spirting forth the proceeds of a large plug of tobacco, which he chewed most unmercifully while under the operation. Near to him was a Frenchman, bellowing lustily, while a surgeon was probing a ball near the shoulder. This seemed to annoy the Englishman more than anything else, and so much so, that as soon as his arm was amputated, he struck the Frenchman a smart blow across the breech with the severed limb, holding it at the hand-wrist, saying, 'Here, take that, and stuff it down your throat, and stop your damned bellowing!' " [10]

On May 25 there was a break in the tedium of outpost duties when the 3rd Dragoon Guards and 4th Dragoons came up with three French cavalry regiments which were advancing across a narrow bridge at Usagre. "My horse galloped so fast down the hill to the bridge that it was like riding a steeplechase," wrote Luard. "I cut down one enemy dragoon who was wearing a tall fur cap, the 4th and 26th being horse grenadiers, while the 20th wore brass casques. They did not stay long to cross swords with us." [11] It had all been very exciting, but the French defeat had been owing as much to their own folly as to the British charge. The leading French regiment, trying to withdraw from the bridge, had been ridden into by the French 26th Dragoons,

[10] *History of the Royal Dragoons.*
[11] The French regiments were the 4th, 20th, and 26th Dragoons.

52

hastening to their rescue, and most of the French casualties were caused by men falling from their horses and being trampled underfoot.

A month later, when returning from outpost duty at the Guadiana fords, John was hailed by his uncle with the news that he had just been gazetted a lieutenant, his father having purchased his promotion for £1,000. The news went a long way toward raising his morale, depressed by the dust and heat and a mild attack of fever, and a few days afterward he brought into camp two French deserters from the 27th Chasseurs who had given themselves up while he was sitting by the river bank sketching the fortifications opposite. They said that "many more would desert, being tired of the campaign, and badly provisioned," the truth being that the French disliked campaigning in Spain just as much as the British, both armies suffering from a breakdown in the commissariat.

Keeping the horses fit was a never-ending problem. The heat, dust, and flies affected their condition, and when winter arrived, the long nights of standing out in rain, cold, and sleet made matters worse. Forage was almost impossible to procure, and Wellington was compelled to import hay from England; at one stage horses were being fed on chopped gorse. All the black remounts brought from England by Luard soon succumbed, and Tomkinson says that the foraging detachments were forced to spend every minute of daylight searching for forage skillfully concealed by the Spanish and Portuguese peasants.

As 1811 drew to a close, the preparations for the assault on the frontier fortresses gathered momentum. Wellington surprised the French at Ciudad Rodrigo by moving his few heavy siege guns over the dreadful Portuguese roads in weather so atrocious that, in Luard's words, "one dragoon actually froze to death while sitting on his horse." Yet, despite the conditions, the guns were dragged all the way from Oporto by teams of oxen and mules, yoked together and urged on by soldiers who were forced to manhandle the guns up the passes. The opening bombardment came as a complete surprise to the garrison. On January 15, 1812, Luard wrote in his journal: "Rode over to see the siege of Ciudad Rodrigo. We were getting on well—opened a heavy battery last night. Our battering train was formed with 40 guns . . . they were brought up so discreetly that the French knew nothing about them and did not know we had breeching guns." Four nights later the town fell to the assault of the 3rd and Light Divisions, Luard riding into the town on January 20. "Examined the breeches and our batteries. A good town, handsome cathedral and good bridge. The town in a filthy state, the garrison consisting of 1400 men, marched out at 11 o'clock prisoners of war."

Badajoz followed suit on April 6, accompanied by the same scenes of rape, pillage, and murder that had been the disgraceful aftermath of the gallant storming of Ciudad Rodrigo, and Wellington could now turn his back on Portugal and advance into Spain. The 4th Dragoons were in the van of that advance, with John Luard "having wagers with my brother as to when we shall catch up with the enemy."

CHAPTER FOUR

The cavalry were first sent in pursuit of Marshal Nicolas Soult, who was withdrawing his army to Seville, his attempt to relieve Badajoz having been halfhearted and ineffectual. The weather was hot, the roads were ankle-deep in dust, and horses and men suffered agonies of thirst. All touch with the retreating French was lost, but Sir Stapleton Cotton, who was in command of the cavalry, learned that the town of Fuente del Maestre had been abandoned by the enemy. He rode into it without any escort and accompanied only by an orderly, whom he sent back to inform the subaltern commanding the forward picket that he might now enter the town with safety, always providing, of course, that he was "sufficiently rested!"

Once Soult was safely beyond the Sierra Morena and back among the palaces and orange groves of Seville, Wellington could afford to move against Marshal Auguste Marmont, whose army was concentrated north of Badajoz, in León. Co-operation between French marshals was usually a matter of expediency rather than choice, and neither Soult nor Marmont evinced much eagerness to assist each other. This made it easier for Wellington to deal with them one at a time, but Marmont was a capable soldier, with an army at least as strong as the British. Throughout the broiling days of May and June 1812, the British and French marched and countermarched across the rolling hills of León, Marmont striving to cut Wellington's communications with Lisbon, while Wellington waited for the right moment to attack.

That moment arrived outside Salamanca on July 22. For more than a week the cavalry of both sides had been on continuous outpost duty, screening their own infantry and reporting each other's movements, and John Luard records that "we always mounted before dawn and were in the saddle until long after dark." The two armies were marching parallel with each other, just out of musket range, but close enough to encourage artillery fire, and the spurts of dust marked the progress of the shot.

On the night of July 21 the two armies posted their sentries and slept by their arms. Parched, dusty, and saddlesore, the 4th Dragoons lay beside their horses, some with the reins in the crook of their arms, while others tied their mounts to farm carts or trees. "I tied my horse 'Bramble' to a threshing machine," wrote John Luard, "and lay down in my cloak a few feet away." Nearby, his uncle Charles Dalbiac had settled down with the intrepid Susan beside an artillery piece, with no other protection than his cavalry cloak to keep off the dew. "At 9 p.m. there was a colossal clap of thunder," wrote Luard, "and this was followed by torrential rain. The thunder panicked the horses and 'Bramble' galloped away with the threshing machine, with me in pursuit. Fortunately my horse stopped after a short distance and I was able to calm him." Susan Dalbiac had a miraculous escape from being ridden over by the stampeding animals; her husband just had time to seize her and roll with her under the protection of the wheels of the gun when more than a hundred terrified horses thundered past, neighing wildly and churning the ground into a quagmire. It must have shaken even Susan, although not enough to quench her ardor; she was in the saddle at dawn and riding off to the flank to get a good view of the battle.

Marmont spent the morning of the twenty-second trying to edge his way around the British and get astride their communications. Wellington waited patiently for his adversary to make a mistake. This occurred at midday. The French were marching in column of divisions, and some divisions inevitably marched faster than others; gradually a gap began to develop between the left wing and the center, and then the latter started to draw away from the left wing. Wellington was eating his lunch when he suddenly realized the French mistake. "By God!" he exclaimed, throwing away the chicken bone he was chewing. "They are extending their line—order my horses!" Then, after ordering the army to be deployed for battle, he galloped three miles to where the 3rd Division, whose commander was Edward Pakenham, Wellington's brother-in-law, was waiting. "Ned," said Wellington, "move on with the Third Division; take the heights to your front and drive everything before you." "I will, my lord," replied Pakenham, "if you will give me your hand." A brief handshake and Wellington was off, the colors were unfurled, and the 3rd Division advanced against the left wing of the French, commanded by General Thomières. The Battle of Salamanca had begun, and, as with most of Wellington's victories, it was fought on a Sunday, and after a night of driving rain.

The cavalry's main contribution to the victory was the charge of General John Gaspard Le Marchant's Heavy Brigade, and John Luard rode in it. It took place about 5:00 P.M. and was designed to relieve the 3rd Division, which had been fought to a standstill. The exhausted infantry had already smashed one French division when yet another loomed up out of the smoke. There was barely time for the British to form square to meet the attack before the French were on them. The battlefield was an inferno of smoke and flame, the dry grass having caught fire and added to the horrors of shot and shell. The cries of the wounded mingled with those of men who were being burned to death. Into this scene of utter confusion, Le Marchant hurled his regiments of heavy cavalry, crashing into the French ranks before they could realize what was happening. John Luard burst out of the smoke to find a team of French artillerymen trying to gallop their gun out of action. "I cut down their leader, turned the horses' heads towards our side, and then galloped on." Hacking and thrusting, the dragoons sabered the French infantry into a rout before they had time to form into square. The enemy division was hurled back in defeat, and the 3rd Division was given time to deploy. The charge had saved the division, but Le Marchant, one of the most promising officers in the army, was killed. Lord Edward Somerset, Luard's commanding officer, was lucky to survive; a shell splinter had carried away one of his stirrups and he fought his way through the enemy ranks with only one. Charles Dalbiac was also reported to have fallen, but this turned out later to be false.

Susan Dalbiac spent the whole night searching the battlefield among the dead and dying for her husband's body. Unfortunately, she lost the 4th Dragoon orderly who was accompanying her and had to carry on the search alone. It was a horrifying experience, not only on account of the dreadful wounds and burns of the men lying out under the stars, but also because of the camp followers and soldiers who had swarmed onto the battlefield to plunder the dead and wounded. "After the firing had ceased," wrote the historians of the Connaught Rangers, "ere you would say

Jack Robinson, all the dead bodies were stript, naked as they were born, by our own troops. They are so accustomed to these things that they think nothing of it whatever. I even saw them pulling the britches off a poor fellow before he was dead." [1]

Susan Dalbiac survived the ordeal and found her husband alive and well the next morning. She rode at his side throughout the triumphant advance to Madrid which followed after Salamanca, and went visiting the sights of the Spanish capital with her nephews George and John Luard as her escorts. John wrote of her later as "one of the wittiest, if not necessarily the most beautiful woman, that I have ever met," and she had the heart of a lioness. Many years afterward, her husband, by then a successful general, had this to say about her in a letter to a friend: "Whenever the Regiment took the field Mrs. Dalbiac accompanied me on horseback and such was the case on the day of the battle of Salamanca, up to the moment when the action commenced. She then remained near the extreme right of our position, whence the heavy brigade of the cavalry had moved for the attack, and she could distinctly discern most of the operations in that quarter, viz. the commencement of the attack by the 3rd Division on the Enemy's left, the movements of the enemy on that flank, the advance and charge of the heavy brigade, and the advance and attack of the right wing of the Allies. Here she had the fortitude to remain during the whole of the action, tho' so completely within cannon range that shots from the enemy's guns frequently raked up the dust near her horse's feet. Of this incomparable wife I will only add that with a mind of the most refined cast, and with a frame alas too delicate, she was, when in the field, a stranger to personal fear." [2]

[1] H. F. N. Jourdain and Edward Fraser, *History of the Connaught Rangers,* London, 1924, p. 200.
[2] *4th Hussar*, p. 123.

Most of the soldiers' wives were equally stouthearted, and Bridget Skiddy was one of them. She was married to a private in the 34th Foot, and carried her man, knapsack, musket, and all, when he could go no farther during a retreat—"an' me back was bruck intirely from that time to this, an' it'll never get straight till I go to the Holy Well in Ireland, and have Father McShane's blessin', and his hands laid over me!" [8] They were the unsung heroines of the Peninsular War, of the British armies in the West Indies, North America, and India, and the wives and mothers of brave soldiers. No story of the British Army, or of any regiment in that army, would be complete without some tribute being paid to the part these women played in encouraging their menfolk to fight—and on occasions doing some fighting themselves.

They were far from being glamour girls, or the vivandières of fiction. They were tough and hard-bitten, often the products of the brothels which sprang up outside every barracks, and no better and no worse than the men for whose needs they catered. Their language was a constant source of tribulation for the more delicately nurtured, their propensity for looting was a perpetual irritation for the Provost Marshal and his staff, and their capacity for involving themselves in the fighting infuriated the commander in chief. And yet Wellington knew that his army could not manage without these brave wenches, who succored the wounded, mended the clothes, cobbled the rapidly disintegrating boots, and who, rough though they may have been, still helped to hold their men fast to the elementary principles of home life and decency.

There were occasions when their courage was more in demand than at other times, and this usually occurred dur-

[8] *Rough Notes,* p. 133.

ing a withdrawal, when supplies ran short, discipline began to crack, and there was a continuous pressure to maintain the pace. Men fell by the wayside, exhausted by hard work on short rations, and their womenfolk fell out beside them; they can surely be forgiven if some of them sought to drown their sorrows in the wine that was stored by the barrel-load in every inn. Such scenes were common during Sir John Moore's retreat from Madrid to Corunna in 1808, and they were repeated again on a lesser scale during the autumn of 1812, when Wellington was compelled to fall back from Madrid to the Portuguese frontier. He had overreached himself, failed to take the fortress of Burgos, which controlled the road northward into France, and exhausted his troops. More cautious than Moore had been four years earlier, Wellington began his retreat before the French were collected in sufficient strength to bring him to battle, although they harried his withdrawal most successfully. The retreat ended at Ciudad Rodrigo on November 19, 1812, and not a moment too soon, for the army's morale had begun to crack and there were some disgraceful scenes of indiscipline. "The men subsisted by shooting pigs, discipline was lost, and men did (in the infantry) what they pleased, unreproved by their officers," wrote Tomkinson, with the lofty disapproval of a cavalry officer whose men were above such misbehavior! [4]

Wellington was so angered by the collapse of discipline that he addressed his commanding officers with some strong words on the subject, and ended by saying, "I am concerned to have to observe that the army under my command has fallen off in this respect in the late campaign to a greater degree than any army with which I have ever served, or of which I have ever read." [5] This caused a great deal of discontent, since, in John Luard's opinion, and in the opinion

[4] *Diary of a Cavalry Officer*, p. 224.
[5] *Ibid.*, p. 225.

of most of his brother officers, the root cause of the disaster lay in "the hopeless failure of the commissariat to deliver supplies during the retreat and in the staff to regulate the marches properly." Wellington's popularity dropped to zero.

John Luard fell ill with dysentery during the retreat. He jolted along at the rear of the 4th Dragoons, lying in a springless cart and soaked to the skin by the incessant rain. He was unable to keep down even liquid nourishment and was alternately freezing with cold or burning with fever. "I was left in a wayside inn outside Ciudad Rodrigo and would probably have died had not Aunt Susan sought me out and rescued me. She was already nursing Colonel Charles Dalbiac and looked after me as well." A few days later, when there were rumors that the French were advancing, all the sick and wounded were evacuated to Almeida. "The river flooded as we were crossing it and we were abandoned in mid-stream. Susan came to the rescue once more and got us safe across." One wonders how they would have got through the campaign without her.

Medical treatment was rudimentary in those days, and John Luard was very ill indeed. Only the devoted nursing of his aunt pulled him through, and it was well into the new year before he was fit for duty. Meanwhile, 1812, which had come in with such triumph, went out miserably. The army was tired and stale, the horses were worn out by the long marches and the bad forage, and there was a crying need for an overhaul of the commissariat system. Wellington had been wise when he decided to abandon Madrid and central Spain and fall back once more on Portugal, but it had not been an easy decision to take. The two years of victory that were to follow would be his reward.

The army that took the field in May 1813 bore little resemblance to the ragged and dispirited columns of the previous November. During the winter it had been completely re-equipped and trained, and morale had been improved by the measures taken to ensure that both officers and men were adequately housed. There had been balls, dances, and amateur theatricals. Wellington hunted his own pack of sixteen couples of foxhounds three times a week, and when hunting was over, there were plenty of black-eyed wenches willing to keep gay young subalterns warm in bed. Leave parties went to Lisbon and Oporto, and the very lucky ones managed to slip across the bay to England. Meanwhile, reinforcements were steadily arriving; the Portuguese Army was being drilled and drilled until it satisfied the exacting standards of its British instructors; and even the so-called "regulars" of the Spanish Army were beginning to march in step.

One hundred thousand men, less than half of them British, crossed into Spain in the early days of May, and as Wellington crossed the Agueda he took off his hat, turned in his saddle, and waved good-by to Portugal, saying as he did so, "Farewell Portugal! I shall never see you again!" He led his main army by way of Salamanca toward Burgos, but the left wing, under General Thomas Graham, marched through the bleak mountains of Trás-os-Montes, in northern Portugal, with the intention of debouching into León behind the French right flank. The French, drawn up to oppose Wellington, were taken by surprise, thrown off balance, and forced to withdraw to Valladolid, where they were followed up so rapidly that they had no time to summon reinforcements, and were pushed back across the Ebro. In the course of their withdrawal, the French, harassed by bands of Spanish guerrillas, whose courage grew with numbers, abandoned Madrid and, shortly afterward, Burgos. Indeed, they were so anxious to escape that they blew up the fortress of Burgos while there was still a garrison of 400 French soldiers within its walls.

The 4th Dragoons, together with the 5th Dragoon Guards

and 3rd Dragoons, under General William Ponsonby, led the left wing through Trás-os-Montes, but John Luard was not with his regiment. He had rejoined in February, before the advance began and while still unfit, but could not compete with the rigors of camp life. His colonel then sent him to command a cavalry depot and hospital at Leria, in Portugal, but the job soon palled. "I passed many weary weeks trying to persuade them to allow me to join the regiment but did not receive permission until July." For an officer who had previously been commanding a cavalry depot, he seems to have been ill-suited with horseflesh, since he had to abandon his horse on the way up to his regiment and bought another from a brother officer named Carleton for a hundred dollars—"to pay when convenient."

The question of payment is significant. Wellington's army was continually in arrears with pay, and so much so that very often officers were reduced to selling their pack animals for food, while the soldiers either stole what they wanted or traded their rations on the black market. Much of the indiscipline, looting, and thieving that occurred during withdrawals, or during rest periods in the rear areas, was attributable to this uncertain pay system. The cause stemmed partly from the need to pay the army in heavy silver coins, since nothing else was acceptable to the local peasantry, which in turn entailed serious manufacturing and transport problems; and partly from the traditional reluctance of the British Treasury to disgorge money, preferring to wait until the very last minute before doing so. Wellington was continually complaining about his shortness of cash, and it is a frequent complaint in every soldier's diary and journal of the campaign.

John Luard's illness prevented his being present at the Battle of Vitoria, fought on June 21, 1813, and one of Wellington's greatest victories. The retreating French Army was caught in the long valley of Vitoria, where the highroad from Madrid to Bayonne runs through the mountains, and only a brilliant stand by Honoré Reille's veteran division saved the French from complete encirclement. The enemy got away by the skin of their teeth but left behind all the booty they had ransacked from the cities and palaces of Spain. Over two million dollars in coin was taken, as well as pictures of priceless value, jewelry, rare books, handsome beds, cutlery, and even furniture. The baton of Marshal Jean Baptiste Jourdan was captured, as were the private papers of Napoleon's brother King Joseph of Spain. The share of Mr. Dallas, commissary of the 16th Light Dragoons, who joined in the loot of one wagon, was over £600. There were mules, parrots, and even monkeys, not to mention several handsome ladies, some more beautiful than good, and also the unfortunate Madame Gazan, wife of one of the French generals.

Perhaps the most famous of all the trophies taken at Vitoria was King Joseph's silver chamber pot. This useful but ornate piece of bedroom equipment was found in the King's traveling carriage by a 14th Light Dragoon, and after various vicissitudes the chamber pot came to rest in the Officers' Mess of that regiment (now the 14th / 20th King's Hussars). The regimental custom on band nights is to fill this considerable receptacle with champagne and pass it around the table, each one drinking as much as he can at one breath, until finally it has to be emptied by some unfortunate designated by the colonel to do so. It is a remarkably heady performance, and one that King Joseph could hardly have envisaged when first he commissioned its manufacture. The British Army, with its strange propensity for nicknames, soon thought one up for the 14th Light Dragoons. They have been known as the "Emperor's Chamber-Maids" ever since.

* * *

"I found it hard to console myself for missing this famous battle," wrote John Luard, who arrived in Vitoria a fortnight later, but at least brother George had done well for himself. He was given a captain's vacancy in the 18th Hussars by Wellington, who was annoyed with both the 15th and 18th Hussars for not pressing the retreating French more vigorously. The 15th got into a scrape when ordered to charge and lost a considerable number of men, while the 18th were caught plundering when they should have been moving forward. As a result, Wellington refused to fill from within the regiment the vacancies created by the death of two captains, and George Luard was given one of them instead.

When John Luard arrived at Vitoria on July 7 the town was still full of wounded French officers. "175 pieces of artillery were lined up beside the road as trophies of war and on the night of my arrival the Town Authorities gave a ball for the Allied officers. The next day I moved out with my regiment to Pamplona where our orders were to cover the investment of that town by the infantry." The capture of Pamplona had been entrusted by Wellington to the Spanish troops, but he thought it essential that the cavalry screen should be British. The Spaniards were haphazard and dilatory, and the siege was not pressed very hard. For this reason the 4th Dragoons spent the winter around Pamplona and San Sebastián and so missed the heavy fighting in the course of which Wellington forced the Pyrenees, crossed the Bidassoa, Nivelle, and Nive, and entered Bordeaux in February 1814. There was a good deal of grumbling among the officers at their being left out of the fighting, but Luard in his journal makes it clear why they did not take part.

"There was harder fighting in the hills, with almost all the Divisions, than at any battle during the war. Our loss was great. Soult was determined if possible to relieve Pamplona—his troops fought most gallantly, some of which were new Levies—but he was beaten at all points and driven back to France with tremendous loss in killed, wounded, losing many prisoners. The cavalry had little to do—the fighting was all in the hills."

There is a sketch by Luard illustrating the advance through the Pyrenees, with the cavalry waiting to ford a river and the infantry marching across the fields preparatory to scaling the heights. Away in the distance, and on top of one of the highest hills, are the tents of Wellington and his staff. Although the cavalry found little opportunity to prove their mettle during this period of mountain warfare, the streams were full of trout, and there was game in abundance. In early November the 4th Dragoons, now commanded by Charles Dalbiac, ably assisted by Aunt Susan, who must surely be the prototype of all "Colonels' Ladies," were billeted in several villages about six miles from Pamplona and enjoyed excellent partridge shooting. They also organized a race meeting in one of the valleys, and a racquets court was discovered in some nobleman's house. Stapleton Cotton himself came down from headquarters to join the subalterns in a game of racquets, and there was much gambling over the cards during the long winter evenings. There was plenty of fox-hunting, in which Wellington joined whenever he could find the time. And when the day's hunting was over there would be a good dinner in some country inn, followed by the drawing up of chairs before a roaring log fire, and the endless reminiscences of this battle and that, amid the comfortable haze of cigar smoke and the sipping of innumerable glasses of brandy and hot water. Not very intellectual entertainment, perhaps, but there are worse ways of passing the time when one is young, healthy, and still alive after five years of war.

John Luard found the army "much better disciplined than had been the case earlier." Apart from a momentary aberration after the storming of San Sebastián on August 31, when the appalling casualties sustained by the stormers were followed by an orgy of loot and murder, the British soldier behaved well during the advance through northern Spain into France. Luard found the Basques easier to understand than the garlic-impregnated peasants of León and Estremadura, and he was agreeably surprised to discover that the Spaniards were at last producing a reasonably well-trained army to fight at his side; only the Spanish officers were still lacking in determination and leadership.

It was the Spanish guerrillas that the British found so difficult to stomach, for their operations were conducted with a ferocity quite foreign to the nature of the easygoing British soldier. Wild, whiskered banditti, hung all over with knives, cutlasses, and even nail-studded clubs, they proliferated like flies as the French gradually lost control of the countryside. Their leaders called themselves "generals," to the disgust of conventional-minded young men like Luard, and they were not averse to cutting up the odd British straggler if they coveted his musket and ammunition. Like the Russian and Yugoslav Partisans and the French Resistance in World War II, they forced the enemy to tie down complete divisions to guard communications centers and keep the main roads tolerably safe. Sorniel, one of the guerrilla chiefs, was a convict in Valladolid jail until released by the French when they evacuated the city. He immediately formed a band of about 600 mounted peasants, whose only pay was plunder, and whose equipment and arms were captured from the French.

The guerrillas hamstrung the occupying French armies until in the end they did not know whom to trust. The French struck back with equal ferocity, hanging, shooting, and torturing, but they only fanned the flames. More and more peasants flocked to join the various bands. "The guerillas at this period," wrote Luard in January 1814, "were a very active body of irregulars. They were cruel, and great rascals, and thought a good deal more of themselves than their country. The figure underneath [a sketch in the journal] is a portrait of General Durang, who called himself general of the guerillas—a little corpulent fellow whose toes only touched the ground when he sat in a chair—how could such a man be of any use in guerilla warfare?" Yet for all Luard's scorn, Wellington's task would have been infinitely harder without the assistance he received from the guerrillas, and many a soldier had cause to owe his life to the fact that the guerrillas had found him wandering and lost in the mountains and had provided both food and a guide back to his own lines.

In March 1814 the 4th Dragoons left their pleasant quarters around Vitoria and Pamplona and moved up to join the rest of the army, now beyond the Adour and advancing through the pleasant wine-growing lands of the Garonne. "On 9 March," wrote Luard, "I rode across the Adour by the bridge of boats." The bridging of this river had been a considerable feat by Wellington's engineers, since there was a bar at the mouth of the Adour and for most of the time there was a strong sea running. Spanish country boats called *Chasse Maries* had been collected, tied together, and planked over. Most of the dragoons found it wiser, and certainly less hazardous, to dismount and lead their horses across the creaking and tossing bridge. The officers remained in their saddles. It was expected of them.

Spain was now far behind, and the news from Paris grew better every day. At the close of every war there are more rumors than reliable information, and wishful thinking reported first that Napoleon was dead, then that he had been sent to Russia in a cage, and, finally, that he had been shot in the Bastille. Actually, he was conducting one of the most brilliant of all his campaigns, refusing to accept the inevitable, and conjuring up to his assistance divisions and armies that had long ceased to exist except in his own imagination. On March 30, when the Russians and Prussians stormed the heights of Montmartre and Paris surrendered, Wellington was discovering that Soult, too, had still a lot of fight left in him.

On March 20 there was sharp fighting near Tarbes, after which the 4th Dragoons galloped for many miles in the hope of cutting off the French retreat. Contact was lost at nightfall, and throughout March 21 the dragoons probed forward in search of the enemy. As darkness fell, John Luard was sent out with a picket consisting of a sergeant and six men; he had been in the saddle since daybreak, but information was needed about a French division reputed to be encamped a few miles away.

"I took up a Frenchman from a cottage on the road side," he wrote, "and mounted him behind one of my men. He showed me a small house where he said there were some French soldiers. I halted my party, dismounted and quickly looked in thro' the window, where I saw several Cavalry men drinking. I placed one man at the gate, and with another, his carbine at the cock, I drew my sword, forced the door open and surprised them. They made no resistance. I took a Corporal and 4 men of the 16th Chasseurs, mounted them on their own horses, and trotted back to my picket with them. There were two or three escaped from the room during the row in making prisoners, so I was afraid a party would be sent after me from the camp not above a mile off. This party of Chasseurs were escorting arms. I upset two waggons in a ditch and left them."

The next day the 4th Dragoons moved forward again, the enemy to their front having vanished during the night. For the next twelve days they trotted slowly through the smiling countryside, waving to the women who came to the doors to stare at them, and chaffing the infantry as they passed them trudging through the dust, weighed down by their knapsacks and heavy muskets. They were a different regiment from the highly polished and brightly uniformed dragoons who had landed in Lisbon five years and over a thousand miles ago. The cocked hats had disappeared, and the helmets that had replaced them were worn and battered. The tight-fitting breeches and jackboots had long since been discarded, and in their stead trousers of every color and kind of cloth, patched and patched again, clad the lower limbs of the 4th, or Queen's Own, Regiment of Dragoons. Scarlet tunics were faded, and sabretaches were tarnished, but weapons were in good order, and so was the saddlery. Officers and men were tanned by the sun, and their eyes were wrinkled into slits from constant searching of the horizon. Their faces were like leather, their bodies as lean and tough as whipcord, and they sat their horses like centaurs. As for the horses, they were like their riders. The weak, the softhearted, and the vicious had long since been cast, and the carcasses of many of them marked the long trail from Torres Vedras, their bones picked clean by the vultures and bleaching in the Spanish sun. It was a hard, fit, and confident regiment which rode toward Toulouse as March ended and April began. The war was not yet over but the scent of victory was in the air.

The news of Napoleon's abdication had yet to reach Soult, and he fought doggedly on. Early in April he dug himself in around Toulouse, with a river between him and the advancing British, and waited for Wellington to shatter himself against the well-constructed defenses. The weather came

71

to his aid, and it rained for days on end, until the Garonne burst its banks and swept away the pontoon bridges so laboriously constructed by Wellington's engineers. At the time the bridges went, John Luard was across on the French side of the river with Beresford's corps of nearly 20,000 men. "Had the French attacked," he wrote, "there would have been no hope of reinforcement but they remained in their entrenchments." Soult had acquired a healthy respect for British musketry, perhaps too healthy, and he allowed the fleeting opportunity to pass. "The French sent large boats down the river in the hopes of destroying the pontoon bridge as the engineers were rebuilding it," but the attempts met with no success, and by April 8 the bridge was rebuilt and the remaining troops of the 4th Dragoons crossed over the river to the town side.

Toulouse was surrounded on three sides by water, but east of the town was the ridge of Mont Rave. Soult had heavily fortified this ridge, since it was the key to Toulouse, and Wellington would have to storm the 600-foot heights if he was to obtain possession of the town.

"10th April. Turned out at 4 a.m. formed in front of our village and then moved on in brigade on the high road to Toulouse," wrote John Luard. "The French occupied a strong position on the southward of Toulouse which Soult had strengthened by throwing up works of considerable strength. The battle of Toulouse began by the Spaniards, about 18,000, commencing the attack on our right when a heavy cannonade opened. The Spaniards went up the heights occupied by the French in gallant style under a tremendous fire of musketry. They gained a ravine from which they did not again advance, but turned and came down farther than they went up and were fearfully slaughtered."

This attack, so gallantly begun but which ended so dis-

72

astrously, was launched at 7:00 A.M. on Easter Day. Once again Wellington was fighting a battle on a Sunday and after a night of drenching rain. The Spanish regulars had begged to be given the honor of storming the ridge, but had rashly launched their attack without any form of support. There were only 9,000 of them—not 18,000, as stated by Luard—but they went up the hill with plenty of *élan,* only to be received on the crest with heavy fire. They broke, started to run, and did not stop running until they were safely out of range. Wellington watched them through his telescope, and then said briefly, "Well, I have seen some curious sights, but I never saw 10,000 men running a race before." [6]

During this attack and subsequent repulse, the 4th Dragoons were drawn up in the rear of the Spaniards, and they remained there for over three hours while the French artillery endeavored to get their range. Because the regiment was moved constantly from one place to another and kept, as far as possible, in broken ground, the casualties were reasonably light: two officers wounded, six men killed or wounded, and sixteen horses killed. The ground was so soft that the cannon balls embedded themselves in the mud, and John Luard regretted the absence of the usual excitement when the balls came bounding along the ground; apparently it was the custom to lay bets on whom the ball would strike or how far it would go before coming to rest.

It was not very exciting for the cavalry in a predominantly

[6] The Prince of Orange was an aide-de-camp at Wellington's headquarters throughout most of the Peninsular War, while General Miguel Alava filled an appointment best described in modern military terminology as Spanish liaison officer. At Waterloo, where both men were present and where the Belgian troops behaved badly, the Prince asked Alava what his Spaniards would have done had they been present. "Your Highness," replied Alava, "I do not think they would have run away, as your Belgians did, before the *first* shot was fired!"

infantry battle, but the 4th Dragoons had a grandstand view as the 6th Division swept into the attack about 3:00 P.M. With their pipes skirling and feather bonnets waving in the breeze, the 42nd (Black Watch) and 79th (Camerons) fought their way through the enemy's defenses. Their casualties were heavy, but the French were forced off the ridge and Toulouse was at Wellington's mercy. Until nightfall the two armies continued to bombard each other, but as it grew dark "the programme of the Easter Sunday was closed; the men lighted the camp-fires and sat around them cooking, and chatting over the ration dinner and *absent* comrades." [7]

Soult abandoned Toulouse on April 12 and laid down his arms two days later; Bayonne held out until April 26, and then, for a space, the guns stopped firing. "On April 13," wrote Luard, "we received intelligence from Paris that Bonaparte had abdicated the Throne, and the French generals and armies of the North had declared for Louis 18th. Lord Wellington appeared at the Toulouse Theatre with a white cockade in his hat, and all the officers of our army wore one. There was a statue of the Emperor Napoleon on the top of the Capitolium which was hurled to the ground in fragments and the white flag waved in its place. Louis 18th was proclaimed without a dissenting voice, for the French people were tired of war, and distressed by the expense of it; scarcely a family had not lost a son in battle."

The 4th Dragoons were quartered in the smiling Languedoc country until the end of May, and for Luard and his friends life was good indeed. There were balls, banquets, and as much horse racing as even a cavalry subaltern could wish. The army received its back pay, which had been continually in arrears throughout the campaign; £55 for six months

---

[7] *Rough Notes,* p. 168.

was the amount due to a cavalry subaltern, and there was a good deal of grumbling because even this miserable sum was subject to income tax. There was no trouble with the local inhabitants, who were delighted to be occupied by an army that actually paid for its provisions, which was more than the French Army had been accustomed to do, and there seems to have been little ill will between the British and their enemies of a few weeks before. The 4th Dragoons were quartered for several weeks at Revel alongside the French 2nd Hussars, one of the regiments they had handled roughly in 1811 in southern Spain, but they forbore to mention the previous encounter, contenting themselves with organizing a race meeting and relieving the French officers of their money by winning all the races.

"Thus ended the Peninsula War, proving the great military and political talents of the Marquis of Wellington[8] and the excellence and bravery of the British Troops. The Portuguese Troops were also very good and brigaded as they were with ours, always behaved well. The Spanish Army was thoroughly bad—the men individually brave but were commanded by bad officers, in whom they had no confidence, and scarcely ever behaved well. They were sent back to Spain and the Portuguese to Portugal. A portion of our infantry, the best soldiers, were sent to New Orleans, for the American War had not yet terminated."

This was John Luard's summing up of the war in which he had taken part in "15 Battles, cavalry affairs and sieges." His brother George had taken part in twenty-two. There followed a leisurely march through France to Boulogne, which the 4th Dragoons reached on July 12. The next day the regiment was inspected by General John Fane, whom John Luard was to meet again in India, and the General

---

[8] Wellington was not created a duke until after the Battle of Toulouse.

was accompanied by a French colonel. The Frenchman had been charged with the task of selecting 300 horses for Louis XVIII, and twenty-two of these were chosen from the 4th Dragoons. The price paid was £25 per horse, and it is interesting that noncommissioned officers' horses were not allowed to be selected. Presumably their horses were government property, whereas the officers' chargers were privately owned.

The 4th Dragoons landed at Dover on July 21, 1814. They had embarked for Portugal on April 16, 1809. It is often thought that the two world wars of this century were unusually long wars, but men like John Luard would dispute that belief, and with good reason. They could also have made the point that they received little or no welcome home, no free issue of civilian clothes, and no other benefit from their service overseas. No bells rang out from the steeples as Colonel Dalbiac led his regiment along the road from Dover to London; a few yokels came to the inn doors to stare, and small boys stood to attention and went through the motions of a salute. But the rest of the nation went about its business; war was bad for trade, soldiers were an expensive luxury, and the sooner things returned to normal, the better everyone would be pleased. A General Order or two to compliment the soldiers on their bravery; an engraved sword or a civic address for some distinguished general; and then as rapid a return as possible to the national pursuit of making money. And, since paying soldiers takes money, the army must be reduced in numbers as soon as possible.

For this reason the 4th Dragoons halted for a few weeks at Lichfield, en route to Liverpool and Dublin, reduced their strength by 200 men, and then moved on to their dreary task of keeping the intractable Irish in some sort of order. As a result of this reduction in the strength of his regiment, John Luard found himself placed on half pay, and he was faced with the prospect of having to support himself on the sum of four shillings a day. He was twenty-four and trained only to be a soldier or a sailor. Feeling more than a little resentful at the treatment he had received from his grateful country, he caught the stagecoach to Northampton and had a long discussion with his father as to what he should do next.

CHAPTER FIVE

On March 2, 1815, and after nearly eight months on half pay, John Luard was gazetted to a lieutenancy in the 16th, or The Queen's, Regiment of Light Dragoons. Although sad to sever his connection with the 4th Dragoons, he was lucky to be restored so soon to the active list. It had required all the Luard and Dalbiac influence to obtain him the vacancy, and his father was £2,000 the poorer as a result.

The 16th were a smart, standoffish, and expensive regiment, having been raised in 1759 as one of the first light cavalry regiments in the British Army, the intention then being to copy the Hussars of Hungary and produce cavalry regiments which united greater lightness, speed, and activity with strength and power. The Honorable John Burgoyne was the 16th's first colonel, and he set a stamp on the regiment which long outlasted his comparatively short period in command. History knows him best as "Gentleman Johnny," the man who surrendered to the Americans at Saratoga, but he was a better soldier than that disastrous episode would suggest. Wit, courtier, and gambler, he filled in the interval between campaigns by writing plays, novels, and poems, his activity with sword and pen only being equaled by his prowess in the boudoir.[1]

In the days when Burgoyne raised the 16th Light Dragoons an almost unbridgeable gap separated officers from men; it was as if they came from different worlds, which to all intent and purpose they did. Few officers even bothered to learn their soldiers' names. In this respect Burgoyne was years ahead of his time, for he issued instructions emphasizing the importance of cultivating a sense of comradeship between the leaders and the led, and he made it clear that this applied as much in barracks as it did in the field.

"To succeed where minds are to be wrought upon requires both discernment and labour; but for an encouragement to the effort it may be depended upon that mechanical valour will always be surpassed by national spirit and personal attachment where discipline is equal. Admitting, then, that English soldiers are to be treated as thinking beings, the reason will immediately appear of getting insight into the character of each particular man."[2]

This was daring stuff—even radical—in 1759, and the military hierarchy deplored the absurd notions of "Gentleman Johnny." Yet the result was a regiment with a sense of comradeship rare in any army during the eighteenth century and which struck John Luard most forcibly when he

[1] He conducted a lengthy liaison with Susan Caulfield, a well-known opera singer. One of their offspring was John Fox Burgoyne (1782-1871), who eventually rose to the rank of field marshal. He entered the Royal Engineers and acquired an international reputation as a military engineer, serving, among other places, in the Crimea, as Lord Raglan's engineer adviser, where he was variously described as "a shocking old dolt" and "a nincompoop." It is only fair to add, however, that he was regarded as a very able officer until senility set in. His statue stands in Waterloo Place in London.

[2] Colonel Henry Graham, *History of the 16th, The Queen's, Light Dragoons (Lancers)*, Devizes, 1912, p. 1.

joined the 16th Light Dragoons in 1815. It has remained a characteristic of the regiment ever since, although it can no longer be claimed that in this respect it is in any way unique.

The 16th Light Dragoons served throughout the Peninsular War, and in November 1814 Lieutenant-Colonel James Hay brought his regiment home from France to the suburban delights of Hounslow, on the outskirts of London. There he anticipated several years of comfortable peacetime soldiering, sufficiently close to the metropolis for his officers to play their proper part in high society and yet far enough out in the country for them to indulge in the other pursuits of the cavalry officer, which meant, of course, hunting, shooting, and fishing.

Unfortunately, all these hopes for a quiet life were dashed by the government's decision to pass the Corn Laws through Parliament. The country at large considered this to be a wholly unnecessary concession to the landowners, and the London mob signified its disapproval by coming out into the streets, pelting the Prime Minister's coach with mud, and breaking windows. The government, with the Gordon Riots still fresh in their memory, rushed troops into the capital, the 16th moving to the area of Westminster Bridge and being booed by the mob every yard of the way. Colonel Hay was a quiet and unobtrusive man, with no desire to involve more than a bare minimum of his officers in what were certain to be extremely unpleasant duties, and when John Luard reported on March 6, he told him to go away and complete his studies at the military college at Farnham, where Luard had enrolled at his own expense the previous November. This military college, the precursor of the Staff College at Camberley, owed its inception to General Le Marchant, who was killed leading the cavalry charge at Salamanca, but in the beginning it was only lukewarmly supported by the military authorities. Among Luard's fellow-students was William Napier, the historian of the Peninsular War.

On the evening of the day when Luard was presenting himself to his commanding officer, a mud-spattered courier clattered into the courtyard of Prince Metternich's palace in Vienna. He carried urgent dispatches from Genoa, and before the day was out, an astounded Congress of Vienna was hearing from Metternich of Napoleon's escape from Elba and that he had already landed in France. As soon as the news reached London all fears of industrial unrest paled before the greater menace, and the army was sent back to its barracks to prepare for war. The 16th marched cheerfully to Hounslow, preceded by their colonel in a cabriolet escorted by twelve light dragoons in blue and silver, while John Luard, "having provided myself with two horses and everything necessary for a campaign," hurried up from Farnham to join them.

Napoleon, had he been free to choose, would probably have preferred peace, but the Allies had suffered too much at his hands, and for too long, to trust him. On March 13 they outlawed Napoleon and bound themselves to fight him to the death, fortified in their resolve by a substantial British subsidy. Three armies were to march by converging routes on Paris—250,000 English and Prussians under Wellington, 344,000 Austrians under Prince Karl Philipp von Schwartzenburg, and 200,000 Russians under their czar, Alexander I. The Emperor had therefore no alternative but to rely on the arbitrament of the sword, and he decided to deal first with the English and Prussians before the slow-moving Austrians and Russians could be deployed along the Rhine. Everything would depend on the speed with which he could assemble and equip his armies, as against the time Wellington and General Gebhard von Blücher would require to

81

concentrate their armies in Belgium. It turned out in the end to be a very close race, or, as Wellington described it, "a damned nice thing—the nearest run thing you ever saw in your life. . . ." [3]

For the English had lost no time in dispersing their army after Napoleon's defeat in 1814.[4] After all their wars the welcome for their homecoming soldiers has seldom outlasted the first few hysterical weeks of victory celebrations, and in less than six months the magnificent army of Vitoria and the Pyrenees had been scattered to the four winds. A few regiments sailed direct from France to the American war, while others were hurried overseas to relieve the fever-ridden garrisons of the East and West Indies. The majority of Wellington's regiments, however, were either disbanded or else reduced to a cadre, their officers placed on half pay, and their soldiers thrown on the streets with neither job nor pension. They hung around the street corners, still in their shabby scarlet jackets, begging a few pennies to drown their sorrows in gin, for this was the period above all in England's history when the devil took the hindmost. Who could be bothered to employ a man who had left a leg behind him in the breech at Badajoz, or whose right arm had been ripped from his shoulder by a round shot at San Sebastián? Had not the poorhouses been created to deal with just such human debris?

Some time, therefore, would have to elapse before an English army could be assembled in Belgium, and, even so, the regiments marching through Kent and Sussex to embark for the Low Countries bore little resemblance to the veteran

[3] *The Creevey Papers,* edited by Sir Hubert Maxwell, London, 1904, New York, 1923, pp. 236-237.

[4] Napier concluded his epic history of the Peninsular War with the words: "Thus the war terminated, and with it all remembrance of the veterans' services."

battalions that had passed that way less than a year before. The drums beat just as bravely, and the fifes squealed out the same old tunes as they had done from Torres Vedras to Toulouse, but the gaps in the ranks had been filled with raw recruits, militiamen, and gin-sodden wrecks from the slums. "It will be admitted that the army is not a very good one," wrote Wellington to Lord Bathurst, and he went so far as to describe his army as an "infamously bad one."[5] Writing to another correspondent on May 20, he said, "I command a very small British army, with a very large British staff, to which my superiors are making additions every day."[6]

It was the comparison with his Peninsular army that worried the Duke; the men might be stouthearted enough, but were there enough of them? And had they sufficient training to take on "Boney"? Thomas Creevey, that incorrigible gossip and celebrity hunter, bumped into the Duke one morning in a Brussels park and proceeded to pump him about his chances of defeating the French.

"Let me ask you Duke, what you think you will make of it?" "By God! I think Blücher and myself can do the thing," replied the great man, blunt as ever. "Do you calculate upon any desertion in Buonaparte's army?" "Not upon a man, from the colonel to the private in a regiment—both inclusive. We may pick up a marshal or two perhaps; but not worth a damn." "Do you reckon upon any support from the French King's troops at Alost?" continued the persistent Creevey. "Oh! Don't mention such fellows! No: I think Blücher and I can do the business." Then, taking Creevey's arm, he pointed at a British soldier who had just entered the park and who was standing there in the sunshine gaping at the

[5] *Wellington at War, 1794-1815*, edited by Anthony Brett-James, London, 1961, p. 306.
[6] Muriel Wellesley, *The Man Wellington*, London, 1937, p. 346.

83

statues. "There!" said Wellington. "It all depends upon that article whether we do the business or not. Give me enough of it, and I am sure." [7]

The 16th Light Dragoons had suffered less than most regiments from the whole-scale reductions in the army, partly because of influence at Court, and partly on account of their proximity to London; the Horse Guards had kept them more or less up to strength for internal-security reasons. Nevertheless, they still had to accept their quota of recruits before they went to war, and there were many uncertain seats in the saddles on the morning of April 9, when Colonel Hay led his regiment out of Hounslow barracks and turned his horse's head toward the Channel and the fields of Belgium beyond.

John Luard, who had been posted to Captain Tomkinson's troop, sniffed the air like an old campaigner as he trotted along the miry Kentish lanes. Few came out to stare or cheer, but there were foaming flagons of ale and cider whenever they halted at an inn, and, of course, the endless reminiscences of Spain and Portugal to beguile the tedium of the march. The 16th embarked at Dover and Ramsgate on April 11 in small colliers, which had been so hastily assembled that there was no time to fit them to carry horses. Ten to twenty-five animals were loaded in each, standing loosely in the holds and at the mercy of any sort of sea. Fortunately, the crossing was calm and there were no casualties. The horses were slung overboard at Ostend and left to make their own way ashore. The few dragoons who could swim followed after them, landing naked on the beach, to the scandal of the locals.

Luard landed in more seemly fashion from a rowing boat with his troop commander, and as soon as the horses were

[7] *The Creevey Papers,* p. 228.

rounded up they made their way to a village six miles distant. There they were given a warm welcome by the inhabitants and provided with excellent accommodation, which even included beds. The contrast with the flea-infested villages of the peninsula was striking; ". . . we did not regret the change," comments Tomkinson, while Private Wheeler, of the 51st Light Infantry, was even more appreciative: "From this [Ostend] we proceeded in boats up the canal to Bruges, landed, went into good quarters, plenty of good grub, gin and tobacco, and as the Flemish man says 'all for nix.' " [8] If this was campaigning in the Low Countries, the British soldier could not have enough of it.

There was, in fact, a curious unreality about the first few weeks of the Waterloo campaign, not unlike the feeling in Britain and France during the "phony war" of the winter of 1939. It was almost as if people were unwilling to believe that war was possible, and that one morning they would wake to find that the whole thing had been a ghastly nightmare. "We passed our time visiting the old churches and museums," wrote Luard, "and there were many balls given in our honour." No doubt the dragoons enjoyed themselves, too, in their own fashion, their feet firmly under the tables of cafés and *estaminets* while they sipped away at their schnapps. As a more serious diversion, Colonel Hay took his officers around Marlborough's battlefield at Oudenarde and asked Luard some searching questions about the role of cavalry in that battle. "It was not a battle I knew anything about," wrote Luard, "and my answers were at best guesses. Since the colonel did not question them I can only conclude he knew little more about the battle than I did."

Tomkinson thought his soldiers better off than he could

[8] *The Letters of Private Wheeler*, p. 160.

ever remember, each man receiving a pound of bread and meat daily, a bed of clean straw at night, and a pint of gin for every six men. Apparently this unaccustomed good treatment was inclined to go to the men's heads.

"The men cannot stand the good treatment they receive from the persons on whom they are billeted," wrote Tomkinson, "and some instances of drunkenness have occurred. The old Peninsular men know their best chance of good treatment is by being civil (which at least they attempt at the first instance), and the inhabitants finding them not inclined to give trouble, generally repay them by something to drink, which, being spirits, sometimes overcomes them in a morning." [9]

Wives were soon coming out to join their husbands, but only a few arrived with the 16th; those who did laundered the regiment's shirts by day and drank their schnapps with the men at night. John Luard deplored a policy that permitted women to accompany their husbands onto the battlefield, forgetting the presence of Aunt Susan at Salamanca, and in after years he criticized Wellington for allowing wives to be present at Waterloo, where at least two of them were wounded trying to assist their injured husbands from the battle. It was, however, a situation that the authorities were bound to accept so long as soldiers were enlisted for what was virtually a life career.

During April and May there was hardly any news about happenings in France. "We heard very little information," wrote Tomkinson, "and the present distribution of the troops appears more like a distribution for winter quarters than for an approaching campaign. It is generally supposed we shall wait the arrival of the Russians and Austrians, and then commence a forward movement. The Prussians are

[9] *Diary of a Cavalry Officer*, p. 275.

closing up on our left, and will have their outposts in the neighbourhood of Charleroi, on the Meuse." [10]

Things were so quiet that Henry Tomkinson, holidaying with his brother, found the whole business rather tame. It was more like maneuvers than a war, and, as a civilian, he had come out to Belgium to see some excitement. All that had happened since his arrival on June 7 was a series of reviews, parades, and balls, the Duke of Wellington being indefatigable in his attendance at the latter, usually with the beautiful Lady Frances Webster on his arm. At last Captain Tomkinson yielded to his brother's persuasion and agreed to arrange a visit to the Prussians, who were at least exchanging the occasional shot with French outposts. John Luard would command the troop in his captain's absence.

This entailed for Luard sitting up very late on the night of June 15 studying the drill manual with his troop sergeant. Major-General Sir John Vandeleur [11] was to review his brigade of the 11th, 12th, and 16th Light Dragoons the following day, and he was something of a martinet. The 16th's commanding officer was an easygoing character who made little pretense of understanding the intricacies of the drill book, and it was perfectly possible that he would give the wrong orders under the stress of Vandeleur's bullying manner. If this happened, it would be every troop commander's duty to hold his men steady and ensure that they performed the correct movement, whatever command Colonel Hay gave, for the 16th had no intention of being ridiculed in front of the 11th and 12th Light Dragoons. Careful preparation was therefore required, while the candles flickered, and the wine glasses were filled, emptied, refilled,

[10] *Ibid.*, p. 277.
[11] General Sir John Ormsby Vandeleur (1763-1849), who commanded one of the cavalry brigades at Waterloo, was Colonel of the 16th from 1830 to 1849.

and emptied again. By the time he went to bed, Luard had a raging headache.

He did not have long to sleep it off; he was wakened at 5:00 A.M. and told that Colonel Hay wanted to see him immediately. Buckling on his sword, he ran out to the farmyard, where his horse was already saddled and waiting, and galloped off to Denderwinche, where regimental headquarters was established in the inn. On the way he passed the two Tomkinsons, riding hard in the direction from which he had just come; they had left for the Prussians an hour earlier, but in Enghien had fallen in with a Belgian dragoon carrying dispatches from the frontier. He told them that the French were on the move and the Prussians were advancing to meet them, whereupon they wheeled their horses and retraced their steps as fast as they could.

Hay confirmed the report when Luard arrived at his lodgings above the apothecary's shop in Denderwinche. Unfortunately, Captain Barra, the adjutant,[12] had chosen that critical moment to fall ill with lumbago. Luard was to take his place and must assemble the regiment at Denderwinche without delay. Then the Colonel went back to his bacon and eggs; he had long since learned the unwisdom of either hunting or fighting on an empty stomach.

The assembly of the regiment took some time, because it was billeted over a wide area and with no thought of the possibility of action. Indeed, several of the officers were on leave, sight-seeing in Antwerp or Ghent, while others had been attending the Duchess of Richmond's ball in Brussels and had not yet returned. The orderlies went spurring up the dusy farm tracks and along the tree-lined *pavés,* starting the larks into the sky as they thundered past with the adjutant's orders for the troop commanders.

[12] At that period the appointment of adjutant was usually filled by a soldier promoted from the ranks, as is the case with quartermasters today.

But the 16th were old campaigners, well used to sudden turnouts on the outpost line, and by 7:00 A.M. the streets of Denderwinche were choked with fidgeting horses, their riders mostly unshaven but with their accouterments complete, checking bits and girths, or enjoying a quiet smoke. What was it all about? No one had the slightest idea, but Cornet Beckwith, newly arrived from England and just sixteen, felt his heart thumping louder than usual; this must be *it,* and if it was, how would he behave when the bullets began whistling overhead?

In the inn Colonel Hay was discussing the situation with his senior officers. These included the six troop commanders, as well as Major George Murray, the second-in-command, Luard, as adjutant, and an improbably named veterinary surgeon, John Jons. Major John Belli was the senior troop commander, a morose, cantankerous man, who had fought throughout the peninsula; he was not popular, but a good man in action.

John Phillips Buchanan commanded Second Troop. He was a Scot, gay, lighthearted, and very much the dandy. The night before, he had been at the ball in Brussels and had ridden back like a madman lest his troop go to war without him. He never returned from Waterloo.

Richard Weyland, handsome and dashing, had been at the ball, too, but he had found time to change. His elegant cavalryman's figure set off perfectly the short blue jacket of the 16th, frogged with silver lace, and adorned with numerous silver ball buttons, while his drawl was the envy of every young subaltern in the regiment.

Tomkinson and King commanded the other two troops. Both were Peninsular veterans, but King was a nonentity, more like a jockey than an officer and little regarded by his colonel. He had risen by his own merits, rather than by purchase, having exchanged from the 11th Light Dragoons

89

some years previously. A man like Colonel Hay would hardly have counted this in his favor.

William Tomkinson was a different case altogether: ". . . one of the best soldiers I have ever met," wrote Luard. His heart was shared by the 16th Light Dragoons, which he had joined in April 1808, and the wide acres surrounding his lovely home near Tarporley, in Cheshire. Quiet and unassuming, yet a man of strong opinions, he was a superb horseman and a born soldier. His men would follow him anywhere, and he had never been seen to blink under fire, not even when a bullet passed uncomfortably close.

With so little information available, there was not much that Hay could tell his officers. There were, however, the usual points of detail to be checked, such as what was to be done with the regimental women, how was the baggage to be protected,[13] and should extra forage be carried in case the march turned out to be a long one? In the middle of the discussion a staff officer arrived with orders for the regiment to march to Enghien, where it would join with the rest of the brigade, and in less than fifteen minutes Hay's trumpeter sounded the order to "Mount!" Then the 16th went chinking out of Denderwinche, leaving poor Major Murray to grapple with the problem of wives and impedimenta, which has always been the lot of unfortunate seconds-in-command.

"The history of a battle," wrote Wellington to Mr. Croker, "is not unlike the history of a ball. Some individuals may recollect all the little events of which the great result is the battle won or lost; but no individual can recollect the order

[13] The baggage train of the 16th was subsequently attacked by Belgian and Brunswick cavalry fleeing from the battlefield. The batmen drew their swords and fought off their erstwhile allies, only Luard losing his kit through the ineptitude of his servant. The 16th were luckier than the 11th and 12th Light Dragoons, who had all their baggage plundered.

in which, or the exact moment at which, they occurred, which makes all the difference to their value or importance." [14] John Luard would certainly have agreed with his commander in chief, since so far as he was concerned the events of the next seventy-two hours were a curious blur, a compound of fatigue, fear, and discomfort, interspersed with moments of wild excitement, and endurable only by virtue of that comradeship which comes from dangers faced and conquered in common. He hardly ever knew exactly what was happening, nor did that seem to matter; all that was expected of him was to obey orders, set an example to his men, and use his common sense. In every war in history the ordinary regimental officer has never been expected to do otherwise.

The truth of the matter was that Wellington had been badly surprised. Neither he nor Blücher had believed that Napoleon could organize and equip an army as rapidly as he had done, and as late as June 13 Wellington was writing to Baron Lynedoch discounting any suggestion that hostilities were imminent. Then on June 15, when the French advance was reported, Wellington misjudged the Emperor's intentions, assuming that he would advance by way of Mons to turn the English flank and sever their communications with the sea. Like so many other British commanders operating on the Continent, Wellington's first concern was his communications with the Royal Navy, and he therefore strengthened his right flank by sending the 4th Division to watch the Mons approach. They never fired a shot throughout the battle.

On the other hand, Napoleon, with all the clarity of his genius, saw that his only hope lay in defeating either the British or the Prussians before they could combine against

[14] *Wellington at War*, p. 319.

him. In this plan he was unwittingly assisted by Blücher, who rushed forward to meet him as soon as the French crossed into Belgium, thereby widening the gap between his own army and Wellington's. Early on the morning of June 15 the news of the Prussian advance was reported to the Emperor, who almost wept with joy. It was the opportunity he had been praying for.

The axis of the French advance was the highway from Charleroi to Brussels, and Wellington was covering that approach to the south of Brussels; he was also watching the alternative routes through Mons and Nivelles. The Prussians were concentrated around Sombreffe and Ligny, more than twenty-five miles to the southeast, a dangerous gap between armies at a time when mobility was measured in terms of the marching capacity of men and horses. If communication between the English and Prussians was to be maintained, it would be essential to hold the crossroads at Quatre Bras, twenty miles south of Brussels on the highway to Charleroi.

Napoleon, better served by his spies than either Wellington or Blücher was by his, was fully alive to the importance of Quatre Bras, but when he crossed the frontier he was still undecided whether to attack the Prussians first or the English. When he learned of the Prussian advance to meet him, he at once decided to deal with Blücher before throwing his whole weight against Wellington, and Michel Ney was accordingly sent forward to seize Quatre Bras, while the rest of the French Army attacked the Prussians at Ligny. Once they had been defeated, General Emmanuel de Grouchy would pursue them to destruction, and Napoleon would join forces with Marshal Ney, bring Wellington to battle, and drive him in hopeless confusion through Brussels into the sea.

Quatre Bras is about twenty miles from Enghien, where

the 16th Light Dragoons spent several hours waiting about on the morning of June 15. There was still no information, and it was not until after midday that they moved on again, a solid mass of jostling, jingling horsemen, down the road that leads through Braine-le-Comte to Nivelles. Bump, bump, bump, they went, now walking, now trotting, without the slightest idea of what was happening or where they were going, grumbling as soldiers always do, pulling at their horses' heads, and easing their aching backsides in the saddles. "What's the bloody hurry?" they shouted, as some gilded aide-de-camp galloped past, aiguillettes flying, and throwing up the dust. "Is Boney after you, or are you hurrying home to mother?"

Laughing, joking, swearing, complaining, and singing unprintable songs, the 16th Light Dragoons jogged steadily on to battle.

At Nivelles, which they entered at 2:00 P.M., they met the first stragglers and wounded from Quatre Bras, who told them that the battle had been in progress for several hours. Now they could hear the booming of the guns, and the sound caused Hay to order his regiment to press on at the trot. Luard rode down the column to tell the dragoons to throw away the bundles of extra forage they had been carrying, for the horses must be brought to battle as fresh as could possibly be contrived. Then Hay, taking Luard with him and following after Vandeleur and his staff, went cantering on ahead of his regiment toward Quatre Bras. "It was just like hurrying to covert side to be there before the fox got away," wrote Luard later.

Napoleon smashed but did not annihilate the Prussians on June 16, two days after the anniversary of his great victory at Marengo; Blücher lived to fight another day—but only just. Ney was even less successful in his mission, failing to appreciate just how weakly Quatre Bras was held.

93

At the outset of the action, the Allies had only 4,500 men and six guns, under Prince Bernard of Saxe-Weimar, holding the crossroads, and Ney could deploy against him his Ist and IInd Corps and the cavalry division of General Charles Lefebvre-Desnouettes. But he took counsel of his fears and thereby threw away his opportunities. Meanwhile, Wellington, surprised but not rattled, rushed up troops as fast as he could lay his hands on them.

"A cabriolet, drawing at a smart pace, passed us," wrote Captain Mercer, hastening forward to Quatre Bras with his battery of horse artillery, "and in it was seated an officer of the Guards, coat open and snuff box in hand. I could not but admire the perfect nonchalance with which my man was thus hurrying forward to join in bloody combat—much, perhaps, in the same manner, though certainly not in the same costume, as he might drive to Epsom or Ascot Heath." [15]

Gallant, undoubtedly, but this was hardly the best way of proceeding to battle, and Wellington experienced some anxious moments until the opportune arrival of Sir Thomas Picton's 5th Division at 3:00 P.M. swayed the balance in his favor. Quatre Bras was held as much by the staunchness of the British infantry, and the unaccountable lethargy of Ney, as by anything Wellington had been able to do to compensate for his previous omissions.

The light was fading by the time the 16th reached Quatre Bras. There was little to see except the debris of the battlefield, the occasional flash of musket or cannon, and the winking fires of the outpost line. The air was acrid with the stink of gunpowder, and the ground was littered with steel breastplates cast aside by the French cuirassiers. Time and again they had hurled themselves against the rocklike in-

[15] John Naylor, *Waterloo,* London and New York, 1960, p. 73.

fantry squares of the 42nd, 79th, and 92nd Highlanders,[16] and on every occasion their gallantry had been in vain. "Of all troops to resist cavalry, where great steadiness, coolness, and obedience to orders is required, I should select the Scotch," wrote Tomkinson;[17] and now, in the gathering darkness, the kilted Highlanders were gathering up the cuirasses to use them as frying pans for the evening meal, while the pipers of the 92nd played a lament for their colonel, who had fallen that day.

John Luard slept that night in a cabbage patch a few miles north of Quatre Bras. Around him the weary light dragoons lay wrapped in their cloaks, worn out by their march of more than twenty miles, stiff and sore after twelve hours in the saddle. The horses, picketed in long lines, and by troops, were equally weary, scarcely able to summon up strength to nibble at the hay spread at their feet. Both men and horses were desperately thirsty after their long and dusty march, but there were no streams, and the few wells had long since been exhausted. Tomkinson tried to draw some water for his charger from a well, but was thrown aside by a crowd of drunken peasants; they, too, were raging with thirst, after plundering a nearby wine cellar.

There was still remarkably little information about what had been happening. Rumor had it that the Prussians had been defeated, and that Blücher had been unhorsed, ridden over by his own cavalry, and left for dead; in fact, he had been wounded, but had managed to regain his own lines. For the most part, however, the British cavalrymen contented themselves with abusing Lord Uxbridge, Wellington's cavalry commander, for his failure to bring them into action in time. They attributed his dilatoriness to his desire

---

[16] The modern titles of the three regiments are the Black Watch, the Queen's Own Highlanders, and the Gordon Highlanders.

[17] *Diary of a Cavalry Officer*, p. 280.

95

to distinguish his own regiment, the 7th Hussars, which he had not been able to accomplish because they had had the farthest distance to travel to reach the battlefield.

June 17 dawned dull and louring. Luard and Tomkinson rose stiffly from their bed among the cabbages, swallowed a crust of dry bread, and rode down the road toward the outposts. There was no sign of movement from the French opposite; only the smoke from their bivouac fires curled lazily up into the still air to show that they were busy preparing their *petit déjeuner*. The enemy had still made no move by ten o'clock, and Wellington himself rode around the outposts to see what was happening.

"Having satisfied himself that the enemy was still quiet," wrote Sir Hussey Vivian, "he then lay himself down on the ground, covered his head with one of the newspapers he had been reading, and appeared to fall asleep, and in this way remained for some time; when he again rose and mounted his horse and rode down to the field in front of Quatre Bras a little distance, and looked about through his glass, and I perfectly well remember his expressing astonishment at the perfect quiet of the enemy. . . ." [18]

All this time the main body of the British Army was withdrawing to a previously selected position at Waterloo, twelve miles north of Quatre Bras and covering Brussels. The infantry went off first, leaving the cavalry and horse artillery to cover the withdrawal, but Ney made no attempt to follow them. It was not until the early afternoon of June 17 that Napoleon learned of Ney's lack of enterprise, and the news infuriated him. "France has been ruined!" he said to J. B. Drouet d'Erlon when that General arrived on the scene with his corps. "Go, my dear General, place yourself at the head of the cavalry and press the English vigor-

[18] *Waterloo*, p. 94.

ously." Then, no longer content to leave the pursuit in the hands of his lieutenants, the Emperor, who had already been in the saddle since nine o'clock, placed himself at the head of d'Erlon's cavalry and personally led the chase after the retreating British.

He was five hours too late. Steadily, and without panic, the British cavalry withdrew in front of him. The horse artillery batteries fired, limbered up, galloped back to the next position, fired again, and went on repeating the process.[19] The French, urged on by the magnetic presence of the Emperor, pressed them very hard, and things would undoubtedly have become serious for Uxbridge's cavalry had rain not come to their rescue. At three o'clock there was a colossal clap of thunder, followed by a moment's silence, and then the heavens opened; down came the rain in an unending downpour, turning the ground into a bog, and quenching the fires of the French pursuit. "It became impossible for the French cavalry to press our columns in any force," wrote one of the English rear guard. "In fact, out of the road in the track of our own cavalry the ground was poached into a complete puddle."[20] The Emperor reined in his horse and stared glumly ahead through the driving rain; it was falling so fast that he could no longer see the British horsemen as they plodded slowly across the sodden fields, hunched over their steaming horses and cursing the elements. They little knew how lucky they had been.

Gradually the pursuit tailed off, and as night fell, the drenched, muddy, and saddlesore cavalry passed through the equally wet British infantry, where they were drawn up on the high ground to the south of the village of Waterloo.

[19] Wellington was particularly well served by his horse artillery, but for some unaccountable reason he never gave the gunners the credit that was their due.

[20] *Waterloo,* p. 99.

It had been the wettest day that most of them could ever remember.

Tomkinson lay down in a clover field, but, "with the horses moving about to get their backs to the rain, and the men walking to feed them and light fires, the clover soon disappeared, and the whole space occupied by the 16th became one complete puddle. I lay down in my cloak, and having been up at 2 a.m. on the morning of the 17th, and occupied throughout the whole of the day, I slept for two or three hours." [21]

The responsibilities of adjutant kept John Luard busy until well after midnight. The troop commanders had to be visited, their strength returns checked, and orders issued about rations and action for the following day. While on his rounds he fell in with a soldier emerging from a cottage with a grandfather clock on his back. It was a curious piece of loot, and Luard inquired what the dragoon intended to do with it. "If you come to our troop, you'll soon see what I will do with it," was the reply. "I'll make the beggar tick." Some time later Luard went back that way and was invited to warm himself in front of a blazing fire, the principal ingredient of which was the clock. When Tomkinson visited Waterloo forty years afterward, and recounted this story, a Belgian peasant forthwith demanded compensation, arguing that the clock had been a valuable family heirloom. He was not paid, of course.

At long last Luard lay down in his cloak, "but it only served to keep the upper part of my body dry. My breeches were soaked and the discomfort kept me awake most of the night, although I was extremely fatigued." For most of the time the rain fell fitfully, growing heavier toward dawn, and finally developing into a deluge. Then, as the gray sky

[21] *Diary of a Cavalry Officer,* p. 287.

slowly cleared, a watery sun came out, and Sunday, June 18, had begun. Unshaven, bedraggled, and covered with mud, the 16th Light Dragoons scrambled painfully to their feet and went off to feed their horses. It had been a hell of a night.

The Battle of Waterloo, according to the historians, started at 11:35 A.M., the time Jérôme Bonaparte's batteries opened the cannonade of the British line; but for the soldiers on both sides it began many hours earlier, when the bugles and trumpets sounded reveille and stirred the exhausted men into some semblance of consciousness. Fires were lit and an attempt made to dry clothing and accouterments. The 16th actually tried to groom some of the mud off their horses, but it was wasted effort. The animals were no sooner dry than the rain came down heavier than ever.

"At nine o'clock I went to Colonel Hay," wrote Luard, "and he ordered me to mount the Regiment, which I did. My horse was so cold and shivered so much that he could hardly stand for me to mount. The Regiment was placed on the left of the position, and we dismounted under a rising ground, waiting of orders." The French were clearly visible, as were their teams of horses struggling through the mud to position the guns, and the sight proved too much for a veteran dragoon named Price, the shoemaker in Tomkinson's troop. Jumping off his horse, the old man hurried away to the rear, no one trying to prevent him, and he did not rejoin his troop until the battle was over. It speaks much for the tolerance of his comrades that they bore him no malice, "knowing as they did the kind of man and his weakness." In most other armies he would have been shot out of hand.

Waterloo was fought within an astonishingly small area. The highway from Brussels to Charleroi passes through the village of Waterloo before climbing a gentle ridge, and

99

then descends again, past the farm of La Haye Sainte, into a valley less than a thousand yards wide. On the far side of the valley the road goes up past the Cabaret La Belle Alliance and through undulating country, by way of Ferme Rossomme, Genappe, Quatre Bras, and Gosselies, to Charleroi. On both sides of the highway the ground was broken by mounds, hillocks, and banks, mostly under wheat, although the crops had been beaten flat by the rain and the passage of the army the night before. The lanes and farm tracks intersecting the battlefield were lined with thick hedges, affording excellent cover for infantry. The heavy rain had made the ground soft everywhere and, in the valley bottom, boggy. From north to south the battlefield extended for less than four miles, and rather less in width. Napoleon's headquarters were established at Ferme Rossomme, about 3,000 yards as the crow flies from Wellington's at the crosstracks above La Haye Sainte. Within this restricted area there were deployed more than 400 pieces of artillery and over 140,000 men.

Until the smoke from the guns obscured visibility, the British were interested spectators of the long columns of French infantry deploying for battle, their drums rattling out the step and their bands playing *"Veillons au salut d'Empire."* Wellington's army was much less visible to the French, since only the outpost line was deployed along the crest of the ridge running at right angles to the Brussels road, not far from Mont St. Jean. The remainder of the army, in accordance with Wellington's tactics, were hidden on the reverse slope, waiting until he decided to bring them into the battle. As to any plan for fighting the battle, he had none. "Plans!" he said to Lord Uxbridge. "I have no plans. I shall be guided by circumstances."

The same was true of Napoleon. The Emperor foresaw no difficulty in blasting his way through Wellington's line.

The French battery of eighty guns, massed near La Belle Alliance, would mow a path through the English; the infantry would then advance in close columns and seize the crest of the ridge; and then the cavalry of the reserve, amounting to nearly 11,000 cuirassiers, lancers, dragoons, and chasseurs, would be launched to drive the enemy in headlong flight from the field. Napoleon had long since abandoned the rapier for the bludgeon. Although still incomparable when it was a matter of bringing troops to the battlefield, he had lost his former touch for maneuvering once he had them there. That was something he had grown accustomed to leaving to his marshals.

About eleven o'clock the 16th moved from their bivouac and took up a position to the east of the Brussels highway. The rising ground to their front was occupied by infantry, and very little happened for the first hour or so. The enemy artillery kept up a steady fire, but the ground was so sodden that most of the shells remained where they fell instead of bouncing along for a mile or more. The reverse slope gave protection; few men or horses were hit, and the dragoons sat about on the damp ground, their reins in their hands, and ready to mount in an instant, but in the meantime smoking their pipes and keeping up their spirits by laughing over the near-misses.

To the right, and slightly forward, a Belgian infantry regiment had formed square just below the crest; they were obviously finding the enemy fire unpleasant, and every now and then a man would break away for the rear, his progress through the cavalry being accompanied by jeers. Beyond the Belgians, the regimental colors of a British battalion could be seen waving amid the drifting smoke, and to right and left a battery of artillery was firing as fast as the gunners could load. The rest of Vandeleur's brigade were drawn up in column of squadrons to the rear of the 16th, also dismounted and waiting patiently for the order to mount. The noise was deafening, the smoke blinding, and Luard found the screams of wounded men and horses "distinctly unsettling." "The noise and confusion was indescribable," he wrote, "and over everything was the smoke, like a fog out of which figures kept appearing, only to disappear as the smoke billowed round them."

To begin with, the struggle was concentrated around the Château of Hougoumont, an outpost of Wellington's lines which, in French hands, would have provided them with an invaluable forming-up position. Every attack by Jérôme Bonaparte's gallant infantry was driven off by the Coldstream Guards with no less gallantry, and by one o'clock a stalemate had developed. Then news reached Napoleon that the Prussians, so far from being annihilated, were beginning to debouch on the battlefield. General Georges Mouton, Comte de Lobau, was dispatched with the VIth Corps and two cavalry divisions to fend off the Prussians while Napoleon redoubled his efforts to break through the British line, concentrating his attack against Hougoumont and La Haye Sainte.

"No man was ever better served by his soldiers," said Napoleon afterward of Waterloo. Unfortunately, they were launched to the attack in column, and this formation was a deathtrap when confronted by English musketry. As the French infantry toiled up to the crest of the ridge, sinking to their ankles in the soft ground, the thin English line rose to its feet and poured volley after controlled volley of fire into the tightly packed ranks of the enemy. The supporting French cavalry were swept away by their panicking infantry in a general *sauve qui peut,* and then there would be a lull while Ney collected together more infantry to repeat the futile maneuver.

On one of these occasions Uxbridge threw in Somerset's

and Ponsonby's cavalry brigades to follow up the French withdrawal. Down the ridge and into the valley thundered the British cavalry, cutting down every man in their way, and cleaving a path through the jaded French infantrymen like a knife through butter. Had they left it at that, all would have been well; but as was so often the case with the British cavalry during a charge, the excitement went to their heads. Men went tearing off in pursuit of individual French soldiers, and in an instant Ponsonby's cavalry brigade had disintegrated into 900 sabers, each following its own particular quarry. Heedless of trumpet calls summoning them to rally, the Royal Dragoons, Scots Greys, and Inniskilling Dragoons hacked and slashed their way through the enemy. And when, finally, their impetus was spent, Napoleon brought up fresh troops and hurled them against the weary and disorganized Union Brigade.[22]

One in three of Ponsonby's men had fallen by the time the French made their counterattack. As the exhausted horsemen struggled to make their way through the mud back to the safety of the crest, they were attacked by French lancers intent on revenge, and their annihilation seemed certain. At this critical moment Uxbridge galloped up to Vandeleur and ordered him to charge and save what remained of the Union Brigade.

The 16th had already been involved in an attempt to break up Durotte's division as it retired across the British front. They had only just returned from this abortive effort when the order to charge was received, and John Luard spurred his horse out to the front of the center squadron, a few paces behind Colonel Hay. Then they were off, sliding, slipping, and slithering down the slope into the smoke-filled valley below, the shrilling trumpet calls muffled by the

---

[22] The brigade contained an English, a Scottish, and an Irish regiment; hence the title of "Union Brigade."

booming of the guns. Luard felt his horse stumble to its knees, clutched frantically at the reins to pull it up again, and at the same moment saw Hay pitch out of his saddle and fall heavily to the ground. Swerving to avoid his colonel's body, Luard passed on into the confusion of his front, cut down a French lancer who loomed up suddenly out of the smoke, and then swung his horse around to avoid a bayonet thrust. Then the 16th were smashing their way through a regiment of French lancers, taken unawares by this sudden onslaught, and the battlefield dissolved into a series of individual combats, isolated by the smoke, the noise, and the state of general confusion. The French broke away, the officers of the 16th rode frantically among their men ordering them to rally, and by some good fortune they were obeyed. Vandeleur's brigade withdrew to their former position beyond the ridge, having saved the remnants of Ponsonby's brigade from destruction, and the battle continued. But in less than thirty minutes Wellington had lost a quarter of his entire force of cavalry, 2,500 of Somerset's and Ponsonby's brigades being left dead and dying on the field.

When they withdrew, the 16th brought in their wounded colonel. He had been shot from behind, almost certainly by a stray shot from one of his own infantry, and the wound seemed mortal; but Hay recovered, and lived to become a general. The 16th had suffered few other casualties. The speed of their charge, and their sudden appearance out of the smoke, had taken the enemy by surprise, and their withdrawal had not been followed up by the French.

The smoke was now so dense that men only knew what was happening to their immediate front—frequently not even that. At about four o'clock an excited aide-de-camp cantered past the regiment, where they were drawn up waiting for orders, "and told us that the Prussian army was arriving on our left." Almost simultaneously a bullet landed with a thud in the head of Luard's charger, and the poor creature toppled forward slowly before crumpling up beneath him. There was no time to unsaddle, for orders had been received for the 16th to move across to the west of the Brussels highway, and so Luard took a troop horse from one of the dragoons, ordering the man to go to the rear. "After the move," wrote Luard, "I saw my brother George, the 18th Hussars being close to us. While in this position I was talking to Lieutenant Philips of the 11th Light Dragoons when his head was shot off by a cannon shot. . . . The Belgians began to give way, the enemy's fire being too hot for them, and we closed our squadrons and would not let them go to the rear. Sir John Vandeleur and I moved to the front and encouraged them. The fire then slackened and they held their ground."

The Belgians were not suffering much from enemy fire, but the battle had been going on for a long time and they were heartily sick of the whole business; given half a chance they would have melted quietly away, leaving a nasty gap in Wellington's line. As Luard and his brigadier were chivvying the Belgians to keep their position, a horseman appeared out of the smoke and took in the situation at a glance. "That's right, that's right!" he called out. "Keep them up! Keep them up!" And placing two fingers to the peak of his cocked hat, the Duke of Wellington, "his face blackened with smoke but otherwise his appearance as neat as ever," cantered away rapidly to shore up some other sector of his battered line.

It was, in fact, the crucial moment of the entire battle. The Emperor had just handed over the Imperial Guard to Marshal Ney for the final assault, less than 600 yards from the English line.

"The battalions marched towards the enemy in review

order, drawn up in ranks 75 to 80 wide, their arms at the present, and the officers in front, swords drawn. Two eight pounders accompanied each battalion, firing as they advanced. By the side of the leading troops rode Ney, until his horse was shot under him for the fifth time that day; he disentangled himself and continued his march on foot." [23]

The Imperial Guard were supposedly, and certainly were in their own estimation, the finest troops in the world; veterans of Marengo, Austerlitz, and Wagram, their mere appearance had been sufficient to clinch the victory on almost every other battlefield. But just before the sun set on that balmy June evening, their reputation for invincibility was shattered forever, destroyed by the superlative fire discipline of the First Foot Guards and Sir John Moore's old regiment, the 52nd Light Infantry. The Guard stopped, reeled, and then recoiled, as the deadly volleys cut swathe after swathe through the ranks. *"La Garde recule!"* exclaimed the horrified French infantry as they saw their champions waver, and then come running back down the slope, bringing with them the contagion of panic and defeat. And as they ran, the man who had saved the day for England rode to the edge of the ridge, took off his hat, and then waved it in the air as a signal for a general advance. "The day was ours!" wrote John Luard many years later, recapturing that moment of relief and excitement as he watched his hero order his battered but triumphant army forward to the kill. Waterloo was won.

The 16th had been brought forward to the crest of the ridge just about the time that the Imperial Guard were thrown back. The slope below Luard was strewn with knapsacks, muskets, and anything else that might hamper the Frenchmen in their flight, and through the drifting smoke

[23] *Waterloo,* p. 168.

he could see the Guard in their tall bearskins running down into the valley bottom. It was a moment of triumph but there was no time to gloat over it. A trumpet shrilled the "Charge!," and Vandeleur's brigade poured down the slope, first at a trot, and then at a canter, swerving to avoid the bodies, smashed guns, upturned tumbrils, camp kettles, cuirasses, riderless horses, and all the other flotsam and jetsam of the battlefield.

At first there was no one to saber. The French were running away too fast. But as the 16th rode up the far slope out of the valley, they could see several formed bodies of the enemy to their front. It was oddly clear after the smoke behind them, and the countryside looked clean and untouched in the rays of the setting sun. Then they came up with the enemy rear guard and the battle started once more.

Vandeleur made no attempt to maneuver his brigade; he was beside himself with excitement. He ordered the 16th to charge the enemy without delay, shouting and waving his sword like a madman.

"The enemy's infantry behind the hedge gave us a volley, and being close to them, and the hedge nothing more than some scattered bushes without a ditch, we made a rush and went into their columns . . . they running away to the square for shelter. We immediately succeeded, many of the enemy immediately throwing down their arms and crowding together for safety. Many too ran away to the next rising ground. We were riding in all directions at parties attempting to make their escape, and in many instances had to cut down men who had taken up their arms after having in the first instance laid them down. . . . I had ridden after a man who took up his musket and fired at one of our men, and on his running to his comrades, my horse trod on them. (He had only one eye (Cyclops) and trod the heavier for not seeing them.) Lieutenant Beckwith, 16th, stood still and

107

attempted to catch this man on his sword; he missed him and nearly ran me through the body. I was following the man at a hand [sic] gallop." [24]

There, in the gathering darkness and amid the wild confusion of cut and thrust, the debonair Captain Buchanan was killed at the head of his troop. Lieutenant Hay fell in the pursuit, as well, as did half a dozen dragoons. It seemed to Luard as if there would never be an end to the killing, for wherever one looked there were the torn and twisted bodies of the dead, and whenever one listened there were the tortured cries of the dying.

Wellington called off the pursuit at about 10:00 P.M., and the Prussians took over the chase. The 16th bivouacked where they had stopped, each man picketing his horse and then collapsing wearily on the ground beside it. Both men and horses were too tired to eat, and there was no water.

Next morning a passing 18th Hussar told John Luard that his brother George was safe: ". . . it is a curious fact," commented Luard, "that throughout the Peninsula War, altho we were between us in every general action from Talavera to Toulouse, and in several cavalry affairs, we were neither of us wounded; at Waterloo we both had our horses shot."

The hand of God must have been on them, because at Waterloo the British lost 15,000 men killed or wounded, while the French casualties amounted to 25,000. "The 27th Regiment (Inniskillings)," recorded Kincaid, "were lying literally dead in square." [25] According to Mercer the ditches around Hougoumont were full of dead.

On June 19 Wellington wrote an account of his victory to the Honorable William Wellesley-Pole. "My dear William," he said. "You'll see an account of Desperate Battle

[24] *Diary of a Cavalry Officer*, p. 312.
[25] *Waterloo*, p. 181.

and victory over Boney! It was the most desperate business I ever was in; I never took so much trouble about any battle; and never was so near being beat. . . ." [26]

It had indeed been a most desperate business, and to the end of his long life John Luard always maintained that his proudest moment was when he charged with the 16th Light Dragoons at Waterloo.

[26] *Wellington at War*, p. 310.

CHAPTER SIX

The 16th Light Dragoons were not one of the lucky regiments selected to form part of the British Army of Occupation in France. After pursuing the retreating French from the Belgian frontier to Paris, where their regimental sergeant-major was wounded at the Pont de Neuilly in the last skirmish of the campaign, the 16th moved by leisurely marches down to Normandy. There they spent several delectable months, poaching the trout streams, coursing their greyhounds, and making themselves comfortable. John Luard, whose proficiency as an artist was steadily increasing, even took steps to enroll himself at an art school in Paris, but unfortunately the Horse Guards had other plans for the regiment. In December 1815 they were recalled from France for garrison duties in Ireland—an unpopular substitution—and they staged en route at Romford, in Essex, so that both officers and men could have some leave. During their stay at Romford the regiment was inspected by the Duke of York, commander in chief of the British Army, who was so pleased with what he saw that he selected the

16th Light Dragoons to be equipped with the lance, a weapon just coming into service in the British cavalry.[1]

It was not until February 1816 that the regiment embarked at Bristol for Dublin, and they could not have chosen a worse month to cross the Irish Sea. A stiff breeze was blowing as they loaded their horses into brigs, hastily converted to horse transports, and it had increased to a gale by the time they set sail. Most of the convoy was forced to put into Milford Haven for safety. The experience of Lieutenant Beauchamp provides an example of the problems which faced a cavalry officer at sea in those days.

"At 10 o'clock the following morning," wrote Luard, "a Brig on board of which was Lieutenant Beauchamp and 18 horses came in—this vessel sailed before I did, and in the gale which drove us into Milford Haven the bales which divided the horses gave way and they were all thrown together. The captain of the Brig said he could not be answerable for her safety unless the horses were destroyed. This was not easy to be done, they could not be shot, all the dragoons except Lieutenant Beauchamp and a Trumpeter were seasick, the sailors were afraid to go amongst the horses; so Beauchamp and the Trumpeter went below and cut all the horses' throats and they were thrown overboard."

It is a matter-of-fact account of what must have been a most grisly affair. The brig was pitching wildly in the gale,

[1] Although the lance was a weapon with as long a history as the sword, the British cavalry did not adopt it until after the Napoleonic Wars, and then largely as a result of their experiences at the hands of Napoleon's Polish lancers. The Poles and the Russian Cossacks had long used the lance, and when the British followed their example they also adopted the style of dress worn by the Polish lancers. The lance cap was modeled on the Polish and was called a *chapka,* the Polish for hat; while the short, double-breasted tunic was called a *ulunka,* and in the German and Austrian armies the lancer regiments were called *uhlans.* The British cavalry finally abandoned the lance after World War I.

the horses were terrified in the darkness of the hold as they struggled to keep their feet, and Beauchamp and his trumpeter were groping in the dark and up to their knees in water as they went about their gory business. A false step would have meant death beneath the flailing hoofs, and there were eighteen fear-maddened animals to be dispatched. There is an equally sad denouement to this story, for Beauchamp, "a most popular officer," cut his own throat not long afterward; not, apparently, from remorse, but shortly after marrying a Miss Ball—from which Luard leaves us to draw our own conclusions.

The 16th spent three years in Ireland, split up in small detachments all over the south, and their task was to keep the turbulent peasantry in some sort of order. It was a distasteful business, on the whole, but this did not prevent the officers from enjoying themselves. "Several of the officers fell in love," wrote Luard. "Lieut Harris and I felt very kindly towards a Miss Reynell—she afterwards married Lord Donoughmore—Colonel Pelly married Miss French —Major Persse married a Miss Moore—it was a very hospitable quarter and the officers of the 16th were paid a great attention." There was plenty of hunting and shooting for what was virtually an army of occupation in the eyes of the Irish, and the horrors of the Great Potato Famine were still in the future; and yet Luard found service in Ireland a poor exchange for the excitements of the Peninsula and Waterloo. "I was gratified therefore when I was selected to attend the Riding School at Buckingham Palace to receive instruction in the lance with which weapon my regiment was about to be equipped," he wrote, and in 1818 he crossed over the Irish Sea and reported to the Horse Guards in London.

His instructor was a Major Peters—"a presumptuous German. He had made himself master of the Lance Exercise and he instructed the men well, and taught a very good riding school drill. At last he bothered the authorities at the Horse Guards so much, wanting so many changes and making so many difficulties, that he was removed, and afterwards appointed to the Greys where he got into some scrape." Soon afterward the title of Luard's regiment was changed, and it became known for some years as the 16th, The Queen's, Light Dragoons (Lancers), which became shortened to the 16th, The Queen's, Lancers. The soldiers, however, continued to be referred to as dragoons until well on into the reign of Queen Victoria.

The fact that Luard had been the officer selected to attend lance instruction shows that he was highly regarded in his regiment as a serious and competent soldier. He was now twenty-eight, a veteran of over nine years' service, an excellent horseman, and an officer who took a keen interest in his profession. His main interest outside the army lay in sketching, at that time a most useful military accomplishment as well, and although he was as steeped in snobbery as most of the cavalry officers of his generation, it is clear that he had no use for those who regarded service in the cavalry as merely a good way of enjoying life. "We regarded our duties seriously," he wrote, "and the 16th enjoyed a high reputation in Ireland."

It must be admitted, however, that many officers did little to raise the army's standing in the eyes of their countrymen. As so often in peacetime, it was the behavior of the lunatic fringe of the community that most attracted attention, and the British Army between 1815 and the Crimean War had more than its fair share of irresponsible extroverts, such as the Earl of Cardigan. Most of the officers were hard-working, keen on their profession, and anxious to improve the efficiency of their regiments, but the machine was against them. At the Horse Guards a succession of commanders in chief, not excluding Wellington himself, set their faces against change, and persisted in the belief that only gentle-men, and by this they meant the aristocracy and landown-ing class, were fit to command men in war; and this despite the oft-reiterated view of the Duke of Wellington that the only way to produce any effect on the British soldier was by the threat of "immediate corporal punishment."

The iniquitous system of buying promotion might have had some use during a war, insofar as it enabled bright young men to purchase their way rapidly up the military ladder, but during a time of prolonged peace it meant that the hard-working but impecunious professional was con-stantly being passed over by the wealthy but unenthusiastic amateur. Henry Havelock,[2] who rose to fame during the Indian Mutiny, and who was a professional soldier if ever there was one, had to wait until he was forty-three before he got his captaincy, "without purchase," and he was sixty-two before he reached the rank of brigadier-general. John Luard was more fortunate. He was gazetted to his troop, *i.e.,* captaincy, on December 22, 1821, at the age of thirty-one.

"I was gazetted to a Troop purchased of Capt. Nixon. I paid considerably beyond the Regulations for it. My father not being able to give me the money, I wrote to Mrs Broadley (who lived at Blyboro on the estate which at her death came to my father), and she very kindly lent me the money, and at her death condoned the debt."

John Luard was still not regretting his decision to leave the navy for the army, although it is probably true to say that the army's popularity reached its nadir during the sixty years following Waterloo. It was virtually relegated to oblivion, save when it was held up to ridicule in Parliament or the press as a collection of ne'er-do-wells and unemploy-

---

[2] Havelock's youngest brother served in the 16th, constantly in debt, and a continual worry to his family.

ables, officered by arrogant and brainless aristocrats. Occasionally some administrative scandal, or the outrageous behavior of someone like Lord Cardigan, would arouse criticism, but for most of the time the army was left to muddle along as best it could, its high command fossilized in the conviction that what had been good enough when they were subalterns remained equally good now they were generals.[3]

The 16th Lancers managed to avoid the scandals and the extravagances. They had their eccentrics, such as Major Persse, a hot-tempered Irishman who was nicknamed "Ninny," and Captain Rowland Smyth. Smyth transferred to the cavalry from the infantry after fighting a duel in Dublin which landed him in jail for twelve months. This did not materially affect his career; he rose subsequently to the rank of major-general and became colonel of his regiment. John Luard thought him "the best horseman I have ever met, and a gentleman of exquisite politeness." He also mentions a Colonel Elphinstone, who exchanged for a short time into the 16th Lancers from the 33rd Foot and who was apparently "a very elegant and courteous gentleman." He was to alter his opinion sixteen years later when he met Elphinstone in less auspicious circumstances.

One result of Luard's service in the navy was to arouse in him "a detestation of flogging as a means of maintaining discipline." He had doubtless had to witness many occasions of flogging during his time in the peninsula, but he was agreeably surprised to find that flogging was rare in the 16th Lancers. This was probably owing to the influence of the adjutant, Charles Cureton, who shared Luard's dislike of

[3] The army reached its lowest pitch in 1841, when its strength was less than 95,000. Administration was hopelessly inefficient, training was virtually abandoned, and officers and men were retained in service until they were virtually senile.

115

the "cat-o'-nine-tails," and who only resorted to it in extreme cases. Cureton had begun his career in a militia regiment, where he fell heavily into debt; his clothing was found one morning wrapped up in a bundle on the beach, and it was presumed that he had drowned himself to escape his creditors. In fact, he had sailed for London, where he enlisted in the ranks of the 14th Light Dragoons, serving with that regiment throughout the Peninsular War with great gallantry and being commissioned in the field. He transferred to the 16th under his own name in 1819, became the adjutant, and eventually rose to the rank of brigadier-general before he was killed at Ramnagar during the Sikh Wars in 1848. Luard mentions him on several occasions and always with admiration and respect.

John Luard was not unique in his dislike for flogging, but was almost certainly in a minority among the officers of his time. He was also in a minority among cavalry officers in wanting to serve in India, since the British Army was sharply divided between those who believed that only home service mattered and those who considered that India was the only place where a military reputation could be won. This was an attitude by no means confined to the post-Waterloo period. One of Wellington's greatest difficulties when he took command in Portugal was that he had made his reputation fighting against the Marathas in southern India. The pipe-clayed old fogies at the Horse Guards referred to him as an "Indian," while Napoleon dismissed him contemptuously as a "Sepoy General." Much the same views prevailed in the British Army right up to the outbreak of war in 1939, the old Indian Army usually attracting officers who found serving in Britain unexciting and expensive, while officers in British regiments had a tendency to regard their fellow-countrymen in Indian regiments as out-of-date and "blimpish."

116

Lithograph

John Luard as a Young Man

Cavilhão, Portugal, 1812

Water Color

Salamanca, 1812

Pencil Drawing

Water Color

Luard's Bungalow, Cawnpore, 1823

Water Color

Mr. Oldfield's House, 9 Russell Street, Chowringree, Calcutta, 1840

Lithograph from Sketches of India

A Budgerow

Pen and Ink

Inside Luard's Budgerow, Ganges, April 20, 1823

Lithograph from Sketches of India

Skirmish of the 16th Lancers, Bhurtpore, 1826

Lithograph from Sketches of India
Assault on the Northeast Bastion, Bhurtpore, 1826

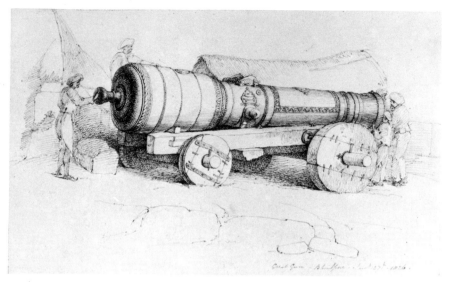

Great Gun, Bhurtpore, 1826   *Pen and Ink*

Gun at Bhurtpore   *Lithograph from* Sketches of India

Pen and Ink

Bhurtpore Rajah's Cheetah

Pencil Drawing

Head of an Albatross

Lithograph from Sketches of India

The *Marchioness of Ely* and the *General Hewitt*

Lithograph from Sketches of India

The Room in which Napoleon Died

Pencil Drawing

Dost Mohammed (on the left) and the Gates of Somnath

Copy of a Sketch by Lieutenant Becher

The Bala Hissar, Kabul

Copy of a Sketch by Captain Seaton

Lahore Gate of the Bala Hissar, Kabul

Copy of a Sketch Possibly by Lieutenant Becher

Khoord Kabul Pass

Water Color

Durbar at Ferozepore, 1842. The Governor-General, Lord Ellenborough, is in the center, with the young Sikh Maharajah, Mr. Maddock, Dhean Singh, and other Sikhs of rank on his right. On his left are Mr. Robertson, Lieutenant-Governor of the North-West Provinces; the Commander-in-Chief, Sir Jasper Nicolls; and Mr. G. Clark conversing with two Sikhs. Behind them are Captain Somerset and Lieutenant Crawley. The Vizier Noor-ood-din is in the chair in the foreground with an armed Sikh behind him.

Photograph

John Luard in Old Age

The British took surprisingly little interest in their overseas possessions during the years that followed after Waterloo. Between 1815 and 1850 there were ten campaigns in India alone, not to mention wars in Burma, China, and South Africa, but these were minor wars which hardly impinged on the everyday life of the nation, the fighting taking place thousands of miles away and at a time when letters and dispatches took six months or more to arrive from the theater of operations. If, however, there was an exception to this lack of interest, it was probably India, that vast and lovely land which had drifted into British possession almost by accident, and despite their better judgment; India, which claimed the lives of successive generations of Englishmen, some of whom counted every day spent there as lost, loathing the climate, despising the Indians, and hating their work. Others loved India so much that they fought for her interests even when those interests clashed with the policy of the home government, and willingly gave their sons, and their sons' sons, to follow after them in the service of the Indian people. "All my life I have wanted to serve in India," wrote John Luard in 1820; he would not have long to wait.

The 16th Lancers were in trouble at Court. Ever since George III had conferred on the regiment the title of "The Queen's," in honor of his consort, Queen Charlotte, the regiment had prided itself on its special loyalty to the Queen of England. That had been well enough during the old King's reign, but when his son came to the throne, the country was treated to the unedifying spectacle of the new King doing his best to avoid having his vulgar and flighty consort present at his coronation. The country was split between those who supported the King, and they were in a minority, and those who supported the Queen, not so much because they approved of her as because they so heartily

117

disapproved of her husband. The officers of the 16th made no secret of their sympathies; so much so that they invited the gentry of the West Riding to dine with them at Sheffield, where they were stationed in 1821, and loudly, and with perhaps unnecessary frequency, toasted the "Queen" in preference to the usual loyal toast. As might be expected, reports of this soon reached the ears of George IV, and in January 1822 orders were received for the regiment to proceed to India. "We are off to Hindoostan," wrote John Luard. "What shall we find when we get there?"

Not every 16th Lancer regarded the prospect of service in India with the same enthusiasm as John Luard. It was welcomed by the ambitious, the adventurous, and the impecunious, since it meant increased opportunities for active service, and hence promotion, while pay went further in India than it did at home. Moreover, the Europeans in India, no matter how lowly their social status, were members of the ruling class and, as such, were regarded with respect, although not necessarily with affection, by the natives of the country.

On the other hand it meant long years of exile in a climate that killed far more swiftly and surely than any bullet. None of the soldiers, and among the officers only those who could afford to pay their own passages, could look forward to a return to England until the regiment was transferred to the home establishment, nor could the man in the ranks expect many creature comforts.

"Life for the ordinary soldier in barracks was very dismal; there were no canteens or reading or recreation rooms; the quarters themselves were squalid and at night lit only by a feeble wick floating in a vessel of coconut oil. Punkahs did not come into use for soldiers until after the [Indian] Mutiny; naturally, under such circumstances, the soldiers sought the bazaars for the lowest of female companionship, always venial, and drowned their wits and sorrows in alcoholic brews of the strongest and deadliest variety. We have heard survivors of the period discourse eloquently of the respective merits of Daroo, toddy, shamsu [in China], and Cape Smoke at the Cape, the best of which could be said that like Hogarth's famous gin alley, one could get drunk on them for four annas, and delirium tremens for a rupee. The only game was cricket, which however could only be played on winter days, a game called handball in the great courts still to be seen in old cantonments, and a curious one called hurling much in favour with the Irish troops, a game which consisted of bowling an iron or stone ball along the roads, he who attained the goal in the least number of 'hurls' being the winner." [4]

It is hardly to be wondered at that many of the officers, and not a few among the soldiers, regarded such a prospect with foreboding. It was easy enough for the officer who wanted to avoid service in India—he had merely to seek out a brother officer whose thirst for military glory or whose imminent bankruptcy made a change of scene imperative, and an exchange between regiments could be easily arranged. Not so for the soldier, however, who was enlisted into the army for an unlimited period and whose regiment was his home. It was rare for the authorities to permit interregimental transfers, and, in any case, commanding officers were usually reluctant to recommend such applications. They preferred to keep "the devil they knew," rather than exchange him for someone else who might well turn out to be even worse. There were, moreover, distinct advantages to be obtained from service in India: service in that country counted one and a half times toward pension, and few soldiers could afford to ignore this at a time when pensions

[4] C. Grey, *European Adventurers of Northern India, 1785-1849*, edited by H. L. O. Garrett, Lahore, 1929, p. 217.

were so wretchedly meager and hedged around with all sorts of impossible conditions. Besides, it was questionable whether the private soldier was any worse off in India than he was at home, where he was regarded as a social misfit and outcast, incarcerated in barracks that were little better than jails, and employed on such distasteful tasks as coercing the Irish peasantry and the downtrodden factory-hands of the Midlands and the North.

There were very few desertions when the 16th moved to Romford to prepare for their move to India, but several officers resigned their commissions, and they included Captain Tomkinson. Others transferred to cavalry regiments on the home establishment, and no one seems to have regarded this as in any way unusual or reprehensible. In the past fifty years a convention has grown up in the British Army that an officer should remain in the same regiment for the majority of his service, although recent changes in the regimental system have made this less, rather than more, likely in the future. However, this certainly did not apply one hundred years ago, when most officers served in two or more regiments during the course of their military service and switched their allegiance with surprising ease.

Regiments on the Indian establishment were nearly twice as strong as those serving at home, and it was therefore necessary to draft men from other cavalry regiments to bring the 16th Lancers up to the permitted strength of 701 officers and men.[5] The sick, the senile, and the worst of the "soaks" were left behind, so far as the commanding officer could contrive to rid the regiment of the latter category, and the horses were handed over to other regiments. It was un-

[5] Only one officer of the 16th Lancers who sailed with it from Gravesend in 1822 was still serving with it when it returned from India twenty-four years later. He was George Macdowell, who went out as a junior captain and returned as a lieutenant-colonel and commanding officer.

usual for a cavalry regiment to take its horses with it when proceeding overseas, unless it was going on a campaign, and the dispersal of horses usually gave rise to a great deal of complaint, each regiment maintaining that it handed over horses in first-class condition, subsequently receiving the most "arrant screws" in their place. It is interesting to note that today, when horses have given way to tanks, much the same kind of complaint is voiced whenever regiments take over from each other.

John Luard left Northampton on May 28, 1822, after saying good-by to his parents. It was the last he ever saw of his father, for Peter Luard died eight years later. Taking a post chaise to Romford, Luard spent a week preparing his troop for the voyage, and then hurried off to London for a hectic week of theaters, concerts, and balls. He left his subalterns to march through the dust with the troop to Tilbury, where he joined them on June 15, half the regiment embarking on the East Indiaman *Marchioness of Ely,* and the other half on the *General Hewitt.* Both ships weighed anchor that same evening and dropped down river, the regimental band played Irish airs, and Sir Harry Darrell, an elderly East India Company civilian (who had left his wife behind at St. Omer), wept so much that he nearly had hysterics. The passage to India had begun.

"I engaged a cabin off the ship's carpenter," wrote Luard, "to share with Lieut. Harris, to pay 60 guineas for the voyage. On the 15th our ship left Gravesend, anchored each night and arrived in the Downs on the 18th—the anniversary of the battle of Waterloo. On the 19th June we weighed anchor, in company with the *General Hewitt:* the next day off the Isle of Wight the Pilot left us and took letters on shore, and we all began to reconcile ourselves to the ship. At our first dinner we found our names written on our plates and we kept those places during the voyage."

121

The journey to India in 1822 was still via the Cape—"one hundred and twenty days in a sea prison, with a plank between one and eternity," as George Bell described it.[6] The government contracted with the East India Company to carry both officers and troops, but the former had to pay for their cabins as well as for their families' passages. It cost George Bell £240 to transport his wife and daughter to Madras in 1825, but this included the cost of furnishing their cabin and their messing. Prices had fallen considerably since Mrs. Barclay paid £400 for her passage in 1780, and Colonel Wood paid the captain of an Indiaman £1,000 for the passage from Calcutta to Tilbury and then died before setting foot on board. Even so, the expense was beyond the pockets of ordinary people. A certain number of soldiers' families were carried free, but a far larger number had to be left behind, and there were heart-rending scenes at the barrack gates and dockside whenever a regiment left for overseas. After 1830 the overland route via Alexandria, Cairo, and Suez gradually supplanted the long sea voyage around the Cape; it cost much the same but was very much quicker.

Only four officers of the 16th Lancers had their wives with them in the *Marchioness of Ely,* but there were several other women passengers: a Miss Gurnet, "a coarse, silly young woman, with an affectation of romance about her," who was traveling out to India with her father in the hope of finding a husband; Miss Rowe, "half-caste and quite harmless," who, despite the fact that faint praise can be damning, nevertheless set several hearts throbbing before the end of the voyage; and little Mrs. Enderby, who was "more like a dry lemon than anything else."

Besides its passengers, the ship also carried forty-four

[6] *Rough Notes,* p. 198.

dozen ducks and hens, fifty-six pigs, and seventy sheep, and, once the weather grew warm, the smell between decks was almost insupportable. Luard, with his memories of the navy, thought it no worse than on board a man-of-war, and wondered why his fellow-passengers found the stench so objectionable. He was much more concerned about the inadequacy of the ship's crew, "Old Die, the boatswain, remarking that if he had been sent through hell with a small toothcomb he could not have picked up a more lousy crew." [7]

Although people were more easily entertained in 1822 than they are today, the boredom of a long sea voyage must have been dreadful. From leaving Gravesend to dropping anchor in the Nicobar Islands, in the Bay of Bengal, the *Marchioness of Ely* was at sea for 129 days without her passengers once setting foot on land. They whiled away the days playing chess or whist, or dancing on the quarterdeck whenever the sea was smooth; sometimes, when the ship was becalmed or was making very little way, the jolly boat was lowered and the younger officers fished for sharks or tried out their marksmanship on the gulls and albatross. The regimental band played most days, and Lieutenant-Colonel Murray, the 16th's commanding officer, kept his officers reasonably busy with routine duties.

"The men were paraded every day to see that they were clean, and in hot weather they were paraded without shoes and stockings to see that their feet were washed and clean; their berths below were inspected daily and their hammocks, unless the weather prevented, were sent on deck. There were drills of sword exercise, and the Arms were constantly inspected."

The officers certainly did their best to keep the soldiers

[7] *The Diary of an Officer of the 16th (Queen's) Lancers,* Calcutta, 1894, p. 4.

occupied, and to amuse themselves, but it was uphill work. Luard held classes in sketching and elementary navigation, and he started to study Persian with a Mr. Parks, of the East India Company's Civil Service, who was on his way to Benares with his wife, the fortunate possessor of the "most exquisitely formed leg and foot" that Lieutenant Lowe of the 16th Lancers had ever seen. There were the inevitable shipboard romances, which helped pass the time, but which also led to quarrels and jealousy. Cornet Mackinnon attributed the "strong matrimonial epidemic which broke out" to the "phosphorescent appearance which we often observe on the ocean, and which must hold some invisible and fiery influence over the minds of those whose business for a time is on the great waters." [8] Mrs. Smallpage, whose husband was a captain in the East India Company's irregular cavalry, was the object of "undue attention" on the part of two young subalterns from Luard's troop, and he had to speak to them "most severely" when they proposed fighting a duel over their charmer. Mrs. Smallpage, although undeniably attractive, was hardly of the social class from which officers of the 16th Lancers were expected to choose their wives, and, in addition, she was a married woman.

Much of the same kind of petty squabbling went on among the soldiers' families. Their accommodation was primitive in the extreme, consisting merely of blankets slung from the bulkhead to provide some privacy from the rest of the troop deck, and the women were expected to use the same lavatories as the men. Down below in the semidarkness, stifled by heat and nauseated by the stench, mothers gave birth to children, wrangled among themselves or with their husbands, conducted affairs with the soldiers or sailors,

[8] D. H. Mackinnon, *Military Service in the Far East,* London, 1849, p. 5.

and, so far as most of them were concerned, longed for the end of the voyage.

"Sergeant-Major Maloney's poor little child that had been ill nearly the whole of the voyage died, and was thrown over the sea gangway," [9] wrote Lieutenant Lowe in his diary on September 4, but he went on to say that, generally speaking, the health of the passengers was good. When, on October 15, they fell in with the *Winchelsea,* bound for Calcutta with the 44th Foot, they discovered that 164 men of that regiment were in the sick bay, whereas there were only twelve men on the doctor's list in the *Marchioness of Ely.*

The voyage dragged on interminably until November 7, when Saugor Island, at the mouth of the Hooghly, was reached. "We then transferred into brigs for the passage up river to Calcutta," wrote Luard, "and on 23rd November we landed at Fort William." It had been a long-enough voyage in all conscience, but they were at least luckier than the other half of the regiment, which had embarked on the *General Hewitt.* They did not arrive in Calcutta until Christmas Eve, having been reduced to a pint of drinking water a day for the better part of the voyage.

[9] *The Diary of an Officer of the 16th* (*Queen's*) *Lancers,* p. 15.

CHAPTER SEVEN

John Luard was to spend the better part of the next twenty-two years in India, and was even to achieve a modest fame from his *Sketches of India,* a book that he published in 1837 and which was considered at the time to be the best-illustrated work on India. It is interesting, therefore, that his first impressions of the country were by no means favorable: ". . . all but the European quarter being indescribably dirty while the natives are either obsequious or outrageously insolent." However, Calcutta society was so gay, and its European inhabitants so hospitable, that the officers of the 16th Lancers were soon able to forget the tedium of the voyage and the squalor of the city, although one of them commented severely on the lack of decorum among the ladies, and the haste with which both sexes entered into marriage.[1]

Anglo-Indian society had, in fact, settled down after the

[1] General Bengough recounts the story of a married man in the 13th Light Infantry who died from cholera. His wife attended the funeral, and on leaving the cemetery was proposed to by another man in the regiment, to whom she had to reply that she was already engaged.

126

wild extravagances of William Hickey's time, forty years earlier, and Emily Eden could find little evidence of immorality or dissipation when she arrived in Calcutta with her brother, the new Governor-General,[2] in 1835. The majority of Europeans worked very hard in an unpleasant climate and can hardly be blamed for enjoying themselves during their off-duty hours. Life for their womenfolk, confined indoors from dawn to dusk owing to an inordinate fear of the sun, must have been desperately dull, and Miss Eden thought they looked "about as fresh as an English corpse."[3] When illness was so common, and deaths were so frequent, it would be churlish to begrudge Calcutta society its attempts at gaiety.

The men of the 16th Lancers certainly found Calcutta a vast improvement on the discomforts of the troop transports. They were camped in tents on the glacis of Fort William, and soon settled down to a routine of polishing and pipe-claying, drilling, and practicing sword and lance exercises; and each evening they would wander down to Calcutta to sample the pleasures and iniquities of a city that could cater to every imaginable vice. "The sooner we are off up country the better," wrote John Luard, although there is no record of any attempt being made by either him or anyone else to keep the soldiers out of the brothels and the drinking dens.

The regiment's destination was Cawnpore, one of the largest military cantonments in the upper provinces, and on January 7, 1823, they embarked and set off up the Ganges in vessels known as budgerows, which, at least so far as the officers were concerned, were not uncomfortable.

"A voyage up the Ganges," wrote Luard, "may be per-

[2] George Eden, Earl of Auckland, Governor-General of India, 1835-1842.
[3] The Honourable Emily Eden, *Letters from India*, London, 1872, p. 210.

formed in boats, as various in shape, as in size; the most convenient is a *Budgerow,* which draws very little water, and is divided into two commodious rooms, which may be furnished at the discretion and the taste of the traveller; a complete establishment consists of a cooking boat, washerman's boat, and a horse boat; in this way, with plenty of books, a good gun, and a fair stock of patience, the upper provinces may be reached without suffering much from ennui. A horse can always be landed of an evening for a ride, or a couple of hours may be passed shooting before dinner; and many parts abound in game, from a snipe to a tiger."

Except during the rainy season, when the current prevented it, these boats were hauled upstream by the crews, known usually as *dandies.* They worked from daylight until dark, often up to the waist in water, pulling and pushing the unwieldy budgerows over the numerous sandbanks. Each night they tied up to the bank, prepared their frugal meal, and rested after the day's toil, while the passengers went for a stroll in the cool of the evening. "As the different stations are reached," wrote Luard, "the traveller visits his friends, or he makes acquaintance by sending his card to the first good looking house, with his compliments to the *Sahib,* requesting he will kindly send him a *dholly* (basket of vegetables)." Occasionally, when the wind was in the right quarter and not too strong, the crew hoisted an immense square sail, and so long as the rotten cordage and sails held, the boat made fair headway; but such attempts usually ended with the sails being blown to ribbons, and the budgerow hard and fast on a sandbank.

It was a very slow means of travel. Ten miles a day against the stream was the usual rate of progression, and joining-time between appointments in India was measured not by weeks, but by months. Three months was the least

128

one could expect to take to reach Cawnpore by the river, and the 16th Lancers took three months and three weeks. It also cost a great deal of money to move troops by this method, amounting to several thousand pounds in the case of a move from Calcutta to Cawnpore, which explains the reluctance of the East India Company to move troops around the country any more frequently than was absolutely essential. But travel by boat was at least comfortable, except on the days when the thermometer inside the cabins rose to one hundred degrees or more. It was then that the soldiers took to the water to cool themselves, many being carried away by the current, while others were seized by crocodiles. The 16th lost more men between Calcutta and Cawnpore than they did between Gravesend and Calcutta—and in less than half the time.

The Grand Trunk Road had yet to be surveyed and laid, and the Ganges was the main highway across India, stretching away into the distance, fringed with jungle and scrub, and winding through country as flat and as uninteresting as a parade ground. Day followed day with the same monotony, the same sights and sounds: women in bright-colored saris up to their knees in water as they pounded their washing on the stones; naked children splashing in the shallows and unmindful of the crocodiles stretched out on the nearby sandbanks; monkeys chattering in the trees; peafowl yowling like cats; parakeets screeching, and the nights made hideous by the jackals. Sweating in their high-necked, thick woolen scarlet tunics, the red-faced English soldiers gazed across the muddy waters at Mother India, swatted the flies, gambled with fast-disintegrating cards, drank pints of the dirty water when no officer was looking, and thought longingly of home and what it felt like to be really cool. And as they traveled farther and farther into the heart of India, the country grew flatter and flatter, hotter and hotter, and more and more dusty. "Hotter than Hades, and a d—— sight less interesting" is how Luard's troop Sergeant-Major described it.

The officers varied the monotony of the voyage by visiting European civilians who were stationed near the river, and their visits were welcomed as a relief in an existence that was as dull as it was lonely. "Two young writers whom we had known in Calcutta came to meet us," wrote Miss Eden of one of these visits. ". . . How some of these young civilians must detest their lives! Mr —— was brought up entirely at Naples and Paris, came out in the world when quite a boy, cares for nothing but society, and Victor Hugo's novels and that sort of thing. He is now stationed at B. and supposed to be lucky in being appointed to such a cheerful station. The whole concern consists of five bungalows. . . . There are three married residents; one lady with bad spirits (small blame to her), and she has never been seen; another has weak eyes and wears a shade about the size of a common verandah; and the other had bad health, and has had her head shaved. A *toupé* is not to be had here for love or money, so she wears a brown silk cushion with a cap pinned to the top of it. The doctor and our friend make up the rest of society. He goes every morning to hear causes between natives about strips of land or a few rupees—that lasts till five; then he rides about an uninhabited jungle till seven; dines; reads a magazine, or a new book when he can afford one, and then goes to bed. A lively life, with the thermometer at several hundred." [4] This is an exaggerated picture perhaps, but there must have been several such isolated stations in India during the first half of the last century.

There were, of course, many Europeans who had come to terms with India and who had adjusted themselves to the

<hr>

[4] The Hon. Emily Eden, *Up the Country,* Oxford, 1930, p. 7.

different standards of life and ways of existence. Luard met one of them at Berhampore, a military cantonment not far from Calcutta. General Stewart, of the East India Company's army, was a remarkable man who had virtually "gone native." He wore his hair long, lived entirely on rice, and never touched wine; he had a harem of Indian wives, numerous children, and professed to be a Hindu. The regime must have suited him, because, although over seventy, he astonished the officers of the 16th by his activity: ". . . after dinner he jumped over a very high chair with slight exertion." Few generals in 1823 were inclined to indulge in such postprandial exercises, and least of all those who had spent their lives in India. Such disregard for convention was not calculated to enhance General Stewart's reputation among more conventional society, and officers who saw too much of him could not expect to be approved of by their superiors. He was nevertheless a remarkable man.

Calcutta, Madras, and Bombay were the main centers of both administration and commerce, but cantonments of varying size and importance were scattered throughout India as far north as the River Sutlej, which in 1823 formed the boundary between the Sikh empire of Maharajah Ranjit Singh and the dominions of the East India Company. The more isolated of these stations contained probably only one or two Europeans, who sought refuge from their loneliness by taking Indian mistresses, some of whom they eventually married, most of whom they loved, and who in their turn loved them. However, as communications with home improved, more and more Englishwomen came out to India, and as the *mem-sahib* extended her influence, so the practice of taking an Indian bibi became increasingly frowned upon. Reginald Heber, Bishop of Calcutta, who traveled through upper India in the 1820's, records that "neither civil nor military have much intercourse with the natives," and goes on to say that "connection with native women, though sadly common among the older officers of the army, is among the younger servants by no means a fashionable vice." In less than twenty-five years it was to become virtually taboo and to remain so until the end of British rule in India. With it disappeared the free and easy relationship that had previously existed between the English and the Indians, and on the European side it was replaced by something akin to arrogance and intolerance— certainly not by all, but by enough to erect an uncrossable barrier between the rulers and the ruled. In their turn, the Indians retired into their shells, putting up with a good deal of hurt to their pride in exchange for peace and security— two commodities that had been conspicuous for their absence ever since the death of the great Akbar.

John Luard considered himself lucky that Cawnpore was to be his first station in India; as upcountry stations went, it was one of the best, and although it was unpleasantly hot in the summer, the winter months were delightful. There was quite a large European community, headed by the Collector, who, according to Lieutenant Lowe, had the reputation of being "the veriest old rogue in India, not an enviable character anywhere, and particularly not in a country where many virtues are made subservient to the love of accumulating wealth." [5] The General commanding the station was not much liked, but he went out of his way to be pleasant to the 16th Lancers, probably on account of his two spinster nieces, who "danced well enough but were uncommonly skinny."

Bachelor officers were not provided with government accommodation in most upcountry stations, and John Luard's first act on arrival in Cawnpore was to find himself a bun-

[5] *The Diary of an Officer of the 16th (Queen's) Lancers*, p. 28.

galow. This, when found, he shared with Captain Greville, of the 16th, and the type of bungalow changed little over the next hundred years. White-walled, and with a thatched roof, it was surrounded by a wide and unrailed veranda, which in the hot weather was hung with screens of khus-khus grass. These were soused at frequent intervals with water in order to lower the temperature within. The ceilings were high, and the rooms were kept in semidarkness, providing a welcome relief from the glare outside but also making a convenient resting place for bats. Punkahs were suspended from the ceiling and were operated by half-naked coolies at a wage of a few pence each week. There was hardly any furniture, and Luard records that the "interior was more like a bivouac than a house." In an attempt to improve on the bareness of the walls, he hung several of his sketches around the place, "but within a short time they had all been eaten by the white ants with which Cawnpore abounded." The beds were string cots, or charpoys, infested by bugs, and scorpions and centipedes added to the hazards of life.

Outside, there were "a few dusty flower beds tended by a gardener who was a lazy rogue," and the boundary of the bungalow compound was delimited by a low wall of crumbling mud brick. In the farthest corner were the servants' quarters, no attempt being made to provide them with any form of sanitation, and opposite them the stables. A tin tub in a dark little room served for the bathing arrangements, and the lavatory consisted of a "thunder-box," which was removed several times a day by the sweeper. It was all very primitive, but not noticeably more so than in an English country house of that period, and there were numerous servants to cater for their masters' slightest whim. There was a butler, or bearer, to act as major-domo, and "who did little else"; several grooms, or syces; two cooks,

133

although most meals were eaten in the officers' mess; a gardener and two assistants; grasscutters for the horses; a boy to look after the dogs; at least two other indoor servants to assist the butler; four coolies to work the punkahs; and a night watchman, or chokidar, to guard the bungalow at night. Luard and Greville had nearly two dozen servants on their payroll, and complained bitterly because their combined wages amounted to nearly £10 a month.

Throughout their rule in India, the British remained slaves to routine, and, according to Lord Auckland, "the staring, round look which everybody's eyes have here is not, as is always supposed, occasioned by the heat and the shrinking of eyelids, but by the knack they have of wondering at everything. The least deviation from every day's routine puts them out." [6] John Luard, by both inclination and training, was a methodical man, and the routine of Anglo-Indian life suited him admirably. His day began about 5:00 A.M., when his butler brought him a cup of lukewarm, oversweetened tea. If, by any chance, the tea was too hot to drink, the servants would blow on it until it was cool enough for the sahib to drink, and would then help him into his tight-strapped overalls with gold stripes, scarlet tunic, and lance cap with flowing plumes. The uniform was almost the same as that which he had worn in Europe, little or no concession being made to the climate, although in the very hot weather a white covering was worn on the lance cap and the plumes discarded. The horses would be waiting outside, walked up and down by the grooms, and it was the fashion to emerge from the bungalow cursing and swearing at the servants. Then a canter down to the parade ground, where bleary-eyed troopers were put through their paces, followed by "stables" around seven o'clock.

[6] *Letters from India*, p. 216.

Officers then went off to breakfast, a leisurely meal which included a variety of cold meats, the inevitable curry, coffee, and beer. About nine o'clock, and by now wearing a loose-fitting jacket and trousers, Luard would drive down to the lines in his buggy and deal with the administration of his troop. Occasionally there would be a conference with the commanding officer, and sometimes a defaulter to be dealt with, but work was over by noon. The men returned to their barrack rooms to get through the rest of the day as best they could, while the officers went back to the mess to enjoy a long and hearty meal, washed down with beer or wine, according to taste. Then came a cigar or cheroot on the mess veranda beneath the punkah, and finally three or four hours stretched naked on one's bed, while the punkah creaked and flapped, "the bats flitted backwards and forwards," and the stale air circulated slowly in the darkened room. It was too hot to read, too hot to think, too hot to do anything. Only in the cool of the evening would Cawnpore come to life.

Around 6:00 P.M. the carriages began to appear in the Mall. "Whose buggy is that [asks Mr. Russel], preceded by two native troopers and followed by five or six armed natives running on foot? — That is the magistrate and collector. — What does he do? — He is the burra sahib or big man of the station. — Who is in the smart gharry with servants in livery? — That is the chaplain of the station who marries and baptises and performs services for the Europeans. — Does he go among the natives? — Not he; he leaves that to the missionaries. . . . — Well; and who comes next, in that very smart buggy with the bay mare? — That is the doctor of the station. He attends the sick Europeans. He also gets, under certain circumstances, head-money for every native soldier in garrison. — Does he attend them? — I should think not. — But why is he paid for them? — Ah, that is another matter. You must attend our system better before you can comprehend things of this sort." [7]

William Russel, correspondent of *The Times,* can hardly be regarded as an unprejudiced critic of British social life in India, but this description of the evening parade along the Cawnpore Mall is not all that wide of the mark. There was a carefully regulated hierarchy, conducting its life with a marked attention to protocol, and quick to take offense if anyone infringed rules of etiquette which had almost the sanctity of Holy Writ. According to Luard, Cawnpore society in 1823 was sadly divided on account of the wife of a colonel in a native regiment; ". . . the lady had not been handed in to supper by a gentleman of sufficient rank and the Company's officers were quick to take her side." The rest of the European community were in opposition, and in consequence half of them drove down the Mall cutting the other half. Trouble had also developed as a result of the dispersal of the assembly room's furniture. The secretary had sent it all off to auction without consulting the Collector, whose wife was furious at the slight. She threatened to bring an action against the unfortunate secretary, insisting that an old window curtain, a warming pan, and one or two other utensils were her property. When Lieutenant Lowe asked her what on earth she wanted with a warming pan in the middle of the hot weather, she turned her back on him and refused to have him inside her house.

It is easy to criticize our ancestors for all this pettiness and snobbery, but it is salutary to remember all they accomplished in the face of disease, the climate, and the appalling apathy of the Indians. The view that good government is no substitute for self-government had yet to be elevated to an article of faith, and India was a good deal safer for the

[7] Dennis Kincaid, *British Social Life in India, 1608-1937,* London, 1938, p. 182.

ordinary man than it had been for centuries past. Devoted work by men like Sleeman was gradually defeating thuggee; highway robbery was on the wane; the constant wars between petty rajahs were ceasing; and a new phase in Indian history was beginning with the construction of roads, irrigation canals, and, in the not too distant future, railways. Seaton, marching from Delhi to Kurnool in 1823, found nothing but continuous jungle swarming with game. When he repeated the march sixteen years later, all the jungle had been cleared and the whole area was under cultivation, and this was happening all over India.

The pace of life was slow, and people found their amusement in simple things. The lighter-hearted members of the community, such as Lieutenant Lowe, were keen supporters of amateur theatricals, Miss Eden recording that in one theatrical performance which she attended the leading lady's part was taken by a muscular young lancer in a long, flaxen wig. John Luard, being of less frivolous disposition, was always busy with his sketchbook, "visiting all the ruins for miles around Cawnpore," and "we were always making up expeditions to go out after the game which abounded within a few miles of the station." A keen horseman and good shot, who could fill in time with his sketchbook, he was less likely to be bored in upper India than the more intellectually inclined, or the seeker after bright lights. There is certainly nothing in Luard's journal to suggest that he found service in India unattractive.

But it is hard to imagine what pleasure the ordinary soldier could find in life. Sergeant Thomas, of Luard's regiment, has left a description of service in India which makes it sound the reverse of entertaining.

"In the first place a troop is huddled together in one barrack to the strength of 87 men. These have continual intercourse with one another as they are ranged at each side of the barrack, two men to each pillar of the building. Each troop is divided into four messes. Each man pays daily five pence, for which he receives 1 lb of bread, 5/7 of an ounce of tea, 1 and 2/7 of sugar, 4 ounces of rice, 2 ounces of salt, and 3 lbs of wood for cooking. Besides this, each man pays 2 rupees 8 annas a month for vegetables. By these means the men mess well for they always have abundance upon the table.

"The duty of a dragoon is very easy on account of the great numbers of followers. Each man has a syce to clean and saddle his horse. Each troop has two barbers, two shoe blacks, two belt cleaners, and eight dhobies or washer-women who wash at 10 annas per month for each man. Thus the men have nothing to do except field service during the cold season.

"The cold months glide rapidly past, and the European is recruited to health and vigour, but he must prepare early in the month of April for his term of imprisonment—the hot winds, suffocating dust and doors closed with tatties, the barrack room being watered from outside by natives to keep them cool.[8] At this time the men know not how to pass away the time unless by drinking or gambling; thus they are led to be drunkards or gamblers before they have been many years in India."

Sergeant Thomas blamed much of this moral collapse on the regimental canteens, which "deprive the soldier of his comforts while realising a fortune in two or three years for the canteen sergeant." He mentions one such sergeant who made £1,400 in the space of eighteen months, and another who died worth 40,000 rupees. In Thomas's view, the government would have been well advised to substitute beer

[8] Punkahs were not introduced into barrack rooms until after the Indian Mutiny.

and wine in the canteens for the rot-gut spirits, and he was a staunch supporter of regimental reading rooms.

When off duty, the soldiers were permitted a considerable degree of freedom, and were allowed to make whatever female acquaintance they chose without the bonds of matrimony, unless their partners were Europeans or Eurasians. No quarters were provided for married men, unless they could hire them from Indian landlords, and the usual arrangement was for part of a barrack room to be screened off for the families. The pay of the ordinary soldier was about one shilling a day, that of the East India Company's European regiments being higher than in the Royal regiments, and in addition there was an allowance of about two drams of rum a day, a dram being about one sixth of a modern whisky bottle.[9]

The mortality in India from the climate, disease, drink, and vice was staggering, and yet men volunteered to remain in the country when the time came for their regiments to return to England. Sixty-eight men of the 51st Light Infantry died in a week from cholera, while on another occasion nearly 450 men, women, and children died in the same period from cholera at Mian Mir. "One might as well be serving a jail sentence," was how one soldier described life in the barrack room during a period of Indian hot weather, and yet there are few references to homosexuality in soldiers' diaries and letters; perhaps the lax attitude with regard to soldiers' morals and the brothels which existed in

[9] The origin of a "peg" of whisky derives from this free issue of rum. "Above the tub from which the men were supplied hung a board, having their numbers painted on it. This number was surmounted by two holes, in each of which as the dram was issued a wooden peg was inserted. When both holes were filled, the man was said to be 'pegged up,' and referred to the board as a proof." *European Adventurers of Northern India*, pp. 217-219.

every cantonment bazaar kept that aspect of prison life in the background. It would also be wrong to try to equate the soldier of Luard's time with his modern counterpart. The conditions from which he came were still primitive and brutal. Men were hung for stealing a sheep or transported to Van Diemen's Land for poaching a partridge. Public executions were popular forms of entertainment; small boys were lowered down chimneys to sweep them clean; and women toiled underground, naked to the waist, as they hauled the coal from the coal face. When all this is taken into consideration, perhaps the life of the soldier in India was not really as bad as it is painted.

CHAPTER EIGHT

India was at peace when John Luard arrived there in 1823. The Maratha Wars were now history, as was the campaign in Nepal, and, like a boa constrictor, the Honorable East India Company had settled down to digest the gains of the past twenty years. "No more annexations!" had been proclaimed by the Directors in London, a decision strongly endorsed by the British government, which was hopeful of obtaining some return for the amount of treasure that had been expended on advancing the frontiers so far to the northwest. The Company now ruled a vast area of the subcontinent, which they had conquered with surprising ease and largely because the majority of the inhabitants had neither the will nor the inclination to defend themselves. They were divided by religion, oppressed by despotic princes, and harried by hordes of turbulent and indisciplined soldiery, most of whom cut better figures in the bazaars than on the battlefield. For this reason, a handful of British soldiers, and a not much larger number of Indian sepoys, trained on the European model and led by British officers and noncommissioned officers, had succeeded in subduing huge areas of territory with surprising ease. Another, and scarcely less important, explanation for the British success was the superiority of their artillery; in days when battles were fought at close quarters, well-handled artillery was a battle-winning factor of incalculable importance, and it is significant that the British came nearest to defeat in India when they came up against the Sikhs, whose artillery was modeled on the European style and equally well handled.

From the year 1800 onward, the steady expansion of the East India Company's dominions must have seemed as inevitable to ordinary Indians as the rising and setting of the sun, but they consoled themselves with the thought that their country would never be completely subdued so long as the great fortress-city of Bhurtpore, in Central India, which they referred to as the "Bulwark of Hindustan," had not passed beneath the invader's heel. Such an event seemed unlikely, for Gerard Lake had made four separate attempts to take the place in 1804, and on each occasion had been repulsed with heavy loss. There was also an ancient prophecy that Bhurtpore would only fall when a crocodile came from across the seas and drank all the ditches dry, and everyone knew that a wide belt of desert and jungle lay between Bhurtpore and the nearest crocodile. It was an unfortunate coincidence that Sir Edward Paget relinquished the command of the Bengal Army to Lord Combermere[1] in 1824. The new commander in chief's name, as pronounced by the Indians, bore a marked resemblance to the vernacular word for crocodile.

Bhurtpore was the capital of the Jats, a race of Hindu yeomen who make excellent soldiers, and was ruled by Rajah Baldeo Singh. He had recognized the wisdom of coming to

[1] Sir Stapleton Cotton, Wellington's old cavalry commander of the peninsula, had been raised to the peerage as Lord Combermere. He had commanded the 16th Light Dragoons in 1807.

142

terms with the powerful Company, but either because he was cleverer than his fellow-rajahs or because the British realized the strength of Bhurtpore, Baldeo Singh had managed to retain his independence. The Company's resident in Delhi, Sir David Ochterlony, retained a watching brief over Bhurtpore, but there was no suggestion that the Company desired to annex the state.

As measured by the standards of those times, Bhurtpore must have been one of the strongest fortresses in the world. A twenty-mile-wide stretch of jungle surrounded the fortifications, and beyond the jungle were the sun-baked plains of Central India. The nearest British garrison was at Agra, thirty-four miles to the west. The city of Bhurtpore, containing more than 100,000 people, was situated in the middle of a level plain, and was surrounded by a high wall of mud brick, strengthened throughout its length by rows of tree trunks buried upright. Beyond the walls was a deep ditch, twenty to thirty feet wide, with perpendicular banks, and fed from a series of swampy ponds some distance from the city. Each of the nine gates was protected by an extensive earthwork, and towering above the walls was the citadel, reputedly the strongest place in India.

The citadel stood on rising ground, protected by a ditch fifty yards wide and twenty yards deep, in which it would have been possible to float a man-of-war. On the far side of the ditch a stone wall rose to a height of over eighty feet, perpendicular, and flanked by forty semicircular towers. An inner wall, seventy-four feet high and equally sheer, completed the fortifications of the citadel, compared with which the fortresses of Ciudad Rodrigo and Badajoz, which had cost Wellington so dear, were almost outworks. Lake had lost nearly 3,000 men killed and wounded in his abortive attempts to storm Bhurtpore, and the inhabitants had afterward erected a Bastion of Victory, paved with the skulls

143

and bones of the dreaded European soldiers who had fallen in the effort to capture the "Bulwark of Hindustan."

Trouble began in Bhurtpore, as almost always in India, when the existing Rajah tried to settle the succession to the throne. Intrigue is endemic in the East, and every Indian court was riddled with it. The matter was complicated by polygamy, which inevitably resulted in there being several claimants to the succession, and all too frequently the business was further complicated by the Hindu custom of adopting sons. Baldeo Singh, Rajah of Bhurtpore, had many wives, and even more concubines, some of whom must have presented him with sons, but in 1824, when his health began to give way and the question of the succession became urgent, the only claimant put forward was his six-year-old son, Balwant Singh. The father did his best to ensure the child's selection by enlisting the support of the formidable Ochterlony, in Delhi, a fabulous old character, who had spent fifty-four years in India and who was probably one of the finest soldiers the British ever sent to India. Ochterlony lived in such state in Delhi that the descendant of the Great Mogul paled by comparison, and whenever he went abroad he was accompanied by two companies of infantry, a troop of irregular cavalry, and a dozen or more elephants: ". . . the whole procession might pass in Europe for that of an Eastern Prince travelling," wrote Bishop Heber, and it was believed that the British Resident's income amounted to more than £15,000 a year. He disbursed most of it on lavish entertainments, and left comparatively little behind him.

Ochterlony agreed to accept Balwant Singh's claim to the throne; and when, early in 1825, the old Rajah died, worn out by too many women, the infant Rajah was duly installed on the gaddi, with an uncle to act as guardian until he came of age. The events that followed were of the usual pattern. A nephew of the dead Rajah, Durjan Sal, won over the soldiery, seized the citadel, and murdered the guardian uncle. He then proclaimed himself the young Rajah's guardian and proceeded to fill all the offices of state with his own creatures.

As soon as the news reached Delhi, Ochterlony reacted with his usual vigor. He denounced Durjan Sal as a usurper, promised support to the Jats if they rose against him, and assembled a force to march on Bhurtpore. Unfortunately, the Governor-General, Lord Amherst, in Calcutta, took exception to his subordinate's actions. He sent an extremely offensive dispatch to Ochterlony, countermanding the military operation and repudiating the British Resident's pledge to the adherents of the young Rajah. Ochterlony, long accustomed to being given his head, and realizing far better than Amherst what was at stake—which was no less than the prestige of the Company throughout Hindustan—resigned, and retired to Meerut, where he died in July 1825. It was a sad ending to a great career.

Amherst's ill-advised intervention lit the fires of rebellion in Central India. They had long been smoldering and needed little to fan them into flame. Less than fifteen years had passed since the formidable Marathas had been defeated; an even shorter period had elapsed since the Pindaris had been hunted down and pacified; while the Rohillas, mercenaries who sold their swords to the highest bidder, were finding the Company's peace a poor substitute for the good old days of murder, rape, and loot. From all over the Deccan, Oudh, Rohilkhund, and Rajputana, the insolent ruffians who had terrorized the villages for centuries past sharpened their swords and spears, polished their rusty armor, unhitched their horses and camels from the plows, and cantered off toward Bhurtpore. It looked as if the good old days were returning.

Charles Metcalfe, who had succeeded Ochterlony in Delhi,

soon recognized the danger, for Durjan Sal had taken advantage of Ochterlony's supersession to oust the infant Rajah and place himself on the throne. "We are bound," wrote Metcalfe to Amherst, "not by any positive engagement to the Bhurtpore state, nor by any claim on her part, but by our duty as supreme guardians of general tranquillity, law and right, to maintain the right of Balwant Singh to the *raj* of Bhurtpore, and we cannot acknowledge any other pretender." It was an argument that was to be repeated time after time during Britain's rule in India—a rule that depended more on prestige than on bayonets. Amherst gave in.

When, in the late summer of 1825, the news leaked out that the Company had decided to settle accounts with Bhurtpore, most Europeans were relieved. It was high time, they thought, for the Indians to be reminded that the Company's arm was a long one. As for the Indians, they were equally pleased, believing as they did that Bhurtpore was impregnable and that a British reverse there might well become the signal for a general uprising all over India. "Go to Bhurtpore; they'll split you up. Go and be killed, all of you!" screamed a wrinkled old hag, rushing out of her hut to abuse the 35th Bengal Native Infantry as they marched to join the Bhurtpore Field Force. The 16th Lancers received their orders to march on November 5, and were delighted to have them, several of the men signifying their pleasure by getting dead drunk. It was always exciting to be employed on active service, and, in addition, the previous hot weather had been singularly trying. There had been five suicides among the soldiers, and Cawnpore had begun to get on everyone's nerves. The regiment had been attacked by a peculiarly debilitating kind of fever, leaving men so weak that they could scarcely find the strength to mount

146

their horses, and at the very moment when the regiment was marching out of cantonments on its way to join the field force, a dragoon in Baron Osten's troop drew his pistol and blew his brains out. It was not a particularly auspicious beginning for the 16th Lancers' first campaign since Waterloo.

Nevertheless, the Bhurtpore Field Force was one of the strongest ever to be assembled in India up to that date: two regiments of British and six of Native cavalry; two battalions of British and sixteen of Native infantry; four troops of horse artillery, and a siege train of 112 guns.[2] Lord Combermere was in command, and the force was separated into two divisions, commanded by Major-Generals Thomas Reynell and Jasper Nicolls. The troops were to assemble at Agra and Muttra respectively, and the 16th took three weeks to march from Cawnpore to Agra. The pace of their advance was largely dictated by the quantity of followers they took with them to look after their wants. "I had nine servants, six bullock carts, and four horses," wrote John Luard, "and this was modest compared with some." The officers whiled away the tedium of the march by stopping at places of interest en route; Luard visited the ancient ruins of Kanoge with Lieutenant Lowe, where they found little of interest apart from the graves of "two Mahommedan saints in a sad state of disrepair." They also spent the night beside a tank, or pond, where legend had it that an old woman had once seduced travelers to spend a night with her beside the tank, whereupon they were at once set upon, robbed, and their bodies thrown into the water. They went shooting

[2] The British regiments were the 16th Lancers (now the 16th / 5th The Queen's Royal Lancers), 11th Light Dragoons (now 11th Hussars), 14th Foot (now the Prince of Wales's Regiment of Yorkshire), and the 59th Foot (now the Lancashire Regiment).

147

after the black partridges with which the country abounded, and Luard says they had some enjoyable sport "hunting the local foxes which were almost as common as hares."

The commander in chief arrived at Agra on December 3, and on the following day he reviewed the cavalry. Lord Combermere was a slow-witted man, a better judge of a horse than of a tactical situation, and new to Indian warfare; even those who knew him well, and liked him, had to admit that he was uncommonly stupid. But, for all his faults, he was brave and generous, qualities more highly regarded in war than they are inclined to be in times of peace, and he made a point of meeting every officer once the review was over. The 16th were delighted to see their old commander of peninsula days, and turned out at midnight to give him "Three Cheers" as he rode past their camp.

They cheered him again on December 8 when he gave orders for the entire force to set out for Bhurtpore. The balls were taken off the points of the lances,[3] the regiment was divided into half-squadrons, and Major Persse, who was commanding the regiment, gave the order "Walk—March—Trot." In a cloud of dust thrown up by their horses, the 16th Lancers set off at the head of the advance, and the infantry came trudging along behind them.

"On the 10th," wrote Luard, "Colonel Murray who commanded our Brigade with 4 guns of Horse Artillery turned out at half past 3 a.m. The infantry remained in camp. We proceeded to Sesma, then brought our left shoulders up and led straight for Bhurtpore. Colonel Murray chequered the Troops by placing alternately a Troop of the 16th Lancers and a Troop of the 6th Native Cavalry. I was ordered to command all the skirmishers, having Lieut. Armstrong of the 16th and Lieut. Farrer of the 6th Native Cavalry under my

[3] The steel tip of the lance was protected by a ball when not in action.

148

command. I was ordered by Colonel Murray to cut off any enemy I could. I led the skirmishers close under the walls to the right, while Skinner's Horse under the command of Mr. Fraser, a civilian, made a sweep to the right. Some of the enemy's horse encamped under the walls retired as we advanced, but another party encamped further out were attacked by Fraser and driven towards one of the gates of the fortress, while I galloped on with my skirmishers, and intercepted them as they approached the gate of the fort. We killed and wounded about 50 and took 100 horses. Mr. Fraser was wounded by a sabre in the face, and Lieut. Armstrong by a musket ball from the walls. Our left squadron under the command of Capt. Cureton came up in support and charged a party more on our right, and had 2 men wounded, 3 horses killed and 3 wounded. The guns from the fort now opened up on our brigade, but only killed one horse. The skirmishers were then called in. Had I been supported by Infantry, I could have galloped into the fort with the retiring enemy horse."

Luard's prosaic account does less than justice to the scene, which was memorable for being the first occasion on which the lance was used in battle by British cavalry. The 16th Lancers had set off while it was still dark, the dry earth smelling damp from the dew, and the air scented by that unforgettable smell of India—the acrid smoke of cow-dung fires intermingled with the perfume of jasmine. As they jogged forward in single file, winding through the jungle and the crops, a dragoon in Enderby's troop fell down a well, horse and man together, which held things up until they could be extricated, which they were, none the worse for their adventure. As the Lancers emerged from the jungle into the plain surrounding the city, they saw the great mud walls of the fortress for the first time, looming up in front of them like cliffs, with the huge bulk of the citadel looking more formidable than ever in the half-light of early dawn.

For a space the open ground between the jungle and the city was a swirling mass of horsemen, with the Jats, taken by surprise, seeking safety within the walls and the British cavalry endeavoring to cut them off. It was hard to tell the difference between the Jats, waving tulwars and shields, and the wild and whiskered irregulars of Skinner's Horse, led by their civilian commander, who had abandoned the drudgery of his desk for the excitements of the field.[4] Luard says he was "an uncommonly good fellow, and always ready for a dash at the enemy." The British and the Native Cavalry were easy to pick out in their scarlet, amid the gaudy yellow of the irregulars and the even gaudier colors of the enemy cavalry. The Jats when cornered fought bravely, one party of four refusing to give up their arms, and being cut down by the lancers as a result. An old man among them turned to his son and forbade him to surrender, saying, "If you don't fight till the last, I will kill you myself."

Combermere's object in sending the cavalry forward was to secure the ponds which supplied the fortress moat with water. This was successfully accomplished, and the Jats were thereby deprived of one of their main defenses. But the formidable walls still remained, and the breaching of them would be difficult. Ordinary masonry could be battered down with round shot, but the cannon balls merely embedded themselves in the mud walls of Bhurtpore, churning the earth into heaps of dust in which men sank up to

---

[4] William Fraser, a member of the Company's Civil Service, had a passion for soldiering. He served as a volunteer in Skinner's Horse from time to time, thereby indulging his thirst for action, and in between times he conducted a paper war with the bureaucrats in Calcutta. He hunted lions on foot with a spear, kept a prodigious harem, and pacified the turbulent peasantry around Delhi by the force of his terrific personality. He was murdered in 1835 at the instigation of the Nawab of Ferozepore.

their thighs; and even when the mud-bricks had been pulverized, the palisade of tree trunks remained standing, protected by the citadel which towered above them.

It was not until December 23 that Combermere's siege artillery could open fire from batteries constructed close to the walls, and although the noise was deafening, the effects were not very impressive. The cavalry were employed in providing a ring of skirmishers around the fortress, in order to prevent bodies of enemy horsemen from slipping away to safety, and the infantry were kept busy digging trenches from which they could assault the walls. Combermere was inspecting the trenches early one morning when he passed the spot where the officers of the 35th Native Infantry were enjoying breakfast; an enemy shell had just landed on the breakfast table, scattering plates, teapots, cups and saucers, but fortunately doing no worse harm. The incident was greeted with loud laughter, causing Combermere to inquire, "What officers are those?" "The 35th, my Lord." "Comfortable dogs, let 'em alone."

The enemy fire grew noticeably more accurate after Christmas Day, and it was soon learned that a Sergeant Herbert, of the Bengal Artillery, had deserted to the enemy and was directing their fire. He was often seen on the ramparts, exposing himself with complete disregard for his own safety as he aimed the guns, and his appearance was greeted with howls of abuse from his erstwhile comrades. "Bad luck to him," shouted an Irishman in the 14th Foot. "He's not content with being a sergeant, but wants to be a jinral!"

All through the last week of December, and the first week of January 1825, the British guns battered away at Bhurtpore. A thick cloud of yellow dust hung like a pall above the city, most of whose inhabitants had slipped away in their thousands to the comparative safety of the jungle, preferring to take their chances with the tigers and the snakes rather than wait for the horrors of the sack that were bound to follow a successful assault. Even the usurper, Durjan Sal, began to lose heart; a mortar shell had landed on the roof of his palace, fallen through four floors, and had burst with a deafening concussion in the courtyard below, killing an elephant and frightening the harem out of their wits. Desertions from the garrison increased daily, especially among Durjan Sal's mercenary Pathan cavalry, who were quite prepared for the cut and thrust of mounted combat, but who had little stomach for a pounding by artillery. Every night parties of these blackguards would slip out from the fortress and essay to cross the open space of half a mile that lay between Bhurtpore and the safety of the jungle, and more often than not they would be intercepted by the British cavalry screen and a splendid free-for-all would ensue.

On one such occasion, Luard says, the 16th Lancers "were engaged by the 1st Light Cavalry, native regiments often being nervous once darkness fell." In the melee that followed, several enemy horsemen took advantage of the confusion to try to break through the cavalry cordon, and some of the officers of the Native Cavalry were wounded by their own troopers. One escaping enemy horseman galloped straight past the guard tent of the 16th Lancers, "but the sergeant of the guard ran the man through with his lance as he galloped past." Lieutenant Lowe, who was in hot pursuit, arrived on the scene shortly afterward, only to find that the wounded man had been stripped to the skin by the grooms and grasscutters who were lurking near the guard tent.

"I dined today with the officers of H.M. 14th" and "We took breakfast with the 11th Light Dragoons" are typical of the entries Luard made in his journal during the siege of Bhurtpore. There was not a great deal that the cavalry could do while the guns were busily leveling the defenses, and so Luard and his friends made the rounds of the various messes and sampled each other's claret. Yet all the time men were being killed in the trenches or were blown to pieces when some mine exploded prematurely. Lord Combermere had a narrow escape on December 28 when three round shot came whizzing through the room in which he was eating his breakfast, carrying away the leg of the native servant who was entering the room with a plate of porridge. His Lordship, quite unperturbed, sent for another plate.

He might have been excused, however, if the situation had begun to worry him, since he knew that the British could never afford to risk another repulse before Bhurtpore. And yet the guns, for all their noise, were doing little damage, and his own casualties grew daily as the enemy's fire became more accurate. At last he decided that the assault would be made, come what may, on the morning of January 7, and in order to minimize the risk of failure he ordered that the storming parties should be principally composed of European troops. Volunteers were therefore asked for from the cavalry to supplement the infantry, the 16th Lancers and the 11th Light Dragoons each being required to provide one captain, two subalterns, and eighty men.

"Major Persse assembled the officers at his tent and read the order," wrote Luard. "I immediately volunteered, Lieut. McConchy did so also, saying he would go anywhere with Luard, and Walker instantly said he would also go; this was very gratifying to me. . . . I paraded my troop and told them I wanted volunteers to go with me and assist at the storm—those who wanted to go were ordered to step two paces to the front. The whole front rank did so, and the rear rank stepped up to them, so I was obliged to select them. All the non-commissioned officers volunteered . . . our orders were to escalade the wall to the right of the

153

breach, by which General Nicolls' division was to storm, gain the rampart, and communicate with General Reynell's division, which was to storm by a breach on our right. We were ordered to be ready for the assault the next day."

Luard paraded his men that same evening and marched them off in high spirits to join the storming party of the 11th Light Dragoons. The men were ordered to remove the pennants from their lances, and carried swords, with pistols stuck through their girdles. One can hardly imagine a worse form of dress for scrambling up a high wall than high-necked tunics, tight strapped trousers, and lance caps; the more so since the wearers would be encumbered with twelve-foot lances and would have to struggle through thick dust and across fallen masonry. In the event, they were not called upon to do so. Combermere postponed the assault as a result of his engineers' protest that the breaches were still unscalable and that they needed more time to spring the mines under the walls. By the time the mines were ready, the Company's 1st European Regiment[5] had arrived from Agra, and Combermere had sufficient infantry to be able to dispense with the dismounted cavalry. When Luard marched his detachment back to camp, the band turned out to march them in, and after he had thanked the men for their willingness to volunteer, "they gave three cheers for each of the officers who had volunteered with them."

Poor Luard seems to have been dogged by the objections of the engineers. General Nicolls asked for a volunteer to swim across the moat and test the depth of the water, and Luard went into the trenches one night to carry out the dangerous task. But the engineers, who were working close up to the walls, prevented him from doing so, arguing that

[5] There were only three European infantry regiments in the East India Company's service in 1825, one in each of the three presidencies—Bengal, Madras, and Bombay. They were increased subsequently.

he might be discovered and thereby bring down fire on their working parties; "they were unnecessarily cautious," he thought.

The assault was fixed finally for the morning of January 18. The storming parties, consisting mainly of the 14th and 59th Foot, supported by the Native Infantry, moved quietly into the trenches while it was still dark, but the engineers were not yet ready with the great mine. As they continued working on it, the storming party of the 14th Foot pressed forward until they were dangerously close to the mine itself. Combermere, anxiously surveying the final preparations, protested to the engineer in charge that the infantry were too close, but was assured that all was well.

Day dawned, light appeared, and still no signal for the assault was given, while the enemy began to appear on the ramparts, and their guns opened fire and raked the waiting stormers. The cavalry, in a cordon around the fortress, waited in tense expectation for the roar of their own artillery as the herald of the assault, but all remained quiet. The minutes ticked by, and nothing happened.

Not until 8:00 A.M. was the mine ready, and Combermere gave the order to explode it thirty minutes later. Ten thousand pounds of gunpowder erupted with an ear-splitting crash, and "the doomed bastion rocked and fell into ruin; a dense cloud of dust and smoke arose, streaked with human bodies, limbs, stores and timber; and masses of earth leaped whirling into the air." [6] Much of this debris fell on the infantry waiting tensely in the trenches, bayonets already fixed and their tunic collars unfastened. Brigadiers McCombie and Paton, who were to lead the storm, were wounded, as, among many others, was Lieutenant Daly of the 14th Foot, whose leg had to be amputated on the spot.

[6] Sir John Fortescue, *History of the British Army*, London, 1923, Vol. XI, p. 363.

Combermere was thrown to the ground by the force of the explosion, but, leaping up, he dashed forward to head the assault. He was restrained with main force by his aide-de-camp. The General fumbled to draw his sword, cursed and blasphemed as he struggled to free himself, and encouraged the stormers at the top of his voice. General Reynell, coming up at that moment, retrieved the situation. "Forward!" he shouted, plunging through the smoke and dust and up into the breach, and with a wild cheer the men of the 14th Foot dashed after him. Behind them, cheering wildly and with their kettledrums rattling out the charge, came the sepoys of the 23rd Native Infantry, the 41st, the 50th, and the 6th; and there were also Gurkhas of the Nasseri and Sirmur battalions, kukris in hand, fighting on one of the first bloody fields they would conquer for England. The assault was on, and the enemy was ready.

The walls surrounding Bhurtpore were high and continuous, and the ramparts were broad. The Jats fought like tigers, but the exploding mines had driven a wedge into the ramparts, dividing one half of the defending force from the other. An immense, yawning abyss separated the defenders, and as the assaulting columns gained the ramparts and then started to fight their way along them, the Jats were forced to retreat toward the gap. Hundreds of them fell into the crater left by the mine, and their thickly wadded tunics, so effective in warding off sword cuts, were highly inflammable. Catching fire from short-range musketry, the unfortunate Jats were turned into flaming torches. As the storming parties of the 14th and 59th Foot met on either side of the gap, after having fought their way around the ramparts, they looked down on a dense mass of burning, screaming, and twisted men, and, sickened by the sight, sound, and smell of burning flesh, they abandoned the ramparts and

156

went down into the narrow streets of the city to rout out all who were left there.

By midday the town was firmly in British hands. The sepoys roamed the streets and looted the abandoned houses, while Combermere brought forward his guns in preparation for an assault on the citadel. This promised to be an even bloodier business, and would undoubtedly have turned out to be so had the Jats continued the fight. But Durjan Sal had had enough. The twelve-pounder guns blew in the great gates, and the place was then surrendered by its garrison. It was 4:00 P.M., and 14,000 Jats had been killed and wounded in the fanatical defense of Bhurtpore. According to Luard, "they fought individually to the last, yielding their guns only with their lives; and the carnage was dreadfully increased by want of talent to direct their courage, or discretion to withold it." As had happened so often before in India, and was to happen again and again, the uncoordinated bravery of the many had failed to withstand the disciplined gallantry of the few.

"All who witnessed the conduct of the Sephoys on this day," wrote Luard, "bear testimony to their gallantry, and the King's officers have declared that their forwardness was not outdone by the British soldier; such conduct is the more praiseworthy, as it is certain that there was a feeling of regret amongst all natives, that the only independent fortress in Hindostan of any note, was about to fall, yet their fidelity to those whose 'salt they eat,' bound them to their duty."

It was a handsome tribute, and handsomely earned, but there is a tinge of sadness about Bhurtpore. It was in many ways the swan song of the old Bengal Native Army, which had served the Company so well and on so many different fields. After Bhurtpore the rot slowly set in, discipline began

157

to deteriorate, and the once-reliable sepoy grew less and less dependable. The fault by no means lay always on the side of the sepoy, but, for all that, Bhurtpore is the watershed. Before, there stretches an unbroken series of victories; after, there comes the slow descent to the humiliation of the Mutiny.

The cavalry's task during and after the assault was to prevent the escape of any sizable numbers of the enemy. Around midday several hundred enemy horsemen had managed to slip out of the fortress and were lurking in the shrub that fringed the jungle. Lieutenant Lowe went in pursuit of one such party and chased them through the trees. "I got on the near side of a horseman, and being within the parry of his spear tumbled him off his horse; another passed and had the speed of me, and as he appeared to be preparing his matchlock for a shot at me, I thought it as well to be beforehand with him. I fired my pistol at him and missed him; he instantly threw away his matchlock, and finding I was now gaining on him, he threw himself from his horse on the off-side, and asked for mercy."

Lowe took away the man's sword and handed him over to his orderly, an elderly dragoon named McCaw, who had just galloped up. McCaw was in no mood to take prisoners, and, bringing his lance to the point, said: "Sure Mr Lowe, wouldn't it be better just to give him a poke!" When Lowe refused to allow him to kill the prisoner, the old soldier rode away grumbling to himself.

Durjan Sal slipped out of Bhurtpore shortly before the citadel surrendered, and was more than halfway to safety before he and his entourage were observed by the 8th Native Cavalry. They pursued him, and a running fight followed, in the course of which the young son of the Rajah was wounded in the hand. John Luard and Lowe came up with them soon after their capture.

"The Rajah rode a large bay Persian horse overloaded with flesh, on which he sat well considering his weight, which must be 18 stone (all fat), he looked dejected, as well he might, but still dignified and important; he had even now the appearance of a man used to command. He had endeavoured to make his escape over the ground where we had been posted till the morning, and was taken after little resistance by an out piquet of the 8th Cavalry commanded by Lieutenant Barber, who now rode in advance of the prisoner with the splendid sword he had taken from the Rajah, stuck in his girdle. The piquet had in the most shameful manner plundered and stripped Durjan Sal, whose dress now consisted of the slightest *dotee,* a pink kummerbund was thrown over his shoulders and could only partially cover his naked body and thighs, and a dirty pink turban was on his head, such as only your lowest caste servants would wear. In this plight he was conducted to the tent of Lord Combermere. His favourite wife followed him, sitting behind her brother on a fine horse; Durjan's son was also taken prisoner and formed one of the party."

Luard, who had early been into the town after the storm, was looking over the ramparts when he saw a splendidly dressed Jat chief, attended by six spearmen, ride out of the gate and make for the jungle. Hurrying down from the walls, he mounted his horse, collected Corporal Tailor and Private Sweeney of the 16th, who were hanging around gaping at the fires and doubtless calculating the chances of loot, and gave chase. "It was just like a fox hunt," wrote Luard, and although the chief escaped, "we cut down four men and took three horses."

The looting went on for several days, and the stench from the decomposing bodies was barely endurable. It does not, however, seem to have worried the 16th Lancers, who established their camp on the edge of the jungle and entertained the rest of the army. Lord Combermere and his staff were their guests on January 23. "The commander in chief was in excellent spirits," as indeed he might well be; it was the first victory he had ever gained on his own account, and he ate like a trooper. Gossip had it that his Lordship's table was not very well supplied, the aides-de-camp complaining that "his beef is white, the mutton lean, and everything sour but the vinegar." Combermere seems to have enjoyed his reunion with his old regiment, staying very late and saying some very complimentary things about the "Gentlemen of the Lancers."

Six days later the army was assembled for a much less pleasant occasion. The artilleryman Herbert, taken during the final assault, was hanged on the northeast bastion. "He was for some time dreadfully convulsed," wrote Luard, and his brother officer D. H. MacKinnon has left a graphic account of the horrors of a public execution.

"The numerous spectators present can bear witness to the prolonged sufferings of the culprit. The rope being adjusted, one native pushed him off a low cart under the gibbet, while two others tugged at the rope to hoist him up. The convulsive writhings of the sufferer long haunted me. They lasted nearly twenty minutes." And throughout this agony, the soldiers would be standing stiffly to attention, their swords at the "carry," while the sweat poured down their faces, and the drums rolled out a long and somber accompaniment to the dying man's convulsions.

People found it hard to account for Herbert's desertion. He was a Waterloo veteran with a first-class record, who regularly remitted home most of his pay for his widowed mother, and he was highly regarded by the officers of that *corps d'élite,* the Bengal Horse Artillery. Two other artillerymen, Irishmen named O'Brien and Hennessey, were lucky to escape with a sentence of fourteen years' trans-
160

portation, an act of clemency that made the rest of the army extremely angry.

The Bhurtpore Field Force was broken up a few days later, and the 16th Lancers were ordered to march to Meerut, a cantonment near Delhi which was reputed to be a vast improvement on Cawnpore. They had reason to look back on their first campaign in India with some satisfaction, since during it they had blooded their lances and had plenty of excitement, with very few casualties. The total British losses amounted to fewer than a thousand, of which more than half were incurred during the actual assault, the 14th and 59th Foot losing 569 officers and men during the storm. The native regiments got off more lightly, as did the cavalry. The 16th Lancers lost no one killed, and they more than re-placed their killed horses by those they captured from the Jats. At an auction held on January 31, Lieutenant Lowe bought an elephant for 430 rupees, which he sold the same evening for double the price; and there were others in the regiment who emulated his example.

The prize money at Bhurtpore amounted to more than £480,000, Lord Combermere receiving £60,000 and thereby laying the foundations of his sizable family fortune. Each lieutenant-colonel received £1,500, and majors £950. John Luard's share was £450, and his subalterns received £250. Every European sergeant was given £12, and the rank and file £4 apiece.

The officers subscribed £1,000 for each of the widows of the four European officers killed in the battle; they also subscribed £1,000 to be distributed among the widows and orphans of the sixty-one European soldiers who were killed at Bhurtpore. By the standards of the time, it was not un-generous.

CHAPTER NINE

When Miss Eden visited Meerut, she described it as "a large European station—a quantity of barracks and white bungalows spread over four miles of plain. There is nothing to see or draw." In the absence of other diversions, and with that interest in the morbid that characterized so many Englishwomen in India, Miss Eden visited the cemetery, where she failed to discover "any one individual who lived to be more than thirty-six."

According to John Luard, however, Meerut was considered to be "the most desirable station in India, and relations between the civilians and military were a great deal more harmonious than in Cawnpore." There were musical parties, balls, and "dinners almost every night," but the most important attraction for Luard was the shooting to be had in the nearby jungles. There was also the thrill of riding down the wild pig, spear in hand and crashing through scrub and steep-sided watercourses on the back of a galloping horse. "Pig-sticking," as it came to be known, was still in its infancy so far as the "rules of the game" were concerned, but the excitement was the same, and John

162

Luard "formed a club with other officers in the 16th which hunted the wild pig around Meerut." There were also visits to places of interest within two or three days' ride, sleeping the night under the Indian stars, and filling the sketchbook by day. For men of Luard's type, India was never dull.

The soldiers also found Meerut an improvement on Cawnpore. Sergeant Thomas, of the 16th Lancers, has left a description of a shooting expedition which provides an interesting example of how some, at least, of the soldiers managed to fill in their time.

"The natives distill a liquor they call Nerem; very mild to drink, but it soon intoxicates. I was once nearly getting into an unpleasant scrape from drinking too much of it when out shooting. A party of us was to meet at Nerellah. Poor Tom Barnby and Tom Graves got leave and started overnight, while me, Tom Stone and Jack Grundle started after the morning duties. We mounted our tattoos (ponies) at about 9 a.m. and galloped off, taking with us plenty of provender in the shape of bacon, bread and onions etc. We got intelligence of the other two at Nerellah and found them about a mile and a half from there up to their middles in a swamp, duck shooting. We joined them in their sport and worked our way to the hut where they sold the native liquor. Such places the Europeans call 'Mud Rack Shops' or 'Smokey Choppers.' Well, we lay down in the shade of some luxuriant lime trees and disposed of a few bottles before the chaps began to talk of being hungry, for the Nerem is rare stuff to create an appetite. The others were for a start back for Nerellah where we had left the provender, but Jack Grundle proposed that he and I should start off to a peacock tope [1] about two miles off.

[1] The Hindustani word for grove of trees, in this case used by peafowl.

163

"So away we started and we had tolerable sport when we got there. We killed one of the finest peacocks I ever saw and this promised glorious sport. But Jack's inward man began to mutiny and it happened that just as we came through a tope we met one of the most tempting little mud rack shops. There could be no passing it, so we dismounted just to have one bottle. Then we thought, hang it, it's no use making a toil of pleasure, let's sit down and enjoy ourselves a bit; 'Come old man, bring us a bottle of the best and let us have it good.' It was good too and Jack and me were soon very easy.

"We sat there drinking and talking over our shooting adventures. Then I found my tongue going very fast and Jack was getting mellow; but he stood it better than I did, being a staunch old toper and well used to it. Well, we stayed there until I was regularly fuzzled. However, I mounted my tattoo all right and didn't find the effects too much until I had been on the road some time. At last to my surprise I found that I would soon fall off if I did not first get off, so I dismounted with exceeding care and laid myself down gracefully on the road, vowing that I neither could nor would move until I had something to eat. But of that there was no chance. Jack, after a most eloquent if semi-intoxicated appeal, in which he showed me clearly that it would be far better for me to come with him than to lie there, (to all of which I gave my unqualified consent, but moved not), dismounted, not for the purpose of accompanying me to the land of nod but to try two or three kicks in my ribs, thinking these no doubt a more forcible appeal. But it was no use and he left me to my fate.

"I was awoke just as the sun was sinking below the horizon by two hussies in the form of native girls, pleasant to the eye withal, who seemed inclined to be kind to me. They brought me water and oat cakes and I gave them grateful smiles and sweet words in return. They found my tattoo for me, and with many thanks I left them and made all speed to be back in barracks by 9 p.m. Poor Jack Grundle has since committed suicide." [2]

Drink, boredom, and the sun soon demoralized all but the best and most levelheaded soldiers. General Mansfield, reporting in 1857 on the British soldier in India, said that after ten years' service in that country the soldier was "less amenable to discipline, he is more slothful, and he becomes incapable of prolonged effort; indeed, it may be said, without exaggeration, of action altogether, except when he is under the impulse of excitement." [3] A total absence of hygiene, whether in camp or in the field, killed men off like flies, a single building serving one squadron of the 16th Lancers as a cookhouse, lavatory, and washhouse. The 44th Foot, who had arrived in Calcutta about the same time as the 16th Lancers, were so reduced by the subsequent campaign in the Arakan that they could only produce twenty-eight fit men on parade when they returned from the operations; they had lost upward of 1,000 men and forty officers, dead or sick, not one of them being killed or wounded in action.

Men drank too much, and ate too much, as seems clear from the supper provided at a ball given by the Bengal Artillery in December 1825. That elegant meal consisted of a large tureen of mulligatawny soup, a huge joint of boiled salt beef, and three plum puddings. The shade temperature was around one hundred degrees Fahrenheit, but Lieutenant Lowe asserted that he had never enjoyed himself more, and had two helpings of everything. Warren, who visited India in 1831, was astonished by the amount the English ate and drank. "My gentle neighbour," he wrote, "calmly

[2] Manuscript letters of Sergeant Thomas in possession of 16th/5th The Queen's Royal Lancers.
[3] *Gallant Gentlemen*, p. 174.

165

disposed of one bottle and a half of very strong beer, alternately with a certain amount of Burgundy. She finished up at dessert with five or six glasses of champagne, very light but very strong. The only effect this appears to have on her was to loosen her tongue and give vivacity to her eyes." [4]

It was certainly an exaggeration to assert, as did Warren, that the Englishwoman in India drank too much; he even went on to say that "as she gets older she often takes to brandy." Certainly the majority of the *mem-sahibs* lived as sober and as strait-laced a life in India as they would have been expected to live in England, but it must have been depressing in the extreme to be so frequently reminded of man's mortality. For every two children they bore in India, the odds were heavily weighted against more than one surviving, and the lack of exercise, the virtual absence of any form of intellectual activity, the concentration on petty etiquette, and the constant dread of illness in the family, all combined to make life in India something to be endured rather than enjoyed. Women aged fast, and, judging from their letters, rapidly became hypochondriacs, although there were of course many who broke away from convention and lived as full a life in India as they would ever have done at home.

John Luard was now thirty-five, an age at which men of his class and generation normally started to think of marriage. It is true that he had dallied with the idea seven years before, while in Ireland, but it was in Meerut that he finally decided to take the plunge. The senior civilian there was Richard Hastings Scott, the judge and magistrate, and his two sisters, Elizabeth and Maria, kept house for him. They were the belles of Meerut society, and every officer in

[4] *Bygone Days in India,* p. 221.

the 16th Lancers who was not already married or engaged set out to woo them. It was not an easy contest, since the General commanding the garrison, Sir Thomas Reynell, was also a suitor, and a general in love was unlikely to look kindly on any captain or subaltern who sought to come between him and the lady of his choice. John Luard was sufficiently in love with Elizabeth Scott to take the risk, and they were married on September 25, 1826. "Sir Thomas Reynell was a most generous rival," wrote Luard, "and never altered his friendship for me, and made Elizabeth a most handsome present of a necklace on her wedding." She was twenty-six, "not very strong in health, but all that any husband could wish for in a wife."

Marriage inevitably involved a change in John Luard's life. Instead of spending most of his free time and leaves on shooting trips, he now found himself taking part in the social life of Meerut. There were calls to be made, and calls to be answered; large and interminable dinner parties which in turn resulted in the Luards being asked back to dinners of equal length and endurance. They were, of course, high in the social register, John as a result of his rank and position in a British cavalry regiment, and Elizabeth as a result of her relationship to Meerut's first citizen —and there was always Major-General Sir Thomas Reynell as a benevolent supporter in the background. There was never enough money, but John Luard had a small private income besides his pay, and this permitted them to maintain the numerous servants and to indulge in the entertaining necessary for anyone who wished to be in the social swim. "Elizabeth was a good hostess and particularly enjoyed music," wrote Luard of the early days of his marriage, from which one may conclude that some form of musical entertainment formed part of the dinner parties they gave. And there were picnics as well, served under the most comfortable of conditions by a retinue of servants, after a leisurely ride out from Meerut on either elephants or ponies. "Elizabeth rode very well," wrote Luard, "and we often made expeditions out into the surrounding countryside."

Their eldest son, Richard, was born on July 28, 1827, and Elizabeth was very ill both before and after her son's birth. Perhaps she had been too long in the sun and her resistance had been lowered, or perhaps it was just that medical attention was too rough and ready; Luard does not say in his journal, but he does write that "Elizabeth was frequently ill after Richard's birth and the doctor said that only a change of climate would cure her." They were then faced with the difficult decision of whether to remain in India, where they were much better off than they would be at home, or to return to England on long leave, which might well entail leaving the 16th Lancers. They took two years to make up their minds, but in the end the problem was decided for them by their child's continued ill-health. Yielding at last to the advice of their doctor, John Luard applied for home leave, and in October 1829 they left Meerut and traveled down to Calcutta by river. The baby "nearly died" on the way, but they reached Calcutta in February of the following year and took passage for England in the *Marquis of Wellington*. Luard was fortunate in being appointed second-in-command of a party of sick and time-expired soldiers who were being shipped home, and he thereby obtained a free passage, but he had to pay £425 for his wife's cabin. This made an appreciable hole in the money they had been able to save in Meerut.

The Luards were preceded home by Lieutenant Lowe. That gay young cavalryman had found it expedient to apply for home leave in order to recuperate his health—either because he found that the pleasures of Meerut soon paled or because of the many irate husbands who were thirsting for his blood. Before leaving Meerut he was kind enough to present each of his lady friends with some farewell lines in shockingly bad verse, and he then set off for Calcutta, breaking hearts in every station where he stopped en route.[5] Lowe was a great wangler, as well as lover, and he found no difficulty in wangling a free passage to England, where he spent the best part of two years in hunting, making love, and forgetting all he knew about soldiering. Then, it seems, the absence of ready cash, and a hint from the 16th Lancers that he was in imminent danger of being struck off the regimental list, compelled his return to the East.

For John Luard, the voyage home was as long, and as tedious, as the journey out. They landed only at Saint Helena, where he sketched the few objects of interest the island possessed, and visited Bonaparte's grave. "We went to see Bonaparte's tomb," he wrote, "under charge of an old sergeant of the 53rd Regiment; it was a disgrace to England and the old house at Longwood was a miserable place. I made sketches. His bed room was converted into a stable and his dinner room where he died was a mill." Lowe also criticized the state of Napoleon's house and tomb. These are interesting examples of the respect and sympathy British officers had for their old opponent. Luard was critical, too, of the high prices prevailing in the island. "Boarded at a Mr Eyres. We had a good dinner and plenty of fish, but were charged enormously. I bought some shoes for little Dick and a black waistcoat for myself, also some eggs and fruit. It cost me altogether for two days nearly 18 £."

They arrived in England on July 3, 1830, eight years al-

<hr>

[5] "When distance puts us, fairest lady
   Think of one, sometimes, I pray thee
   Who whate'er his fortune be,
   With fondness will remember thee."
   —*The Diary of an Officer of the 16th (Queen's) Lancers*, p. 144.

most to the day since John Luard had sailed from Tilbury. To his great sorrow he learned that his father had died the previous May, leaving the estate at Blyborough to John's eldest brother, and his West Indian property in Saint Kitts to the youngest children. His brother George, to whom he was devoted, had been compelled to leave the army as a result of a hunting accident, and for the past five years had been enduring a pain-racked existence in a wheel chair. The family fortunes were not very rosy, and even had Luard wanted to leave the army, the time was hardly propitious for such a step. But before the end of his leave he would have to make up his mind whether or not to return to India and his regiment, or arrange an exchange into another regiment which was garrisoned at home. When it came to the point, he chose the latter course.

The Luards took a house in London for their leave, but spent a good deal of their time visiting relations. John Luard did not take kindly to doing nothing, and so spent days preparing for publication his book *Sketches of India*. These were sketches drawn on stone and accompanied by descriptive pieces on scenes of Indian life, and they were eventually published in 1837 with a great deal of acclaim. He was also extremely interested in the history of uniforms and employed much of his leisure in collecting material which subsequently formed the foundation of his *History of the Dress of the British Army*, which he published in 1852. These, with hunting and shooting, filled in the days; John Luard was not the type of man who ever allowed time to hang heavily on his hands.

On November 16, 1832 he exchanged his captaincy in the 16th Lancers with a Captain Maunsell of the 30th Foot. It was not done without a good deal of thought, and even more heart-searchings, for Luard, as his journal makes clear, was a devoted 16th Lancer. He never ceased regarding himself as one, even though he never served with the regiment again, and on his return to India he took the liveliest interest in the regiment's fortunes during the Afghanistan campaign. But this was all in the future, and for the next eight years he passed his time in what we today would describe as staff appointments, and the Luards lived in London for most of the time in a rented house in Baker Street.

There were no staff officers as we understand the term in the British Army today; every general officer had a personal staff of aides-de-camp, military secretaries, and so on, filling the appointments with such of his own relations and friends as he wished to oblige. Sir Charles Dalbiac, John Luard's uncle and commanding officer of Peninsular days, now held the appointment of Inspector General of Cavalry, and it was only natural that John Luard should avail himself of the General's influence. Dalbiac did not fail him and appointed his nephew as his aide-de-camp. It was not a very onerous post, for seldom has military thought been more stagnant. Bumbling old generals were rooted in the past, fearful only lest any reformer should succeed in altering regulations that time had hallowed. At the outset of the Crimean War, the British Army had thirteen generals with over seventy years' service, thirty-seven with between sixty and seventy years', and 163 with between fifty and sixty years'.[6] Until advancing years blurred even their eyesight, they were swift to detect any deviation in dress or drill movements, but their knowledge of tactics had advanced not at all since their days as subalterns. However, this barely signified, because there had been few changes in weapons, and a knowledge of close-order drill was far more important than any study of field craft.

Staff work was merely a matter of writing the general's

[6] *Gallant Gentlemen,* p. 199.

letters for him, and any original ideas were rapidly stultified by the red tape that clogged every military department. Old men commanded old soldiers—recruits being hard to come by—and men served on until they had almost to be assisted onto parade. The working population of that time did not play organized games, or even watch them as they do today, and there was therefore no requirement for the officers to interest themselves in their soldiers' leisure. "Beer and baccy" was all the soldier required to keep him happy, or so people thought, and the officer was free to leave his soldiers to amuse themselves. But it would be a mistake to assume that this laissez-faire attitude gave cause for resentment. There was a genuine comradeship between officers and men in most regiments, the soldier being as quick then as he is now to detect the spurious and the inefficient. A good officer like Luard would have no difficulty in persuading his men to follow him in action, however unpleasant the consequences for all concerned, and some of the soldiers were just as staunch supporters of privilege as was their commander in chief.

"In truth they do not make good officers," said the Duke of Wellington in 1836, when giving his views on promoting men from the ranks. "They are brought into the society and manners to which they are not accustomed; they cannot bear being at all heated with wine or liquor. . . . I think in general they are quarrelsome . . . and they are not persons that can be borne in the society of officers in the Army; they are men of different manners altogether." [7] This was reactionary, maybe, but many a private soldier would have endorsed the Duke's sentiments.

Since few of the officers, and certainly hardly any in the cavalry, were dependent solely on their pay, it was com-

[7] *Ibid.*, p. 207.

172

paratively easy for an officer to adjust his military career to suit his private requirements. John Luard, for example, went on half pay on joining his uncle's staff; he was therefore not carried on the establishment of any regiment, and there was no limit to the time he would be able to do this. It gave him time to look around and decide about his future. He was also able to purchase an unattached majority in 1834 for the sum of £3,000—"£1500 less than a majority in the 16th Lancers would have cost"—and four years later he was given a brevet lieutenant-colonelcy, the reward for being on the staff of the Inspector General of Cavalry at the time of Queen Victoria's coronation. He was ascending the military ladder at a respectable pace without any of the tedium of serving with troops or of enduring the inconvenience of overseas service, and he was being spared the discomfort of the hot weather in Meerut, where his old regiment was suffering a great deal from illness; 364 of them, out of a strength of 580, were in hospital, and cholera had killed forty-eight.

There was now a growing family of three sons and a daughter to be provided for, Elizabeth Luard bearing with fortitude the lot of every godly matron of her day, which was to produce a child every twelve or eighteen months. In the fourteen years of her married life, she bore John Luard four sons and two daughters, her pregnancies interspersed with miscarriages and ill-health. Luard, who was a devoted husband, was fully aware of the danger to her health that a return to India might produce, but he was finding it increasingly difficult to make ends meet in England. As aide-de-camp to Sir Charles Dalbiac he was forced to maintain an establishment of horses and carriages, as well as a house in London, while uniforms were growing more and more elaborate and expensive. It was therefore with something approaching relief that he opened a letter from his old commander of Bhurtpore days, Sir Jasper Nicolls, in May 1838, and read that Nicolls was going out to India as commander in chief of the Madras Army, and would be glad if Luard went with him as military secretary. After long hours of anxious family consultation, for the three eldest children would have to be left behind, Luard decided to accept; and on July 13, with "my dear wife, with Freddy and Charley, and a servant Eliza, I went from the Gloster Hotel, Dover Street, in the Rocket Coach to Portsmouth, and boarded the East Indiaman *Carnatic,* that same evening." The three elder children never saw their mother again, and Richard, the eldest, was not yet eleven.

Lieutenant-General Sir Jasper Nicolls, who came aboard the next morning, together with his wife and "two very charming daughters," first came to notice during the disastrous British expedition to South America in 1805. As Major Nicolls of the 45th Foot, he had been one of the few to achieve distinction during the fighting in Buenos Aires. He had added to that reputation in Spain, where he had commanded the 14th Foot, and again at Bhurtpore as a divisional commander. Now, after more than forty-five years' faithful service, he was to receive his reward in the command of the Madras Presidency Army, an appointment that would bring him more comfort than glory, but one in which he could be relied upon to do nothing to upset the existing order. He was old, shrewd, and opinionated, but a man of character with a deep suspicion of civilians and all their ways. This was later to bring him into conflict with two successive governors-general, Lords Auckland and Ellenborough, for both of whom he had the profoundest contempt, regarding the former as a nincompoop, and the latter as an arrogant idiot. They might both have cut a better figure in history had they heeded the advice of the cantankerous and taciturn old General.

Luard has left an account of the expense involved in setting up house in Madras. He had to employ twenty-four servants at a cost of nearly £20 a month—which hardly seems excessive in view of the numbers involved—and maintain an establishment of four horses, a pony, two carriages, and a buggy. His pay amounted to nearly £125 a month, exclusive of his half pay, which continued to be paid in England, and his salary does not compare unfavorably with a lieutenant-colonel's pay today, taking into consideration the higher purchasing power of the pound at that time and the much lower rate of income tax; there were also certain "perks" which went with his appointment as military secretary. On the other hand, there were no houses provided by the government at nominal rents, and John Luard had, therefore, to buy his own bungalow, which was "large and roomy with a pleasant garden," and then furnish it. When Sir Jasper Nicolls was unexpectedly transferred to command the Bengal Army after less than a year in Madras, Luard had to foot the bill for the transfer of his goods and chattels to Calcutta, as well as pay for the passage of his wife and children to Bengal.

Sir Jasper's promotion, for that is what his appointment to command the Bengal Army amounted to, was the result of his friendship with Rowland Hill, the commander in chief of the British Army. Lord Hill was determined to give the principal military command in India to someone in whom he had confidence, and that meant a veteran of Hill's old division in the peninsula. The fact that the appointment of an officer of the Royal Army to be commander in chief entailed passing over the claims of many senior officers in the Company's army carried no weight with Lord Hill. The important thing was to put a "safe" man in the job, and who could be safer than old Nicolls?

The General, his staff, and their families were lucky to

175

reach Calcutta safely. They sailed from Madras in an old tub called the *Golconda,* which was virtually unmanageable in a heavy sea; she stuck on a sandbank while being towed up the Hooghly by a steamer, developed an alarming list, and very nearly capsized. Later, when refloated on the tide, she was carried downstream in a "crab-wise motion which made all the ladies very ill," and narrowly missed running ashore. Luard considered it to be the most alarming of the many voyages he made, and was extremely thankful when eventually they reached Calcutta. The *Golconda* disappeared without trace the following year while on passage from Madras to Rangoon with half a battalion of Madras infantry.

Calcutta, the seat of the Governor-General, was a very different kind of place from provincial Madras. When the Luards arrived there toward the end of 1839, nearly all the conversation was about the war in Afghanistan which had begun the previous year. As military secretary to the commander in chief, and, as such, his confidential factotum, John Luard now found himself dealing with matters of high policy, a fascinating if sometimes frustrating experience. Not surprisingly, his views on affairs tended to reflect those held by his master, and Sir Jasper left no one in any doubt of his opinion that the campaign in Afghanistan was misguided, and probably doomed to failure; "unfortunately," wrote Luard, "he proved to be right."

The threat of an overland invasion through Persia and Afghanistan had long existed in India; Alexander the Great had come that way, and it was through the passes of the Hindu Kush that Nadir Shah and other conquerors had swooped down on Hindustan. Napoleon, at the height of his power, had sent emissaries to Persia to spy out the way, and French and British agents had flitted around Central Asia, risking death by hideous torture, in a romantic en-

176

deavor to seduce the local khans to their side. Napoleon's defeat had removed any threat from France, and the Honorable East India Company might therefore have been reasonably expected to relax its fears, but it was prevented from doing this by the steady advance of Russian power in Central Asia. As each barbaric emirate was swallowed up, so the fear of Russian dominion over Persia and Afghanistan increased in Calcutta and London, and some time early in the 1830's a belief grew among those soldiers and civil servants concerned with high policy that Russia's ultimate ambition was to possess herself first of Afghanistan, and thereafter of India.

Matters were complicated for these honorable, and by no means unintelligent, men by the nature of the Afghans and the other races of Central Asia. In general they were wild, fanatical, xenophobic, and fiercely independent. They lived in oases or fertile valleys, separated from each other by barren desert or savage mountains, and were as harsh and cruel as the countries in which they lived, owning allegiance only to those of their rulers who were even harsher and crueler than they were themselves. In Afghanistan, for example, the sirdars, or tribal chiefs, were constantly at war with one another, one of their practices being to put out their captives' eyes, or to incarcerate them in lightless dungeons for years on end. Europeans who ventured into such regions did so at the peril of their lives, and the majority left their bones there. Occasionally the tribes would unite under a strong leader and burst out from their mountains and deserts to found some transient empire, which would endure for a few generations and then disintegrate from internecine feuds, self-indulgence, and individual ambitions.

One such empire had been the Durani empire of the Afghans, founded by Ahmad Shah in the early eighteenth century, which at one stage contested the dominion of India with the Marathas and the English. On several occasions the bloodthirsty Afghans poured down through the north-western passes as far south as Delhi, sacking the villages, forcibly converting the inhabitants to Islam, and sending back to Kabul, Kandahar, and Herat the spoils of conquest. "Pearl of the Age," or *Dur-i-Durân,* was the title assumed by Ahmad Shah on his coronation, and so long as he lived the Afghans were a great military power; his empire, however, disintegrated rapidly after his death. The frontiers rapidly receded, until they approximated more or less to those of Afghanistan today, Ahmad Shah's descendants found themselves waging war more with their own subjects than with the Persians or Indians, and the country relapsed into its usual state of anarchy.

Simultaneous with this collapse of the Afghan empire came the rise of three other empires, the Russian, the East India Company's, and the Sikh. The last was the creation of Maharajah Ranjit Singh, a man of genius, with a taste for debauchery unsurpassed in India at that time, and an ambition to make his Hindu warrior sect the principal power in India. He was, however, clever enough to appreciate the strength of the East India Company and he early resolved never to cross swords with the English. Instead, he turned his attention to the northwest, where the Afghans were busily fighting among themselves, and partly by battle, but mostly by intrigue, he possessed himself of all the former Afghan territory up to the Khyber Pass. His ambition would scarcely have stopped there had he not realized that his Sikhs were no match for the Afghans in their native mountains, and so he settled down to consolidate his newly won empire by sowing discord among the Afghans.

The materials for doing this were ready to hand. Another strong man had appeared in Afghanistan in the person of

Dost Mohammed, who had experienced little difficulty in ousting the legitimate ruler, Shah Shuja, from the throne. The latter took refuge in Lahore with Ranjit Singh, and the wily Sikh proceeded to strip Shah Shuja of all his jewels and treasure, which included the famous Koh-i-noor diamond, before agreeing to assist the exile to win back his throne. A combined Sikh and Afghan expedition then advanced as far as Kandahar, where it was ignominiously defeated by Dost Mohammed, and Shah Shuja once more fled to India. Profiting from his previous experience at Ranjit Singh's hands, he did not stop traveling until he reached British territory, where he placed himself under the protection of the Company. And, after a short period to recover his breath and his equilibrium, he reopened his intrigues to overthrow Dost Mohammed, and in circumstances that were unexpectedly propitious for his cause.

The steady Russian advance toward the Oxus was creating great alarm in Calcutta. Lord Auckland, the Governor-General, was a well-intentioned, languid, and irresolute English aristocrat with an inclination to pay undue attention to the opinions of a few selected advisers. These were all clever men, but extremely opinionated, and none more so than William Macnaghten, whose appointment in the Indian government can best be described as that of foreign secretary. Macnaghten had gone out to India originally as a cadet in the Company's army, but had early set out to master several of the Indian languages, including Persian, which was then the language of Eastern diplomacy, just as French was in the West. A curious, aloof, and self-centered man, Macnaghten held the conventional military mind in contempt; what he had seen of his brother officers during his comparatively short period of military service had not impressed him. He preferred and trusted those young military officers who had taken the same course as himself, which was to escape as rapidly as possible from the army and become "politicals." They were fluent in native languages, knowledgeable about native customs, and as convinced as experts often are that their opinions were the only ones worth heeding, irrespective of other considerations.

Miss Eden described Macnaghten as *"our* Lord Palmerston, a dry sensible man, who wears an enormous pair of blue spectacles, and speaks Persian, Arabic and Hindustani rather more fluently than English." Her brother, who found governing the East India Company's territories a tedious and perplexing business, leaned heavily on Macnaghten's advice. Luard thought this advice "to be ill-considered and often wrong," while Lieutenant Lowe, who had gone campaigning with Macnaghten, thought him "dry as dry, like an old nut, and so reserved as to be rude."

There were, of course, other advisers, such as those who composed the Governor-General's council in Calcutta, but at the crucial moment, when Shah Shuja approached the British for aid, Lord Auckland was three months' march from Calcutta, touring the upper provinces, which were in the grip of an appalling famine, paying a courtesy visit on Ranjit Singh, and enjoying the climate and the amenities of Simla. There, among the deodars, with the Himalayas always in view, the Russian threat to Afghanistan must have seemed less remote than might have been the case in Calcutta, and, in any case, the dispatches from London were full of warnings of possible Russian intentions. Macnaghten, on the available evidence, had already made up his mind that a friendly ruler in Afghanistan was a vital requirement; there was no other way, short of annexation, that could guarantee the northwestern frontier. Despite the advice of Sir Alexander Burnes, a flamboyant young political officer who had already visited Kabul and been favorably impressed by the so-called usurper, Dost Mohammed, Macnaghten came to the conclusion that Shah Shuja was the man for the British. Whereas Dost Mohammed, for all that Burnes said in his favor, was at loggerheads with the Sikhs and seemed disinclined to give a firm guarantee against receiving a Russian mission in Kabul, Shah Shuja was prepared to promise anything. Pacing the mountaintops around Jakko, peering through his blue spectacles at the enormous pile of files on his desk, discussing the pros and cons with his chosen "politicals" until far into the night, Macnaghten eventually persuaded Auckland to sign a tripartite treaty with Ranjit Singh and Shah Shuja, which, among other clauses, promised the latter armed assistance for the recovery of his throne. There was thus set in train a series of events which was to culminate in the most disastrous campaign that Britain was to wage in the East until she was defeated in Malaya and Burma by the Japanese in 1942—exactly a hundred years later and under equally humiliating circumstances.

At the time Auckland was trying to make up his mind whether or not to support Shah Shuja, Sir Jasper Nicolls and his staff were out of touch with great events. They were still in Madras, which was an immense distance from Simla in 1838, and, in addition, the commander in chief was newly arrived in the Presidency and fully occupied visiting and reviewing the regiments under his command; what went on in the far northwest was the business of the Bengal Army, not of that of Madras, and it was not until he arrived in Calcutta in October of the following year that Sir Jasper found himself responsible for conducting a campaign of which he heartily disapproved, not least because there were far too many civilians mixed up with it, some of whom, like Macnaghten, he disliked all the more because he had never made their acquaintance.

His open disapprobation could not have been more unwelcome to the Governor-General, who had returned to Calcutta from Simla glowing with self-satisfaction. He did not find it easy to weigh conflicting opinions and make up his mind, and when he had brought himself to do so, and with apparently happy results, it was all the more irritating to feel that his principal military adviser was against the whole affair. "Sir Jasper Nicolls did not approve of the government's policy in Afghanistan," wrote Luard, "and frequently counselled against our involving ourselves further." It must have been an insufferable bore for an aristocrat like Lord Auckland to have his decisions questioned by a gruff and glowering old soldier, who was probably no more articulate in council than most generals of his time. Meanwhile, from beyond the Hindu Kush, came dispatch after dispatch from Macnaghten, hailing the advance into Afghanistan as one of the most brilliant operations of all time, describing the enthusiasm of the Afghans for the return of the conceited and dim-witted Shah Shuja as precisely what he had foretold all along, and attributing much of the success to the able handling of the situation by the bright young political officers who had accompanied him to Kabul. So far as Lord Auckland and his devoted sisters could see, there was no cause for concern, and indeed every reason for congratulation.

CHAPTER TEN

For most of the next four years John Luard was to find himself inextricably involved in events in Afghanistan. Despite Sir Jasper Nicolls' disapproval of the whole concept of the campaign, the old General had inherited the plan from his predecessor and had no alternative but to see it through. Initially in Calcutta, and later in the upper provinces, which were nearer to the seat of operations, John Luard had to toil through dispatches from Kabul, Kandahar, and Jalalabad, some absurdly optimistic and others full of warnings of disaster, sifting truth from rumor in an attempt to provide his general with a dispassionate background to the events which were taking place more than a thousand miles away, behind the barrier of the Hindu Kush. He had, moreover, a close personal interest in the campaign, since many old comrades in the 16th Lancers were deeply involved in the fortunes of the war, and he must often have wished himself with them instead of poring over dispatches far into the night in the steamy heat of Bengal. For this reason, although the campaign was already over a year old before Luard arrived in Calcutta, some idea of what had occurred previously is essential in order to see the campaign through Luard's eyes.

Orders for the assembly of an army to invade Afghanistan went out during October 1838. "The probability of a campaign beyond our North-West Frontier has been for months the general topic of conversation," wrote Lowe on October 30, "but till the beginning of August it was not decidedly known our Government had determined to march an army down the left bank of the Indus, while a force from Bombay would march up the right bank and meet us at Shikarpur. After the free navigation of the Indus has been established, the united forces proceed through Candahar to Caubul, depose Dost Mahommed from the throne of Caubul and reinstate Shah Shujah. It is supposed all this will be effected by the summer of 1839, and the force is to pass the hot weather in Guzni or some of the Highlands of Afghanistan. We are then to proceed to Herat (at a rough guess I suppose 2,000 miles from our territories) now besieged by the Persians, aided by Russia, and recapture the fort . . . should it have fallen." [1]

The plan of campaign was much as Lowe surmised. There were two possible routes of invasion from India into Afghanistan: the one, direct on Kabul through the Khyber Pass, and the other, a more roundabout route, by way of Baluchistan and Kandahar. The military planners, if such there were in India at that time, chose the latter route on two counts. Firstly, because the Khyber Pass, although more direct, was a serious military obstacle, and there were other difficult passes between the Khyber and Kabul; and secondly, because the lines of communication by the Khyber route would run through Ranjit Singh's territory, and were

[1] *The Diary of an Officer of the 16th (Queen's) Lancers*, p. 280.

therefore liable to interruption at the whim of that unpredictable and capricious despot. The advantage of the route down the Indus and thence through Baluchistan was that it would open up the Indus to navigation and would not be so liable to interference by the Sikhs. The fact that it would entail a march mostly through desert, where the scarcity of water and forage posed a most serious problem to an army encumbered with tens of thousands of civilian followers and baggage animals, was quietly ignored. The British in India were not inclined to look for difficulties in their projected operations; they preferred to launch them and then allow the difficulties to manifest themselves.

The main army, grandiloquently named the "Army of the Indus," was to be composed of two divisions of the Bengal Army; it was to assemble at Ferozepore, on the Sutlej, early in November, and would then be reviewed by Lord Auckland and Maharajah Ranjit Singh. A division of the Bombay Army would meanwhile move up the Indus from Karachi, and the two forces would combine at Shikarpur before advancing into Baluchistan. The 16th Lancers received their orders to join the Army of the Indus on October 16 and started off for Ferozepore four days later, everyone in high spirits at the prospect of active service, although Lowe (now a captain) was hardly convinced of the justice of their cause.

"Sir Alexander Burnes and all European travellers who have visited his Court speak of Dost Mahommed as a fine soldier of high character, governing his country mildly and beneficially for all classes, and well-disposed towards our Government. One of the best actions of his life, undoubtedly, was kicking Shah Shujah for his many misdeeds out of Afghanistan. Our protegé Shah Shujah is, we understand, universally despised as a coward and a tyrant in the country he lost. . . . The policy of Government cannot be fathomed, and we can only surmise that there must be certain intelligence of Russia intriguing with Dost Mahommed for a passage of troops through Afghanistan for the invasion of Hindoostan." [2]

There was in fact no such "certain" intelligence, and not for the first time, or for the last, the robust common sense of the ordinary officer was a good deal nearer the heart of the matter than were the imaginings of his political masters.

The 16th Lancers took nearly a month to cover the 270 miles from Meerut to Ferozepore; behind them trailed a vast caravan of noncombatants, without whom they could scarcely have existed. There were men to pitch the soldiers' tents, since no European in India could be expected to pitch his own; grooms to tend the soldiers' horses, and grasscutters to cut grass for the animals; drivers to twist the tails of the patient bullocks as they plodded through the dust, dragging the creaking carts piled high with camp furniture, boxes of mess plate, crates of crockery, boxes of wine and cigars, and every other luxury needed to take the sting out of a campaigner's existence; men to lead the long strings of camels, lurching and swaying under the bales of hay carried for the horses; other men to drive the officers' carriages and buggies, to cook the food, to cut the hair, to draw the water, to clean the camp sites, to sell the soldiers food, drink, and women. In all, there were nearly 5,000 followers to minister to the needs of a regiment less than 800 strong, and the number soon swelled to around 30,000 men, women, and children as the Army of the Indus set out for Afghanistan. How any army managed to fight a campaign with such an incubus is hard to comprehend—but they did.

On November 29 the army staged a grand review for Lord Auckland and the Company's newly acquired ally,

[2] *Ibid.*, p. 281.

Maharajah Ranjit Singh. The "Lion of the Punjab" approached the British camp at the head of a vast retinue mounted on elephants and escorted by squadron after squadron of gorgeously clad and "indifferently mounted" cavalry. Auckland rode out to meet him, mounted also on an elephant, and then the Sikh entered Auckland's howdah, embracing him as he did so, and breathing a mixture of garlic and country spirits down the noble lord's neck. Later they dismounted and went into a splendid durbar tent pitched specially for the occasion, but so darkened to keep out the glare that Ranjit stumbled over a heap of cannon balls piled in the entrance as part of the Company's gift to their new ally. Miss Eden, who had painted a picture of Queen Victoria for Ranjit, described him as "exactly like an old mouse, with grey whiskers and one eye." [3] Lieutenant Mackinnon was less flattering: "The maharajah was rather below the middling stature, slight in form, and his face expressive of the shrewdest cunning. The leer that occasionally escaped from his single optic seemed to tell a clear tale of debauchery." [4] Ranjit Singh was about fifty-six at the time, but looked much older; his addiction to a special brew which burned like "liquid fire" had begun to affect even his iron constitution. Yet he was, according to his lights, a great man, and the Sikhs have yet to produce a greater.

Two days later Ranjit Singh returned the compliment by staging a review of his own. The Sikh infantry greatly impressed the British spectators, and their nobility were splendidly attired, several of them wearing epaulettes composed entirely of pearls. Ranjit, on the other hand, was plainly dressed. He had been so impressed by the Company's army when first he encountered it that he had engaged foreign adventurers to train his own along the same lines,

[3] *Up the Country,* p. 198.
[4] *Military Service in the Far East,* p. 62.

187

and there could be no doubt about the success of their efforts. "It is a horrid thing, which we none of us own publicly," wrote Miss Eden, "but there is every reason to believe that Runjeet Singh's troops are quite as well disciplined as ours." [5] The Sikh army was undeniably the most formidable native force in India, and yet Lord Auckland was launching an army into Afghanistan entirely dependent on the good will of the Sikhs for the safety of that army's lines of communication. "It was a foolhardy enterprise," Luard was to write later, "and one which no soldier could easily condone."

Shah Shuja was absent from these ceremonies, doubtless having no desire to resume acquaintance with the man who had relieved him of all his finest jewels and humiliated him in the process. He had already set off down the Indus on the first stage of his journey back to Afghanistan, and Lowe saw him some weeks later when the cavalry brigade was paraded for his inspection at Shikarpur.

"The Shah passed down the line in a litter borne by numerous bearers dressed in scarlet, and wearing high scarlet caps; for his age he is one of the handsomest men I ever saw; very fair, with a beard as black as the raven's wing, reaching down to his girdle. It is quite provoking to see a man with such an exterior, and to reflect he should have the character of being a coward and thoroughly worthless." [6]

Macnaghten would probably have disagreed, but the shrewd Captain Lowe was not wide of the mark. Shah Shuja had a fine presence and an inordinate sense of his own importance, but he lacked the character to sustain either. He was vain, pusillanimous, and cruel; he only believed what he wanted to believe, and that was invariably anything that was in his own favor. He took with him down

[5] *Letters from India*, p. 114.
[6] *The Diary of an Officer of the 16th (Queen's) Lancers*, p. 308.

the Indus a motley crowd of cutthroats and adventurers, who made up what was euphemistically known as the "Shah's Army." This rag, tag, and bobtail, sharked up from every bazaar and broken-down rajah's court in Upper India, had been drilled into some semblance of order by officers and noncommissioned officers lent from the Bengal Army for that purpose, but its military value was negligible. It amounted to 6,000 infantry, cavalry, and artillery, and many of the Bengal sepoys were lured into its ranks by the promise of higher pay and quicker promotion. "It was said at the time," wrote Sita Ram, who joined it as a havildar, "that this army was paid by the Company Bahadoor. All I know is, that when the Shah regained his throne, he could not pay his own guards." [7] Brigadier Abraham Roberts of the Bengal Army had the unenviable task of commanding this rabble; although he was distinguished enough in his own right, probably his main claim to fame is that he was the father of Field Marshal Earl Roberts of Kandahar, V.C., the best-known and certainly best-loved of all the commanders in chief of the old Indian Army.

The original intention had been that the Army of the Indus should be commanded by Sir Henry Fane, the elderly, irascible, but respected commander in chief of the Bengal Army. However, once it was known that the siege of Herat had been abandoned by the Persians, there was no longer any requirement to send two divisions from the Bengal Army into Afghanistan. One division from Bengal, together with one from the Bombay Army and the Shah's own troops, would suffice, and the over-all command was given to Major-General John Keane, commander in chief of the Bombay Army, who was about to advance up the Indus from Karachi with his division. This was a very un-

[7] Sita Ram, *From Sepoy to Subedar,* translated by Lieut. Col. Norgate, Lahore, 1873, p. 75.

popular decision, because Keane was universally disliked. He was a coarse, blustering, and bullying Anglo-Irishman, whose nickname since Peninsular War days had been the "Fortunate Youth," the inference being that he owed his success more to luck than to ability. He belonged to the Royal Army, having next to no experience of Indian warfare, but made up for this lack of knowledge by an open and undisguised contempt for the Company's officers. An apt, clever officer, but hardly deserving the name of general, was Havelock's summing-up of this much-disliked officer.

Major-General Sir Willoughby Cotton, who commanded the Bengal division, was a totally different character. He, too, was an officer of the Royal Army, but with long experience of India; debt, incurred as the principal dandy in the Guards, compelled him to try his fortunes abroad, where he was more successful in making friends than in improving his finances. Cotton must have been very high-spirited in his youth; while a boy at Rugby School he led a rebellion and burned the headmaster's desk and schoolbooks in the Close. He was a typical example of the British officer who was equally at home in camps or at Court, having fought through Spain with the Guards, been a boon companion of the Prince Regent, and held a command in Burma during 1824-1825. A *bon viveur,* whose rotund shape was visible evidence of his fondness for high living, he endeared himself to Ranjit Singh by his ability to drink that ruler's hell brew, and not only quaff it at a draught, but come back for more. "He came back of course very tipsy," wrote Miss Eden, "but they said he was very amusing at dinner." Cotton was a great talker, popular with both officers and soldiers, and even the Company's officers liked him. He was polished and dignified, shrewd and tactful, and commendably prompt in dealing with business. He could, however, be exceedingly irritable, no doubt as a result of his excessive wining and

190

dining, and he was not overkeen on responsibility. "I don't think," wrote Sir Henry Fane, "that Cotton has a mind which carries away much of verbal instructions," but this did not prevent him from entrusting Cotton with command of a division.

The other senior general was William Nott, a Company officer with over thirty years' service in the Bombay Army. A solid and very dour man, who combined an almost fanatical devotion for his sepoys with a robust and imperturbable common sense, Nott came out of the Afghan War with a better reputation than any of his brother generals. Unfortunately, he was a bad co-operator, liverish rather than quick-tempered, contemptuous of the Royal Army, which he considered inferior to the Company's, and jealous of the Bengal Army, which he thought inferior to that of Bombay. Nott took over command of the Bombay division when Keane was promoted to the command in chief, and thereafter neither pressure from the Governor-General nor the pleadings of his own officers could persuade him to act against his better judgment. Constant, cautious, and crotchety, Nott was fifty-six at the outset of the campaign, Keane was fifty-seven, and Cotton fifty-five. They were young as generals went in those days, and between them they possessed sufficient military experience to make short work of the Afghans. Their judgment, however, was clouded by mutual antipathy and parochial jealousies, and perhaps the only thing they really shared in common was a deep-rooted suspicion and dislike of the political officers with whom they were saddled.

It is impossible to understand the sequence of events that finally culminated in disaster in Afghanistan without some knowledge of the relationship that existed between the military commanders and their political advisers. "The interference of the political officers in military matters is quite intolerable," wrote John Luard eighteen months later, and he was only echoing the opinions of men like Nott and Cotton, whose dispatches were full of complaints. There has, of course, always been a conflict between the military and the political mind, and perhaps the most famous example is the wrangling that went on between the "frocks" and "brass hats" during the 1914-1918 war. But the First Afghan War is worth study as an example of the inability of those responsible for the political direction to understand the military implications of their policy, and of the generals' failure to convince their political masters of the military dangers.

Matters were undoubtedly additionally complicated by the character of Sir William Macnaghten, who had been chosen to represent the Governor-General at Shah Shuja's court. He had little use for army officers and a sublime faith in his own judgment, preferring the advice of young captains only recently transferred to the Political Department, to that of generals and colonels who had spent their life in the army. "The gentleman employed to command the Army" was how Wellington contemptuously described Macnaghten, and it is certainly true that the Army of the Indus was completely under the thumb of the Political Department. Macnaghten dismissed as unsound any suggestion that the Afghans, who had already twice thrown Shah Shuja out of their country, would hardly be likely to welcome his return, and military operations were conducted solely with political considerations in mind, even though those considerations were founded on false assumptions. Macnaghten's highhanded attitude was faithfully reflected by most of his subordinates.

The political officers, riding Arab ponies and often appearing on the battlefield in black frock coats and top hats, had begun their careers as soldiers, and most of them had transferred to the Political Department because they believed it would provide a more interesting and worthwhile career than soldiering. They were all young, ardent, and self-assured, convinced in most cases that they would have made extremely good generals had they remained in uniform, and prepared equally to command a division or govern a province. Some of them went completely native, donning Afghan dress, adopting Afghan customs (and Afghan wives, if they could get them), and talking away in the vernacular while the soldiers stumbled along in halting Hindustani. Senior army officers, on the other hand, considered them mere upstarts, careerists who thought only of themselves and who were completely ignorant of military matters. It was hardly a propitious beginning for one of the most difficult campaigns the army was to fight in the East.

The march down the Sutlej and Indus to Shikarpur, where the Army of the Indus was to cross the river and enter the Baluchistan desert, took nearly two months. The weather was fine, neither too hot nor too cold, there was plenty of game to be shot, and the inhabitants, although wild, were not unfriendly. Only the absence of supplies for the vast horde of followers seemed ominous, the path of the army being marked by dead bodies with bones bleaching in the sun, as vultures and jackals grew fat on this unexpected largesse. The camp at Shikarpur soon became loathsome from the stench of dead camels, lying in clusters of three and four around the perimeter, and forage was also running short for the horses. Commissariat officers scoured Baluchistan and Sind to find replacements for the animals, and for forage with which to feed them, since the worst part of the march still lay ahead. Between Shikarpur and Kandahar, the army's first objective in Afghanistan, lay 375 miles of desert and mountain passes, the first 150 miles, as far as Dadur, being across a blighted waste which claimed far more victims in the Afghan War than all the Afghan bullets. The water was brackish, causing diarrhea among both men and horses, and wreaking havoc among the followers who left the protection of the column to perform their natural functions and were promptly murdered by the local tribesmen, who hovered around the horizon waiting for just such opportunities. And when the army reached Dadur, at the mouth of the Bolan Pass, the place was hardly calculated to raise their spirits. It was a small walled town, dominated by a citadel of crumbling mud-brick, whose inhabitants were accustomed to ask each other why Allah had bothered to create hell when there already existed Dadur. The shortage of supplies led to a storm of protest from the officers, who blamed the unfortunate commissariat for the failure, but the generals, better informed than the captains, blamed neither the commissariat nor their own staffs. Their wrath was directed at the "politicals," whose responsibility it was to persuade the local inhabitants to provision the army, and they wrote bitter letters to their friends in Calcutta, complaining of Macnaghten's arrogance and his subordinates' incompetence. Their protests increased in volume as the distance from India grew greater.

The Bolan Pass could have been a very serious obstacle had the wild Baluchi tribesmen chosen to dispute its passage, but in the event they contented themselves with cutting out camels and murdering stragglers. The entrance to the pass is nearly a mile wide, but it rapidly narrows, the track following the shingly bed of a river, and winding its way upward beside beetling crags, devoid of any vegetation and radiating heat. Torrential rain which fell during the night added to the miseries of the army, turning the dry river bed into a torrent, saturating the tents, and lowering the temperature to around the freezing point. The mountains ahead were sheathed in glistening rime, looming out of the mist and boiling drift, cheering the Europeans after the heat of the plains, but casting dread into the sepoys and followers who had never seen snow before. It took nearly eight days to traverse the pass, rising from sea level to almost 6,000 feet, and every yard of the way was marked by an abandoned camel, a foundered horse, or a follower dying from exhaustion. Tents, camel trunks, wine chests, cooking pots, bundles of blankets, and overturned bullock carts marked the progress of the Army of the Indus through the Bolan Pass, as the shore is littered with sea wrack after a storm.

"The country we came through surely was on the confines of hell!" wrote Sita Ram. "It was a land of stones, with no green thing but the *jowasser* (camel-thorn), not a bird but the vulture, which feasted on the dead bodies of our carriage cattle, and the dead comrades we were unable to bury. There were no animals in that vile country till our army came; for what had they to live on? Troops of jackals followed in our track right through the desert and got sleek and fat by their attendance. . . . Now I understand why it was forbidden to cross the Indus; truly the fate of those who ever do so is bad; and our misfortunes were increased by the thoughts of having done that which was forbidden by our religion." [8] But far worse lay ahead.

From the Bolan the army marched to Quetta, a small fortified town lying in the middle of well-irrigated and fertile fields, and there was now a halt while the political officers endeavored to discover what was happening in Kandahar, and to ascertain the sympathies of the local chieftain, the Khan of Kalat. The tribesmen around Quetta were fiercer and more truculent than those on the plains, murdering any straggler and swooping down from the nearby

[8] *Ibid.*, p. 81.

195

mountains to raid the great herds of camels which grazed around the camps. Keane aroused considerable indignation among his officers by ordering the execution of a wounded tribesman who had been taken prisoner in one of these forays, and there were even suggestions that his name should be Ketch, and not Keane. But although this was rough justice, it was the only thing the tribesmen would understand. Keane was hundreds of miles from his base, his army dependent on the camels, which alone could withstand the heat and lack of water, and it was vital that they should be protected. Even so, he was compelled to reduce the ration of flour from two pounds to one per day for the soldiers, while the unfortunate followers only received half a pound. This was particularly hard on the high-caste Brahmans, who formed such a large part of the Bengal native regiments, since they were accustomed to cook their own food, and their religion forbade them to eat in messes. When a well-intentioned lancer offered Sita Ram some of his bread, the starving sepoy had to decline, or face eternal damnation.

The last main obstacle between the army and Kandahar was the Khojak Pass, a narrow and precipitous defile about seventy miles northwest of Quetta; it was more easily defensible than the Bolan, and there was every reason to suppose that Dost Mohammed, who had a sizable army at Kandahar, would dispute its passage. Macnaghten, however, had convinced himself that Shah Shuja's return would be so popular with his former subjects that not even a token resistance would be offered, and relations between Keane and himself were not improved by the way he urged this opinion. At last Keane gave orders for the advance to begin on April 7, 1839, the start of the march being signaled by an outburst of musketry, not the enemy's, but that of the cavalry slaughtering those horses too weak to continue. Fifty of the jaded creatures were shot that morning, and the process was to be repeated daily all the way to Kandahar.

The infantry, with some sappers and miners, went on ahead under Colonel Arnold of the 16th Lancers to reconnoiter the pass, but ran into a party of Afghans who exchanged shots with them and then tried to cut off their retreat. The Afghans were driven off, much to Shah Shuja's annoyance, for he told Macnaghten that they were a party from Kandahar come to pay homage to their sovereign. Arnold, when admonished by Keane for opening fire on "friendlies," replied that if that was the normal method of exchanging compliments in Afghanistan, he hoped that next time the Shah would receive his friends in person. It was of a piece with the muddle and cross-purposes that marked the relations between the Shah and Macnaghten, on the one side, and the soldiers, on the other. In this case, however, the Shah may well have been right, since the army made its way through the Khojak Pass with no other impediment than the appalling road and the failing strength of its animals. The guns continually stuck on the steep slopes, the bullocks and camels yoked together in long teams were incapable of moving them, and in the end the 16th Lancers were forced to take off their jackets and lever the guns upward a few yards at a time. It was 4:00 P.M. before the guns had been pushed and dragged to the summit of the pass, and after all that labor there was hardly any water for the men to drink; the horses got none at all. Meanwhile, looking back down the gorge, the exhausted troopers could see what looked like ants, stumbling and staggering through the rocks, falling over the precipices, gasping for water, and crying out for help, as the unfortunate followers made their way in the army's wake. "How many of them," wondered Mackinnon, "will ever see Hindustan again?"

The descent next day into the plain that led to Kandahar was just as bad. There was still no water, and more horses had to be shot. The heat was overwhelming, and the army began to lose what cohesion it had possessed up till that moment. Men went wandering off searching for water, failed to find any, and lay down to die. Camels were laden until they foundered in the sand with those too weak to walk any farther, horses collapsed and gasped out their life for lack of water, and even the pet dogs which followed the British officers were dying from thirst. It was as well that the Afghans had not chosen such a moment to attack. British gold and the Shah's lavish promises, however, had succeeded in sowing dissension among them. There was certainly no love for Shah Shuja, but Dost Mohammed was far away in Kabul, and—who knew?—his star might be on the wane. It was probably just as well to come to terms with the Shah; if Dost Mohammed succeeded in defeating the English, it would be equally easy to betray the Shah. And so Hadji Khan, the principal citizen of Kandahar, rode out to greet the advancing Shah and surrendered the keys of the city. Kandahar fell without a shot being fired; but, even so, the behavior of a turncoat like Hadji Khan, who was renowned for his faithlessness, would hardly seem to justify Macnaghten's description of Shah Shuja's entry into the city as a "triumph." Alone, it seems, among all who had marched that far with the Army of the Indus, Macnaghten steadfastly believed in the Shah's popularity; but even old Sita Ram, a humble sepoy, knew better.

There was now a two months' lull in operations while the army settled down at Kandahar to recoup its strength, but, instead, it grew weaker. The Afghans soon overcame their initial respect for the soldiers and developed a skillful technique for murdering them whenever they wandered far from their tents. Detachments were sent out under control of the political officers to pacify the surrounding countryside, but the weather was very hot, the hostility of the Afghans increased daily, and morale was low. Jaundice and diarrhea were rife, and some of the soldiers started to distill rough spirits and died from overindulgence in their own brews. The Shah was crowned on May 8, the troops were reviewed, and the officers then waited on the Shah as a measure of respect. Each officer was expected to present the Shah with a *nazarana,* or present, which in the case of field officers amounted to five gold mohurs, and two for captains and subalterns. The mohurs were provided by the Company, but this did not prevent General Nott from complaining about the farcical ceremony. He had marched the Bombay division into Kandahar early in May, after some furious wrangling with the political officers, and he soon took good care to let Macnaghten know his views on Afghanistan in general and Shah Shuja in particular. Relations were little better between Keane and Macnaghten, the latter's scholarly and refined nature finding little to like and much to deplore in Keane's coarse language and personal conduct. The heat grew worse, and tempers likewise, an average of two men a day were dying in the hospitals, and the dreaded cholera was beginning to appear among the followers. Macnaghten pressed Keane to move on to Kabul, arguing that there would be no resistance, while Keane hesitated to take the plunge. Finally, on June 27, he acceded to Macnaghten's request and marched out of Kandahar with the Bengal division, intending first to capture Ghazni, and then advance on Kabul. Nott remained in Kandahar with the Bombay division, belaboring the political officers with his tongue, and penning vituperative letters to his correspondents in India. "Sir William Nott remained throughout dissatisfied with the conduct of operations," wrote Luard later, possibly a little wearily after perusing such a string of complaints.

Ghazni, the capture of which earned Keane a peerage, was taken as much by treachery as by the gallantry of the infantry stormers. The town was reputed to be impregnable, barring the road between Kabul and Kandahar, and was defended by a garrison pledged to defend the citadel to the death. When Havelock warned Keane of the danger of trying to take the place without adequate siege artillery, his advice was brushed aside; perhaps by this time Keane thought he had taken the measure of the Afghans, or had been unduly influenced by Macnaghten. Certainly in this case boldness paid, although much was due to the action of an Afghan traitor who deserted the cause of Dost Mohammed and joined forces with Shah Shuja outside Ghazni. He advised Keane to assault the town by the Kabul gate, since it was indifferently defended, and in the absence of siege guns the British could not hope to batter a breach in the walls.

Ghazni was successfully stormed in the early hours of July 23, 1839, the storming parties being found from the 2nd, 13th, and 17th Foot, and from the Bengal European regiment; no native regiments were employed in what might well have turned out to be a really forlorn hope. The day before the assault there had been an encounter between the cavalry and some Afghan tribesmen, and prisoners were taken. To the fury of the English, the Shah ordered the immediate execution of the captives, and they were horrified by the zest with which the Shah's minions went about their bloody work: ". . . they were laughing and joking and seemed to look upon the work as good fun."

The Kabul gate was blown in two hours before dawn, and amid scenes of hideous confusion the stormers fought their way up the debris, resisted by fanatical Afghans who believed a death in battle to be the surest way to paradise. As often in night operations, there was order, counterorder, and disorder. Robert Sale, the gallant old colonel of the 13th Foot, commanded the troops who were to follow after the stormers. When he arrived outside the Kabul gate in the half-darkness before dawn, an excited engineer officer told him the breach was choked with debris and the dead, and that the stormers had failed to force an entrance. Whereupon Sale ordered the "Withdraw" to be sounded, but a few minutes later he fell in with yet another engineer, who had contrary information. While Sale was still havering—a not uncertain state for him—the "Advance" was sounded by an unknown bugler, and the 13th advanced at the double, cheering as they came, scrambling up the broken masonry, forcing their way across the dead and dying, bayoneting, firing, and clubbing with their musket butts. Sale was swept forward by the onrush, and as the sun came up above the rim of the surrounding hills, the strongest fortress in Afghanistan fell to the powder-blackened and blood-spattered British infantry. Sale was wounded in the face while waving his men on with his sword; he was always being wounded, and the 13th loved him for it.

The storming of Ghazni was not followed by the usual orgy of looting, rape, and drunkenness. Sita Ram was particularly impressed by the treatment of the governor of the town. When Hyder Khan was taken before Shah Shuja, who was most reluctant to spare his life, he was both defiant and dignified. "Kill me if you like," he said, "but if you ever let me go, I shall ever be found as your enemy, and will do all in my power to excite the people against you." Keane treated the Afghan with respect and even admitted that he admired his sentiments. "Again I saw here the curious customs in war with the English," says the mystified Sita Ram. "Had this man said half as much before a Nawab or Rajah, he would have been cut to pieces on the spot; still here, in open durbar, the very Sahebs who had fought against him cried out, *Barekilla! Barekilla!* (Bravo! Bravo!) This was wonderful! Why do they fight! Not to kill their enemies, but to have pleasure of capturing them, and then letting them go! It is true, their ways are unaccountable!"[9]

Once Ghazni had fallen, the Afghans lost their stomach for the fight. Dost Mohammed, deserted by many of his chieftains, fled to the mountains of northern Afghanistan and abandoned Kabul to the British. At 4:00 P.M. on August 7, Shah Shuja, accompanied by Macnaghten, Burnes, and General Keane, and escorted by a squadron of the 16th Lancers and another from the 4th Dragoons, made a state entry into his capital. He was mounted on a white Persian horse, splendidly dressed in black velvet with a magnificent glittering sword belt, and looked every inch a king. The ominous thing was that this magnificent apparition raised hardly a cheer from the spectators, and the silence hung like a storm cloud as he rode into the ancient fortress-palace of the kings of Afghanistan, the Bala Hissar. It was clear to everyone, apart, of course, from Macnaghten and his besotted political advisers, that the British had backed a loser.

Be this as it may, Keane and his officers had some reasons to congratulate themselves. The Army of the Indus had marched 1,500 miles across desert and through barren mountains, where a few determined men could easily have held up an army; it had defeated the Afghans on every occasion when they had chosen to make a stand; and it had successfully accomplished its mission of restoring Shah Shuja to his throne. The time had now come to enjoy some well-earned rest in a pleasant and well-watered countryside, where the women were handsome and in some cases forthcoming, the inhabitants not noticeably unfriendly, and where food and drink were plentiful. There were worse places than Kabul, thought Mackinnon as he rode out with a friend in the

[9] *Ibid.,* p. 86.

202

4th Dragoons to lay out a racecourse, while Captain Lowe wrote out a challenge to the officers of the Bombay Army, wagering that the Bengal officers would defeat them at cricket. The pacification of the rest of Afghanistan could now be left to the native regiments, split up in detachments and placed under control of the political officers, while the European regiments relaxed; it was the usual pattern of a British expedition in the East. Only, from Kandahar came the warnings of old Nott, and after the successes of the past few weeks his pessimism seemed to be curiously misplaced.

Although everything seemed fine on the surface, the fires kept smoldering beneath. Shah Shuja had learned nothing and forgotten nothing; his ostentation and arrogance offended even those who were prepared to be his friends, and his cruelty to his opponents revolted most of the British. Macnaghten, as if taking his cue from the King, was equally arrogant and disinclined to listen to advice. He insisted on laying out a military cantonment not far from the city walls, and its predominant characteristic was its defenselessness. The soldiers urged him to turn the Bala Hissar into a British-held fortress, but any such suggestion was spurned by Shah Shuja as an abrogation of his sovereignty, and Macnaghten refused to press the point. Even an attempt to repair the crumbling walls of the citadel was resisted by the Shah, who preferred that the money should be spent on embellishing his hall of audience. And so with races, cricket, shooting parties, and visits after dark to the not unwilling Afghan ladies, the British officers of the Army of the Indus filled in their leisure hours. There is no record of how the soldiers filled theirs, but a particularly potent kind of wine was brewed in Kabul, and there were plenty of brothels. A few officers, of whom Havelock was one, worried about their soldiers' souls, but the majority had better things to do with their time.

The 16th Lancers buried their colonel in Kabul. He had been ill ever since leaving Kandahar, and was carried most of the way from there in a litter. His death was due to an abscess on the liver. The Colonel's effects were auctioned a few days later, and the prices fetched are indicative of the shortage of luxuries in Afghanistan: sherry fetched the equivalent of £5 a bottle today, bottles of sauce almost as much, and mustard in square bottles reached nearly £7 apiece. The amenities of Kabul soon palled, in fact, since they existed only by comparison with the march from Baluchistan and Kandahar. For more than a year the army had been living either under the sky or in tents, rising every day before dawn, and living for most of the time on hard-tack. At the end of it all, they had arrived in a country of "rocks, savages and starvation," whose inhabitants took pleasure in murdering the unwary. Yet the political officers maintained that the country was now pacified, apart from a few of the wilder and more inaccessible regions, and although few of the soldiers believed them, it was as good an excuse as any to press for a return to India.

On October 8, 1839, a General Order was published formally breaking up the Army of the Indus. Several regiments, including the 16th Lancers, were ordered to return to India by way of the Khyber Pass, and General Keane, awarded the G.C.B. for his capture of Ghazni, marched with them. Cotton was left to command in Kabul, and Nott remained in Kandahar. Sir John Keane was suffering acutely from gout, an occupational hazard among senior officers of his time, and his popularity had not increased. Nevertheless, a grateful Queen, doubtless on the recommendation of an equally grateful Governor-General, raised the gallant General to the peerage as Baron Keane of Ghazni and of Cappoquin, in County Waterford, and conferred on him a pen-

204

sion of £2,000 a year. For a man who owed most things to luck, he had not done too badly, but Nott nearly had a fit when they told him.

The march back to India took nearly four months. They went via Jalalabad, the winter capital of Afghanistan, and the Khyber Pass, and apart from some desultory sniping there were no untoward incidents and India was safely reached. Ranjit Singh had died the previous June, and the Sikh empire was fast collapsing into anarchy, but nothing succeeds in the East like success, and the Company's prestige was high. Despite scowls and a certain amount of saber-rattling on the part of the Sikhs, the British were allowed to cross the Punjab without opposition, and Luard records with satisfaction "the safe return of the 16th Lancers to Meerut, and with them some fox hounds they had taken with them when they set out from that place."

Behind them in Afghanistan the British garrison had settled down to make the best of a bad job, and as has always been their way in such circumstances, they laid out gardens, built a club, and began to agitate for their wives and families to join them. Before long Lady Macnaghten, Lady Sale (her husband had been knighted for his conduct at Ghazni), and several other officers' wives were on their way across the Punjab and up the Khyber Pass to join their husbands. By camel-litter and on horseback, they jolted their way past the beetling crags, braving the elements, the tribesmen, and the absence of any sort of creature comfort, to join their husbands in a hostile land, and, not surprisingly, Lady Sale took with her some packets of sweet peas and assorted "hardy perennials." They were soon followed by Shah Shuja's own harem, 600 women, children, and eunuchs, escorted by a fiery young major of the Madras Army, George Broadfoot, who found the whole business

205

rather ridiculous. So did John Luard, who thought it "quite wrong to send women to Afghanistan under the conditions which existed there and in view of the hardships of the journey." We may safely assume that Sir Jasper Nicolls thought likewise, but his opinion, if asked for, must have been ignored.

CHAPTER ELEVEN

General Nicolls had assumed his appointment too late to exert any influence on the policy to be adopted in Afghanistan; that had already been decided long before by Lord Auckland on Macnaghten's advice, and the then commander in chief had not opposed it. As early as October 1840, however, Luard had drafted a memorandum for the Governor-General's council which set out the commander in chief's views on the Afghanistan affair, in the course of which Nicolls took leave to doubt most of Macnaghten's optimistic assertions. Shah Shuja could remain on the throne only if he was supported by British bayonets, and to assume otherwise was to discount the reports of such sensible and experienced officers as General Nott. The Shah's own forces, even though they were officered by the British, were of no value without the British Army to sustain their morale, and in Nicolls' view, Afghanistan would require a permanent garrison of three European regiments and ten Native. These could be provided only by reducing other garrisons in the Company's territories, and the risks were unacceptable. Therefore, additional regiments must be raised, or else, like wise men the world over, the government must cut its losses and withdraw from Afghanistan.

Such pessimistic forecasts contrasted forcibly with the opinions of Macnaghten, now installed with some state in Kabul as the Governor-General's envoy at the court of Shah Shuja, and whose reports on the situation were full of good cheer. Indeed, it is true to say that, despite Shah Shuja's obvious unpopularity, the first eighteen months of the occupation passed pleasantly enough. Dost Mohammed had voluntarily given up the struggle in the autumn of 1840, surrendering himself to Macnaghten in person while the Envoy was enjoying a ride outside Kabul. He was sent back to Calcutta in honorable captivity, and everyone found him a good deal pleasanter to deal with than the arrogant Shah Shuja, especially when he asked his European visitors why the British should have bothered about a country as poor as Afghanistan when they ruled a city as splendid as Calcutta? But his departure did nothing to reconcile the Afghans to the rule of a king they so heartily despised and whose authority was dependent on foreign bayonets. Sporadic insurrections kept the occupying forces completely busy, and Ranjit Singh's death had placed in jeopardy the long lines of communication across the Punjab. Despite these obvious dangers, Macnaghten remained full of optimism, referring to those who disagreed with him as "croakers" and "old women."

John Luard records that he was kept extremely busy throughout the summer of 1840, "mainly on account of events in Afghanistan," and in October of that year his troubles were increased by a severe personal tragedy. Elizabeth Luard had never been strong, and long periods in India, accompanied by frequent childbearing, had seriously undermined her health. The Calcutta hot weather can be trying to the healthy, and far worse for the sick. Elizabeth went "into a decline," although John Luard does not specify the cause of her illness. It appears, however, to have been a comparatively short one, and she died on October 31, at the age of forty-one. John Luard was devoted to her and was heartbroken by her death. In December he sent his three younger children home to join their brothers and sister, engaging a soldier's wife to look after them during the voyage. Not long afterward he went upcountry with Sir Jasper Nicolls on a tour of inspection, and on their way up the Ganges they stopped at Monghyr, where twelve years before John Luard had spent a few days with his wife and baby son on their way back to England from Meerut. They had stayed at Monghyr with a Bengal civilian who had married Elizabeth's sister, and now both sisters were dead, as was Maria's husband, "and I a widower with six children." He could not have been a very cheerful traveling companion that winter.

His morale was not improved by the arrival in India of his old commanding officer of the 1820's, for Major-General William Elphinstone had come out from home to take over the command in Kabul from Sir Willoughby Cotton. Elphinstone's career is a good example of a general who had risen largely through influence, for his family was a distinguished one, his relations were all admirals, generals, and members of Parliament, while he had started off in the approved fashion by serving in the Guards. At Waterloo he had commanded the 33rd Foot, Wellington's own regiment, and with some distinction; a few years later he had exchanged into the 16th Lancers, and commanded them for less than a year. He left when they were ordered to India, climbed the ladder steadily on half pay, and in the autumn of 1840, gouty, prematurely old, and desperately homesick, he set out for India much against his own wishes, but mainly because he had always been brought up to do his duty; and also, perhaps, because his old friend the Duke thought that India could do with a few more of his Waterloo veterans.

"General Elphinstone passed through camp today in his palanquin," wrote Miss Eden. "He is in a shocking state of gout, poor man—one arm in a sling and very lame. . . . He hates being here. . . . He is wretched because nobody understands his London topics, or knows his London people. . . . He went off with a heavy heart to his palanquin. He cannot, of course, speak a word of Hindoostanee, neither can his aide-de-camp." [1]

This was the man whom Auckland had determined to appoint to the Kabul command; they had many friends in common, the same aristocratic background, and no doubt Auckland enjoyed the General's London gossip. Luard was horrified when he learned of the Governor-General's intention and implored the commander in chief to resist it. "Feeble in health as well as in mind," he wrote, "wanting in resolution and confidence in himself, no experience in warfare, he was totally unfitted to command the Force at Cabul. He was appointed to command in opposition to Sir Jasper Nicolls' wish. I had known Elphinstone when in command of the 16th Lancers as a very gentlemanly and agreeable person, but from want of decision and never trusting to his own opinion unfit to command even a regiment." He was certainly the last man to stand up to the imperious Macnaghten or exert any control over his arrogant and ill-mannered second-in-command. This was a Brigadier Shelton who had lost an arm in the Peninsula and who later commanded the 44th Foot. He had arrived in Kabul with his regiment, who heartily detested him, but shortly afterward was given command of a brigade in Kabul. He was quarrelsome, vindictive, and moody, a petty martinet who

[1] *Up the Country*, p. 289.

aroused little loyalty and a great deal of ill feeling, and who was not likely to be amenable to Elphinstone's feeble control.

"Sir Jasper Nicolls constantly urged Lord Auckland to strengthen the garrison," wrote Luard about the situation in Afghanistan during 1841, but Auckland, although uneasy, still procrastinated. Throughout 1839, 1840, and the early part of 1841, a constant stream of optimistic dispatches from Macnaghten told of the increasing popularity of Shah Shuja, the strengthening of his grip on the country, and the improving relations between the British and the Afghans. Dost Mohammed's surrender to Macnaghten must have seemed a triumph to Auckland, amply vindicating his bold decision to invade the country, and silencing the grumblers like old Nott who foretold disaster in every letter they penned. It was true that the stories of conflict between the military commanders and their political advisers had given Auckland much cause for concern, especially since some of the officers had chosen to ventilate their differences in the columns of the London and Calcutta press. "We had a good deal of trouble as a result of ill advised correspondence in the Calcutta newspapers," wrote Luard, "much of it directed against the direction of the war, and thus giving Sir Jasper Nicolls much food for concern. It is altogether a bad business when officers write to the newspapers."

By the middle of 1841, however, matters appeared sufficiently well in hand for Macnaghten to receive his reward for all his labors. He was appointed governor of Bombay in September and told to return to India the following month. The same dispatch expressed the concern of the directors of the East India Company in London at the continuing and increasing cost of the Afghanistan expedition, and Auckland directed that economies must be made forthwith, notably by reducing the subsidies paid by Macnaghten to the tribal chiefs as a form of Danegeld. Macnaghten's entire policy was based on buying the good will of the powerful Afghan sirdars, and he vehemently protested against the Governor-General's fiat. But to no effect, and the result was rebellion in the more remote areas, which spread with the rapidity of a bush fire until it was menacing Kabul itself. Sale's brigade, which was due to leave shortly for India, was ordered to clear the defiles that lay between Kabul and Jalalabad on the route back to India, and Major George Broadfoot was ordered to accompany his force.

Broadfoot was an officer of proved ability and courage, and the difficulty he experienced in trying to obtain clear instructions regarding his task is an indication of the divided counsels, indecision, and jealousy that hung like some evil miasma over the British operations in Afghanistan. He first sought an interview with Elphinstone, but the General was so exhausted after getting out of bed to receive him that it was half an hour before he could summon up enough strength to talk. He then said bitterly that Macnaghten completely ignored him, and that he had been degraded "from a general to the Lord-Lieutenant's high constable." Broadfoot had far better get his orders from Macnaghten direct.

Broadfoot then went to Macnaghten, who was "peevish" and accused Broadfoot of being an "alarmist." The Envoy lost his temper, and Broadfoot responded in kind. He returned to Elphinstone, had a brush with the latter's adjutant-general, who was both discourteous and incompetent, and then left with Elphinstone's words ringing in his ears: "If you go out, for God's sake clear the passes quickly, that I may get away; for if anything were to turn up, I am unfit for it, done up in body and mind!" As Luard commented later, these were hardly words calculated to encourage a junior officer's confidence in his superior commander.

On October 11, 1841, Broadfoot marched out from Kabul

with Sale's brigade, fully expecting that Macnaghten would follow a few days later, together with Lady Macnaghten, Lady Sale, and Sale's daughter and son-in-law. In the event, matters were to turn out far differently.

Sale had to fight every inch of the way to Jalalabad, and kept up his record by getting wounded early on during the operations. The defiles through which his troops had to pass were picketed by the Afghans, and the brigade had received severe casualties by the time it cleared the passes and reached Gandamak, about halfway to Jalalabad. There Sale halted on October 30 to await further orders from either Macnaghten or Elphinstone, but none were received, and Sale then summoned a council of war to make up his mind for him. The majority voted against a return to Kabul, arguing that even worse casualties would be incurred, but Broadfoot and one or two other forceful characters argued even more hotly for a return to Kabul. It would be unthinkable, they urged, to abandon the Kabul garrison to its fate, and one might have expected that Sale, whose wife and daughter were still in Kabul, would have chosen to fight his way back to their side. However, he decided to continue his march to Jalalabad, supposedly to join up with reinforcements which were reported to be on their way from India, and by this decision he virtually condemned the Kabul garrison to annihilation.

Meanwhile, in Kabul life continued much as before in the hopelessly indefensible cantonments laid out by Macnaghten not far from the city walls. Lady Florentia Sale continued to weed her vegetable garden and fussed lest her peas should be killed by the early frosts; she also continued a paper war with that "obnoxious fellow" Brigadier Shelton, who was asserting his rights to Sale's bungalow now that he was the senior brigadier in Kabul. She had received news of Sale's recent wound, but it does not appear to have worried her unduly; he was fifty-one and was always getting himself wounded, and, in any case, Lady Sale was an admirable soldier's wife who was accustomed to taking the rough with the smooth. Only the constant delay on Macnaghten's part to set off from Kabul irritated her. Boxes were packed, pack animals hired, and there was only chipped crockery to eat from. She wished the Envoy would make up his mind, pick a date, and stick to it. Conditions were growing steadily worse; news had reached Kabul that Sale's force had been defeated, and the bazaars were seething with rumors and unrest. Individual Europeans, who had grown accustomed to wandering around Kabul without molestation, were insulted and attacked, and Captain Sturt of the Bengal Engineers, who had married Miss Sale a few months previously, was set upon while visiting Shah Shuja's palace and nearly stabbed to death. Only his wife's and his mother-in-law's devoted nursing saved his life.

November 2, 1841 was the day on which the mob rose in Kabul. They first attacked the house of Sir Alexander Burnes, Macnaghten's intended successor, murdered him, and set the place on fire. Burnes, who had always been a protagonist of Dost Mohammed, had gained a bad reputation as a result of his amours with highborn Afghan ladies, and his friendship with many of the leading sirdars failed to save him when the time came. With him there died George Broadfoot's brother, both men fighting to the last, and then the Kabul mob went sweeping through the streets and noisome alleys, howling for blood, and working itself up into a frenzy of hate. Every European they caught was murdered and burned, or the bodies were dragged through the streets and subjected to every possible indignity. The British out in the cantonments crowded the roofs of their bungalows and listened anxiously to the angry roar from the city; soon they would be virtually besieged and even Macnaghten would be compelled to admit that the Afghans had risen against the King and his British supporters. And yet the Envoy still obstinately refused to persuade Shah Shuja to allow the British to withdraw behind the stout defenses of the Bala Hissar, and as a result they were forced to fight it out from behind the miserable entrenchments that were hastily thrown up around the straggling cantonments.

"The news from Cabul around this time was very scanty and disturbing," wrote John Luard. He was camped, with his commander in chief, somewhere in the upper provinces, and engaged in the unrewarding task of trying to piece together a coherent and reasonably accurate picture of events from information that was often conflicting, always inadequate, and invariably out of date. Dispatches from Kabul and Kandahar took weeks to arrive, coming by pony, camel, or runner, preceded by rumor, and very frequently followed by quite contrary reports of the situation. Political officers with their own axes to grind said one thing; the soldiers usually said the opposite. General Nott continued glumly to prophesy disaster; Sale could throw no light on anything from Jalalabad; and Elphinstone apparently had given up the unequal struggle. It was hard to produce worthwhile reports for Sir Jasper Nicolls out of such a jumbled mass of information, but Luard did his best. Meanwhile, the old General sat glowering to himself, now and again indulging in the pleasure of reminding Lord Auckland that he had told him so.

Morale was low in Kabul. "It is more than shocking, it is shameful," wrote Lady Sale in her diary, "to hear the way that officers go on croaking before the men; it is sufficient to dispirit them, and prevent them fighting for us." Or again, "Colonel Oliver is one of the great croakers. On being told by some men of his corps that a certain quantity

215

of grain had been brought in, he replied, 'It was needless, for they would never live to eat it.'" Lady Sale goes on to say, "Whatever we think ourselves, it is best to put a good face on the business." The conduct of poor General Elphinstone also comes in for criticism. "Grand dissensions in military councils. High and very plain language has been this day used by Brig. Shelton to Gen. Elphinstone; and people do not hesitate to say that our chief should be set aside. . . . The poor General's mind is distracted by the diversity of opinions offered; and the great bodily ailments he sustains are daily enfeebling the powers of his mind. . . . Our soldiery like to see their officers bear their part in privation; it makes them more cheerful; but in going the rounds at night, officers are seldom found with their men."[2] One cannot help feeling that Lady Sale would have been a much more effective commander than old Elphinstone.

Her son-in-law, Captain Sturt, appears to have been one of the few exceptions to the general lethargy and indecision. He was up from his sickbed within a week, although hardly able to speak from the knife wound in his jaw, and, as the only engineer officer in Kabul, was hard at work all day long. His accounts of Elphinstone's councils of war make incredible reading. Few decisions were ever reached, and, when they were, usually turned out to be wrong. Shelton was so disgusted that he used to roll himself up in his cloak and go to sleep on the floor. Halfhearted efforts were made to break through the ring that was gradually closing around the cantonments, but the troops had little stomach for the fight. Shah Shuja's troops were worse than useless, and when Brigadier Shelton eventually formed his brigade up for an attack, he was handled quite severely by the Afghans.

[2] Lady Sale, *Journal of Disasters in Afghanistan,* London, 1843, p. 121. Colonel Oliver commanded the 5th Bengal Native Infantry.

Neither the 44th Foot nor the 37th Native Infantry managed to distinguish themselves on this occasion.

"It would only have required a resolute commander to put some heart into the troops," wrote Luard, but Elphinstone spent most of the day in bed, Shelton refused to accept responsibility without proper authorization, and Macnaghten still clung to the belief that he could negotiate a settlement with the Afghans. It was the last desperate resort of a man who was a negotiator and not a soldier, and he sent out overtures for a parley with Akbar Khan, a son of Dost Mohammed, who was directing the Afghans' operations. These do not seem to have been pressed very hard, and the garrison was able to go about its daily business without much concern, save only when anyone sought to venture beyond the cantonment defenses. Lady Sale watched the operations from the roof of her bungalow, dodging from time to time behind the chimneys to avoid the bullets that came whizzing past, and fretting that old Sale was not there to put some heart into the defenders.

On December 23 Macnaghten made a last desperate attempt to negotiate a safe-conduct back to India for Shah Shuja and the British garrison. His attempts to persuade Nott to advance from Kandahar to relieve Kabul had failed, that cautious commander fully realizing the folly of exposing his small force to attack by Akbar Khan, and, anyway, he had been bombarding Macnaghten for months past with warnings of rebellion. Macnaghten therefore decided to deal direct with Akbar Khan, and they met at a secluded spot not far from the cantonments. They had been in conversation only a few minutes when Akbar Khan himself cut down Macnaghten and another of his party, and that was the end of an extremely clever and able man, who had utterly failed to appreciate the full consequences of the

217

policy he had urged upon the Governor-General. Short-term gains in politics are seldom likely to be profitable if their ultimate consequences have failed to be properly assessed. Shah Shuja had not long to wait before he, too, paid in full for Macnaghten's mistaken policy.

On December 27 Lady Sale notes that the council—Elphinstone, Shelton, and three others—had ratified a treaty with the Afghans. "No one but themselves exactly knows what this same treaty is; further than that it is most disgraceful! 14½ *lakhs* to be given for our safe conduct to Peshawar; all our guns to be given up save six; and six hostages to be given up on our part. . . ."[3] There was nothing left but to await the orders for the march, and to hope against hope that the Afghans would let them go. "Wisdom seemed to have departed from every one," wrote Sita Ram, "and the usual energy displayed by English officers was gone."[4]

The British Army has long been inured to disaster and forlorn hopes, as often the result of political mismanagement as of incompetent generalship, but on few occasions in its long history has it faced a more forbidding prospect than did Elphinstone's little army on January 6, 1842. Its commander was dying on his feet, or, rather, in his litter, since he was too unwell to either ride or march. The only European regiment, the 44th Foot, was reduced to half its strength, and the Indian regiments were suffering from a lack of British officers and the extreme cold. Neither British nor Indians had distinguished themselves during the siege of the cantonments, always excepting the Bengal Horse Artillery, the cream of the Company's army, which alone emerged from the operations with laurels untarnished. Moreover, the troops were greatly hampered by the large number of families and followers who accompanied the column.

[3] *Ibid.*
[4] *From Sepoy to Subedar,* p. 98.

The temperature was well below the freezing point, the snow lay thick on the ground, and the route to Jalalabad and beyond to India lay through some of the starkest mountains in the world, pierced by steep and narrow gorges, and inhabited by tribesmen who had given even Alexander the Great cause to pause. Even Lady Sale's unconquerable spirit quailed a little at the prospect that lay ahead.

"Previous to leaving cantonments, as we must abandon most of our property, Sturt was anxious to save a few of his most valuable books. Whilst he selected these, I found, amongst the ones thrown aside, Campbell's poems which opened at Hohenlinden; and strange to say, one verse actually haunted me day and night:

> 'Few, few shall part where many meet,
> The snow shall be their winding sheet;
> And every turf beneath their feet
> Shall be a soldier's sepulchre!'

I am far from being a believer in presentiments; but this verse is never absent from my thoughts. Heaven forbid that our fears should be realized, but we have commenced our retreat so badly, that we may reasonably have our doubts regarding the finale." [5]

There was over a foot of snow lying as the garrison marched out of the cantonments. Lady Sale, her daughter, who was pregnant, and the other European families rode with the advance guard, most of them on horses, but some in *kujavas,* which were panniers slung from either side of a camel. Progress was terribly slow, and it took them two and a half hours to cover the first mile. Hours were wasted while the sappers endeavored to repair the pontoon bridge

[5] *Journal of Disasters in Afghanistan,* p. 226.

over the Kabul River, although it was easily fordable, and the whole road was littered with men, women, and children who had lain down in the snow to die. After covering only six miles, the column halted and settled down for the night. It was 4:00 P.M.

"There were no tents, save two or three small palls that arrived. All scraped away the snow as best they might, to make a place to lie down on. The evening and night were intensely cold; no food for man or beast procurable. . . . Captain Johnson, in our great distress, kindly pitched a small pall over us; but it was dark, and we had few pegs; the wind blew in under the sides, and I felt myself gradually stiffening." [6]

When morning came, they woke to find several men frozen to death, and the Horse Artillery had been forced to abandon their six-pounder guns. The road was strewn with baggage, and, so far as the native troops were concerned, there was an end to a disciplined retreat. The intense cold had completed what hunger, distance from their native land, and lack of faith in their officers had begun.

The force had left Kabul with five and a half days' rations and forage, which should have been sufficient to take it as far as Jalalabad had the withdrawal been pressed with vigor and determination. As it was, only five miles were covered on the second day before the order to halt was given, as early as 1:00 P.M. "Here, again, did evil counsel beset the General; his principal officers and staff objecting to a further advance; and Capt. Grant, in whom he had much confidence, assured him that if he proceeded he risked the safety of the army!" By the third day of the retreat, the force was completely disorganized, and most of the soldiers were paralyzed by the intense cold and the shortage of food.

[6] *Ibid.*, p. 227.

Hostile bodies of tribesmen hovered around the flanks, firing into the mass of followers and troops, and cutting off any stragglers. The sepoys had burned their caps, accouterments, and clothing in an attempt to keep themselves warm, and the ground was littered with boxes of ammunition, private baggage, and regimental plate. Some of the artillerymen were drunk with the brandy handed out from the 54th Native Infantry's officers' mess stores, and even Lady Sale enjoyed a mild tipple. "For myself, whilst I sat for hours on my horse in the cold, I felt very grateful for a tumbler of sherry, which at any other time would have made me very unlady-like, but now merely warmed me, and appeared to have no more strength than water!"

Slowly the column staggered on, and, as discipline disintegrated, the hovering Afghans grew bolder. Sturt rode back down the column, and his horse was shot under him; before he could disentangle himself, he was shot in the stomach. His wife's pony was wounded in the neck and ear, and Lady Sale "had fortunately only *one* ball" in her arm; three others passed through her sheepskin coat without damaging her. By nightfall 500 soldiers and about 2,500 camp followers had been killed, while hundreds more straggled off into the snow to die.

Lady Sale, her daughter, and her mortally wounded son-in-law spent the third night of the retreat in the shelter of a bivouac tent, into which thirty people packed, with no room to turn. No attempt was made to scrape away the snow, and although Sturt's wound had been dressed, it was clear that there was little hope of his recovery. Dr. Bryce of the Horse Artillery had "kindly cut the ball out of my [Lady Sale's] wrist and dressed both my wounds," but he could do little for poor Sturt. He lingered through the freezing night, and next morning they found a camel litter for him. For a few more hours he endured the intolerable agony of being jolted by a camel, and then he died, and "we had the sorrowful satisfaction of giving him a Christian burial."

The fourth day's march saw the final disintegration of Elphinstone's force. Only the remnants of the 44th Foot and the Bengal Horse Artillery, without their guns, were capable of standing up to the enemy. There was hardly any control, "the only order appearing to be, 'Come along; we are all going, and half the men are off, with the camp followers in advance!'" The animals had been without food for four days and nights, the native soldiers could hardly put foot to ground they were so exhausted, and the Subedar-Major of the 37th Native Infantry had deserted to the enemy. The much-maligned Brigadier Shelton had, however, come into his own, fighting like a lion as he sought to rally his old regiment, now in charge of the rear guard, and then dashing forward to put some life into the advance guard. He never slept, was always first into action, and if the energy of one man could have saved the Kabul army, Shelton would have been that man.

But it was too late for heroic gestures; the army was defeated. The tribal chiefs, who had promised Elphinstone a safe-conduct to Jalalabad, had lost control of their tribesmen, either intentionally or by default. The Afghans hung around the flanks of the retreating troops, murdering and pillaging soldiers and followers alike. Akbar Khan then offered a safe-conduct to such European women and children as remained alive, providing they were given up as hostages, and to this Elphinstone was forced to agree. Akbar also demanded the surrender of Elphinstone, Shelton, and some of the other senior officers, in return for a safe passage for the remainder of the force to Jalalabad, and after hours of agonizing soul-searching, the dying Elphinstone gave himself up to the enemy. With him went Shelton, in an honorable attempt to spare the lives of his men. No man had fought better than the one-armed Shelton before he finally had to surrender. As for the rest of the army, it staggered on through the defiles in a last desperate effort to reach Jalalabad.

By 8:00 P.M. on January 12, 1842, six days after leaving Kabul, all that remained of Elphinstone's army were about twenty-five artillerymen and 120 officers and men of the 44th Foot; not a single sepoy remained at duty, and almost all the followers had fallen by the wayside. Ahead of these remnants of an army lay the formidable Jagdalak Pass, up which the track winds its way through a narrow gorge, commanded throughout its length from the heights above, and in places so narrow that three horses could barely get through it abreast.

As the battered and exhausted soldiers fought their way up the 9,000-foot pass, they were subjected to a continuous fire from the tribesmen on the crags above; and when at last they gained the summit, it was to find the track blocked by a barricade of boulders, logs, and branches of trees. From behind this barrier came the tribesmen, crazed with blood lust, hacking with their long knives and carving with their tulwars, as the soldiers fought back with bayonet, rifle butt, and even fists. Less than half the column broke through to reach Gandamak, at the foot of the pass, and there, on a small knoll, what remained of the 44th Foot turned at bay and sold their lives dearly. Six officers managed to get beyond Gandamak, and, of them, only one, Dr. Brydon, succeeded in reaching Jalalabad. He brought with him the story of the Kabul disaster; of the 4,500 soldiers who had set out, one had reached the destination. There had also perished 12,000 camp followers and thousands of horses, camels, and donkeys.

Sale's first action on hearing Brydon's story was to hoist the Queen's Color of the 13th Foot on the flagstaff above the Kabul gate in Jalalabad; he intended by this to demonstrate that the British still held the winter capital of Afghanistan and meant to stay there. His next was to send his cavalry to scour the surrounding countryside for stragglers, but all they found were the mutilated bodies of Brydon's companions. At night lamps were hung above the gate, and every quarter of an hour the "Advance" was sounded by two buglers from the southwest bastion as an encouragement for any who might have escaped the carnage in the passes. "The terrible wailing of those bugles I shall never forget," wrote Captain Seaton, "it was a dirge for our slaughtered soldiers, and, heard all through the night, it had an inexpressibly depressing effect." [7] How much worse it must have sounded to old Bob Sale as he paced the ramparts the long night through, staring out through the darkness toward the mountains, beyond which his wife and daughter were the prisoners of a cruel and ruthless enemy.

The news of the disaster reached Calcutta toward the end of January. Lord Auckland was within a few weeks of completing his tenure as Governor-General, and the news virtually broke him. Almost his last act was to appoint Major-General George Pollock of the Bengal Artillery to the command of the troops on the northwest frontier, adding that he hoped that some means might be found to relieve Sale's brigade, now besieged in Jalalabad by Akbar Khan, before it, too, was overwhelmed and massacred. Although Sir Jasper Nicolls approved of Pollock's appointment, he was, according to Luard, "averse to any further adventures in Afghanistan." He admitted that there would be advantages in recapturing Kabul, releasing the prisoners, and demonstrating to the Afghans that the Company's arm was long, but he doubted whether the effort involved would be justi-

[7] Maj-Gen Sir Thomas Seaton, *Cadet to Colonel*, London, 1866, p. 283.

fied. His instructions to Pollock, a capable soldier whose father had been George III's saddler, limited him to relieving Sale, and Luard wrote to a friend on Pollock's staff informing him of the fact. "When General Pollock came to hear of this," wrote Luard, "he was very angry with me and sent me a strong rebuke."

Edward Law, Lord Ellenborough, who had succeeded Auckland as governor-general, disagreed with his commander in chief. He wanted Pollock to advance at least as far as Kabul, release the prisoners, join hands with Nott, who was to advance from Kandahar, and then the whole force was to withdraw to India. "India was won by the sword, and must be maintained by the sword," he had proclaimed grandiloquently before taking up his appointment, and he saw perhaps better than Sir Jasper Nicolls that the British had received a blow to their prestige which could not be allowed to go unanswered. Meanwhile, as Lady Sale and her fellow-captives were being led farther and farther into the interior of Afghanistan, her husband sallied out from Jalalabad and defeated Akbar Khan with such ease that one cannot help feeling that the attempt might well have been made earlier. On April 16 Pollock marched into Jalalabad, and the "Illustrious Garrison," as Ellenborough described Sale's brigade, was relieved. Somehow or other they scraped together a band, and Pollock's troops were greeted with the Jacobite song "Oh! but ye've been lang o' coming."

There was then a pause while Pollock gathered together more pack animals and was plagued with contrary instructions concerning his next move. Sir Jasper was still for withdrawal, and Lord Ellenborough blew hot and cold, but the matter was clinched by the Duke of Wellington, who insisted that a severe blow should be struck against the Afghans. General Pollock's "Army of Retribution" moved forward again on August 20, traversing the same route as

225

Elphinstone's wretched army, whose bones lay whitening in the sun, and on September 17 British troops once again encamped outside Kabul. Two days later Lady Sale was reunited with her husband.

"It is impossible to describe our feelings on Sale's approach. To my daughter and myself happiness so long delayed, as to be almost unexpected, was actually painful, and accompanied by a choking sensation, which could not obtain the relief of tears. When we were arrived where the infantry were posted, they cheered all the captives as they passed them; and the men of the 13th pressed forward to welcome us individually. Most of the men had a little word of hearty congratulations to offer, each in his own style, on the restoration of his colonel's wife and daughter; and then my highly-wrought feelings found the desired relief; and I could scarcely speak to thank the soldiers for their sympathy, whilst the long withheld tears now found their course." [8] And when she, her daughter, and the baby born during their captivity were escorted toward her husband's tent, the guns of Captain Backhouse's mountain battery boomed out a salute. Such an honor may not have been in strict accordance with regulations, but at least she deserved it more than the generals.

Nott joined Pollock in Kabul, still grumbling about the "politicals," and soon the two Generals were barely on speaking terms. He disagreed with Pollock's action in blowing up the Kabul bazaar, he objected to the order of march back to India, and he had grown so used to prophesying disaster that he took the gloomiest view of the army's chances of forcing its way through the Khyber Pass. Pollock, for his part, conducted a long-range war with Nicolls' staff, objecting to interference from a distant headquarters, and

[8] *Journal of Disasters in Afghanistan*, p. 437.

226

the First Afghan War ended as it had begun, with divided counsels, endless recriminations, and lost tempers. Lord Ellenborough held a grand review of Pollock's and Nott's force when they reached the River Sutlej on November 16, Sale crossing the river first at the head of the 13th Foot and 35th Native Infantry from Jalalabad, and close behind came Lady Sale, riding on an elephant. The band of the 16th Lancers played "Lo! The Conquering Hero Comes!," guns boomed out salutes, and the Governor-General and Sir Jasper Nicolls rode out to greet the returning troops. It was all very splendid, and the Indians may have been impressed, but Luard felt that "the course of the war in Afghanistan did not justify such celebration." The bones of Elphinstone's army lay bleaching in the passes, and there were hundreds of sepoys still enslaved in remote mountain villages.

All Lord Ellenborough's eloquence, and the honors he awarded so lavishly, could not gloss over the complete failure of British policy in Afghanistan. It is true that in the end the Company's authority had been restored for a space in Kabul, but at the cost of much blood, treasure, and prestige. The blood of soldiers, as we well know, is expendable, and as for treasure, it can be replaced. But prestige, especially in the East, is hard to regain once lost. The disasters in Afghanistan sapped the morale of the Bengal Army, hitherto the means whereby the British maintained their rule over the greater part of India, and they sowed the seed that germinated in the dark days of the Mutiny. Nor, in Luard's opinion, was anything gained by the decision to court-martial Brigadier Shelton and certain other senior officers who had come to grief in Afghanistan. The real culprit, Macnaghten, was dead, and so was poor old Elphinstone, who had remained a cipher throughout. Luard had a great deal of sympathy for Shelton, although he admitted that he was not "an agreeable or useful second-in-command, objecting mostly to all that was proposed to be done by his Chief, but seldom or never aiding him with advice." In Luard's view, Shelton, who was eventually acquitted, was treated very harshly by a government that was vainly seeking scapegoats to cover up its own errors of judgment. He kept up a correspondence with him until his death, which took place some years later, in Dublin, when his horse reared up and fell on him on the barrack square. Martinet to the end, he was cheered by the soldiers he commanded when they heard the news.

Sir Jasper Nicolls certainly had no doubts about the causes of the disaster. In his tent beside the Sutlej he dictated a dispatch which Luard wrote down, ascribing the failure to the following:

1st. Making war with a peace establishment.
2nd. Making war without a safe base for operations.
3rd. Carrying a native army out of India into a strange and cold climate, where they and we were foreigners, and both considered as infidels.
4th. Invading a poor country, and one unequal to supply our wants, especially our large establishment of cattle.
5th. Giving undue power to political agents.
6th. Want of forethought and undue confidence in the Afghans on the part of Sir William Macnaghten.
7th. Placing our magazines, even our treasure, in indefensible places.
8th. Great military neglect and mismanagement after the outbreak.

It was a verdict that could be applied in some degree to a great many campaigns before and since, but there was one other cause which may have had a greater effect than Sir Jasper realized at the time. The manner in which the

British, headed by Sir Alexander Burnes, made free with the women of the country gave rise to passions that can perfectly well be understood, particularly in an Eastern country, where the woman's place in society is more carefully regulated than in the West.

From the moment that the Army of the Indus left Ferozepore in December 1838 until the Army of Retribution withdrew down the Khyber Pass during November 1842, the story of the Afghan War is one long chronicle of errors in judgment. The hesitations of the commanders were matched all too often by the irresolution of the soldiers; generals who had won their spurs under Wellington lost their reputations in Afghanistan; and regiments whose colors were blazoned with victories faltered and broke before the Afghans. The final epitaph of the campaign was written many years later by Sir John Fortescue, when he compiled his *History of the British Army*. "From beginning to end," he wrote, "it brought nothing but disgrace." John Luard would certainly have agreed with him.

CHAPTER TWELVE

John Luard was fifty-two years old by the time the Afghan War was over, and by the standards of today would be far too old for such an active command as a battalion of infantry. However, no such considerations applied in 1842. The military authorities worked on the theory that experience counted for a good deal more than physical vigor, and in the native regiments of the Company's army in particular, it was not unusual to find commanding officers in their late sixties. Havelock was forty-eight when he got command of the light company of the 13th Foot, the most physically exacting appointment in the regiment, and he was sixty-two when charged with the relief of Lucknow at the height of the Indian summer. John Luard had always kept himself fit, partly by being naturally abstemious in a country where Europeans, by and large, tended to drink too much, and partly by following his favorite outdoor pursuits of riding and shooting. His neatly trimmed beard, mustaches, and side whiskers may have been flecked with gray, but he still had the trim figure of a cavalryman. There was therefore no reason to suppose that he would not make a good commanding officer of the 10th Foot, the regiment to which he had been gazetted in 1842 as a lieutenant-colonel, and since the 10th Foot's existing commanding officer was a martyr to gout and virtually senile, any change could only be for the better.

Nevertheless, there were other considerations that passed through Luard's mind, and foremost was the fact that he had not seen his children for nearly four years; they were fast growing up without knowing their father, and their mother was dead. He probably felt like the Bengal civilian who, a few years later, sent his son home at the age of four and had not seen him again by the time he reached thirty-four, "and I should not know him if I passed him in the street." Nor did India improve with the years. The climate grew more, rather than less, trying, the longer one spent in the country, and "the tedium of the social life became increasingly hard to endure." Moreover, Sir Jasper Nicolls had no intention of being saddled with the task of clearing up the mess made in the army by the policies of two successive governors-general, and he was therefore agitating to vacate his appointment. With Nicolls gone, Luard would be without a patron, an all-important requirement for military advancement in those days, and for all these reasons he decided to quit India with his chief and retire from the army. It was a decision he was to regret for the rest of his life.

On October 31, 1843, the third anniversary of Elizabeth Luard's death, the commander in chief, his family, and his staff embarked on a fleet of boats which had been assembled to carry them down the rivers Sutlej and Indus as far as Karachi. There was a large boat for Nicolls, Lady Nicolls, and their two daughters; one for the aides-de-camp; one for Luard; a baggage boat, a guard boat and a cooking boat. It was the start of a leisurely progress that was to take John

Luard by way of Karachi, Bombay, Egypt, Italy, France, and Germany, until he finally arrived in England during June of the following year. Nowadays officers, even when retiring, are expected to move from one appointment to the next at the fastest possible rate, often finding when they reach their destination that their arrival is as unexpected as it is unwelcome, and they may therefore be forgiven if they envy at times the more gentlemanly pace of the past century. War in John Luard's time was still regarded as quite a sporting affair, and the intervals between wars were expected to be filled as agreeably as individual taste and length of pocket dictated. John Luard did his best to comply with the existing and civilized rule by filling his sketch-books at Luxor, Cairo, Naples, and Rome, in the course of which he acquired an abiding love for Italy; ". . . from that time onward," he wrote, "I never missed an opportunity to visit that country."

However, leisure, if it is to be filled in any way profitably, does cost money, and as England loomed up out of the summer haze, John Luard must have asked himself whether he had been entirely wise to abandon the more or less secure life of a senior army officer for the uncertain hazards of the civilian world. He was far from being a rich man; such private means as he did possess came from his dead wife's small estate and his share of the West Indian properties bequeathed by his father. He had not been able to save from his army pay—how many soldiers can?—and his only means of adding to his income was through his skill as an artist; and there were many artists in days when the camera and the cinema were things of the future. In 1837 he had published his *Sketches of India,* which came out in ten parts, and which was acclaimed as "the best illustrated work on India," and this had earned him a modest reputation in the world of art, without materially adding to his income. He now set out to produce his *History of the Dress of the British Army,* illustrated by himself, which involved a great deal of research without much expectation of commensurate reward. Even in an age when light reading was as likely to be a volume of sermons as anything else, Luard's book about uniforms was hardly likely to appeal to a very wide audience, and the sketches seem to us today to be surprisingly amateurish. Yet apparently it got a favorable reception from the critics. However, it was as an expert on India that he seems to have been most in demand, and in 1852 he made the drawings for, and superintended the execution of, "The Diorama of the Ganges," which was exhibited in Baker Street and attracted admiring audiences.

Army regulations of those days permitted an officer to go on half pay for an indefinite period, and during the time that he was on half pay an officer was still liable for promotion in existing vacancies. It was therefore quite possible for a half-pay lieutenant-colonel to be promoted through the intervening grades until he reached the rank of major-general, whereupon he might be required to return to active duty in order to assume command of some expedition destined to land on hostile shores. Since this might not occur until the officer concerned had reached the late sixties, and had been out of touch with military affairs for fifteen years or more, it is hardly surprising that so many blunders took place. While on half pay a lieutenant-colonel drew eleven shillings a day, providing an income of around £200 a year, which, when added to a private income of £500 a year or more, was sufficient to maintain a modest establishment.

However, an officer could always sell out, in which case he sold the value of his commission either to the Horse Guards or to some other officer anxious to purchase a step in rank, and this could mean an increase in capital of anything from £6,000 to £14,000, depending on the rank and appointment of the seller; a lieutenant-colonel in the Guards might expect to receive upward of £14,000 for his appointment, while the Earl of Cardigan is reputed to have paid more than £40,000 for the privilege of commanding the 11th Light Dragoons. Luard, as a lieutenant-colonel in the infantry, received nothing like so much, but even so his bank account was increased by nearly £7,000 when he sold out his commission in 1848.[1]

Yet he never ceased to regret his retirement from the army, and almost the last entry in his journal reiterates his regrets. "In truth the great mistake of my life," he wrote in 1863, "was leaving the army. I ought to have returned to India and taken command of my regiment, then the 10th Foot, and remained in the service until I became a Major-General, or remained on half pay until arriving at that rank." Had he done so, however, it is as certain as anything can be that he would never have lived to reach the coveted rank, since the 10th Foot were virtually decimated in the bloody battle of Sobraon during the Sikh Wars. Few of the regiment's officers survived that desperate action.

Perhaps he was lucky that he left when he did. The army was fast sinking into a morass of inefficiency and bumbledom. Recruits were becoming harder and harder to find, barracks were collapsing for want of money to shore them up, and the soldier has seldom been more unpopular in the eyes of his fellow-citizens. In one of the many debates about the abolition of the slave trade, one of the arguments advanced *against* abolition was that slaves in the Middle

---

[1] This compares quite favorably with the compensation terms offered to redundant officers in the British Army under the retirement scheme which has operated between 1959 and 1962, popularly referred to as the "Golden Bowler." It was possibly even better, since, in terms of purchasing power, £7,000 was worth a good deal more in 1848 than it is today.

Passage had more air to breathe than the average British soldier in his barracks, where men slept four to a cot; while a soldier, writing to *The Times* about his pay, complained that his shilling a day was reduced to twopence by the time he had paid for rations, laundry, and essential cleaning materials. The infantry were finding it increasingly difficult to attract officers, and the cavalry had become so expensive that parents were unwilling to permit their sons to enter that branch of the service. A cornet's commission cost more than £800, and living had reached such extravagant and costly proportions that an officer required nearly as much again in private income if he was to be kept out of the hands of the moneylenders.

Those officers who did desire to study their profession soon found themselves engulfed in the quagmire of tradition which stifled any original military thought. The British Army did not seem to be in the slightest bit interested in weapons development, although this was the period when the Prussians were experimenting with the needle gun, and the French with the chassepot rifle; and tactics in 1844, so far as the Horse Guards was concerned, had altered little if at all since Waterloo. That had been the greatest battle of all time, and what had been good enough for the British Army in 1815 must necessarily be equally good for it in 1845.

And yet in the world outside the army a complete revolution was taking place, particularly with regard to the means of transportation. The railways were spreading out their tentacles all over England, and it seems barely credible that the soldiers did not realize what sort of effect this must have on future warfare; though it is only fair to add that there were a good many sailors who still pinned their faith on sail, as opposed to steam. It required the Crimean War, and the series of administrative blunders that dogged the course

235

of that war from beginning to end, to awaken the British to the shortcomings of their military organization, but even so, Colonel Luard, three of whose sons fought in that war, saw no reason to criticize the authorities in his journal. The generals had all won their spurs under the Duke of Wellington, and that was good enough for John Luard.

Of course, it is easy from this distance in time, and with the advantages of hindsight, to be critical of a man with Luard's intelligence for his failure to equate technical advances with their effects on the military profession, but soldiers are invariably forced to operate within the limitations imposed on them by the politicians; what may all too often be militarily desirable is unable to be implemented for political considerations, and it is a truism that defense is never a popular subject in peacetime. During the early years of Victoria's reign, England had no enemy she need fear; France had been beaten, Germany was still divided, while Russia was more feared for her ambitions in Asia than for any designs she might have in the West. Home affairs, industrial development, and trade dominated the British political scene, and there were as few then as there were in the years immediately following World War I who could be bothered to concern themselves with defense. Thus the army languished, and its officers took refuge in the minutiae of their profession, such as parades, uniforms, and an unnecessary and inordinate attention to rules and regulations of the most bureaucratic description.

With four sons serving in the army, and with frequent and lengthy reunions with his old Waterloo comrades, John Luard never really lost touch with the profession to which he had given his heart and the best years of his life. When the time finally came for him to settle down and find a house, he chose one at Farnham, in Hampshire, not far from Aldershot, which prides itself on being the "Home of

236

the British Army." When the wind was in the right direction he could hear the long-remembered bugle calls, and on a fine day he could travel in his carriage to Laffan's Plain and watch the cavalry squadrons being drilled to the sound of the trumpet. He was proud of the successes which three of his sons were having in the army, although the career of his fourth son, John, gave him much cause for anxiety. That young man had entered the 82nd Foot from Sandhurst and had early shown that he had inherited his father's skill as an artist. He soon abandoned soldiering for painting, but was a feckless individual who got badly into debt. There is an entry in Luard's journal which shows that he had to pay £139 to settle some of these debts, and among the creditors is an entry of £19 as due to Millais. The young artist acquired some fame from his paintings of the Crimean War—"The Welcome Arrival" and "Nearing Home" were hung in the Royal Academy—but he succumbed to some kind of mental disorder and died at the age of thirty.

After an early, and financially unfortunate, attempt to farm, Luard spent most of the years of his retirement in travel, never without his sketchbook, and usually accompanied by one or the other of his two daughters; they never married, but devoted themselves to the care of their widowed father. He taught himself sculpture, and the fonts of several village churches in the neighborhood of Farnham, and one at Alderton, in Suffolk, are the result of his work. He added to his income by a directorship of the London and South-Western Railway, traveling all over the south of England on railway business, "and distinguished himself by his regular attendance to the duties of his office." [2] It seems clear from his journal that his income was sufficient for his needs; he paid his cook, Hannah Kerridge, £18 a year; his maid,

[2] *The Surrey Advertiser & County Times* of Saturday, November 13, 1875.

Jane Ward, £16; and his gardener and groom received a cottage and ten shillings a week apiece.

"In the enjoyable pursuit of art, and with the constant companionship of his youngest daughter, he spent the greater part of his latter years abroad," wrote the *Surrey Advertiser* in its edition of November 13, 1875. "His nature ripened to perfection. He was a man of liberal parts, his high courage was tempered with gentleness, and though he maintained, and if necessary, defended his own convictions, he had the largest tolerance for those of others. His character was great enough to be simple; his manners were frank and courteous alike to rich and poor; and his appearance was that of a noble soldier, and a distinguished English gentleman. Almost the last act of his life was to be present at the School of Art opening and concert at Farnham, which had been established partly by the exertions of his daughter, seconded as they always were by his counsel and the love of many friends. . . ."

Although one must always make allowances for the superlatives that tend to creep into obituary notices, it seems clear that John Luard was a highly respected member of the local community when he died at Farnham in 1875 at the age of eighty-five. His long life had spanned some of the greatest events in his country's history, and in his lifetime he had seen his country grow in stature until she had become the greatest power in the world. "For this great mercy," he wrote, "we have much cause to thank the Royal Navy, but the Army too has played its part." It was always his pride that he had served in both.

One of the last acts in his life was to drive over to Aldershot to watch a review held for the Duke of Cambridge, in the course of which his old regiment, the 16th Lancers, took part in a mock charge. What memories it must have roused in the old man as he sat there in his carriage, covered

238

with rugs, reliving that afternoon sixty years previously when young Lieutenant Luard, at the head of that self-same regiment of Lancers, had charged down the sodden ridge from Waterloo and completed the rout of the once-invincible "Old Guard." Times had changed since those days—not always for the better—and the army had changed with them. He was by no means certain that discipline was as strict as it should be, and perhaps the officers lacked the dash of his young days; indeed, the only lesson that seemed to him to have emerged from the recently concluded Franco-Prussian War was that war had become much too complicated and altogether too ungentlemanly. It was even possible that the increasing emphasis being laid by the military authorities on the need for officers to study their books might result in an army led by clerks, instead of by gentlemen. Certainly no British army would ever be quite the same as the one which had marched and fought its way across Spain and Portugal, stormed the Pyrenees, wrested Toulouse from Soult, and sent Bonaparte fleeing from Waterloo. They had been giants in those days, and had gone beyond recall. But then, it has always been the privilege of old soldiers to acclaim the past, just as it has always been the task of the younger generation to safeguard the present and to attempt to assure the future. Military organizations may change, but the good officer and soldier do not alter.

INDEX

Mansfield, General, 165
Maratha Wars, 141, 145, 178
Marchioness of Ely, 121, 122, 123, 125
Marengo, Battle of, 47, 93
Marmont, Auguste, 56, 57
Masséna, André, 42, 43, 44
Maunsell, Captain, 170
Meerut, 161, 162-63, 166, 167, 168, 173, 186, 205, 209
Mercer, Captain, 94, 108
Metcalfe, Charles, 145, 146
Metternich, Prince, 81
Moore, John, 61, 106
Mouton, Georges, 102
Murat, Joachim, 30
Murray, George, 89, 90, 123, 148, 149
Muttra, 147

Namur, H.M.S., 12
Napier, William, 81, 82 *n.*
Napoleon, 3, 12, 30, 36, 70, 81, 82, 91, 96, 97, 116, 176; abdication of, 71, 74; in Battle of Waterloo, 100, 101, 102, 103, 105; escape from Elba, 81; grave of, 169
Needle gun, 235
Nelson, Horatio, 14, 19, 23
Ney, Michel, 92, 94, 96, 102, 105, 106
Nicolls, Jasper, 147, 154, 174, 175, 181, 182, 183, 206, 207, 209, 210, 211, 215, 224-31
Nott, William, 191, 192, 199, 203, 204, 205, 207, 211, 215, 217, 225, 227

Ochterlony, David, 143, 144, 145, 146
Osten, Baron, 147

Paget, Edward, 142
Pakenham, Edward, 57
Pamplona, capture of, 66-67
Paris, surrender of, 70
Paton, Brigadier, 155
Peninsular War, 24, 73 *n.,* 75, 80, 81, 82 *n.,* 116

Persia, 176, 177, 184, 189
Persse, Major, 115, 148, 153
Peshawar, 218
Peters, Major, 112
Philips, Lieutenant, 105
Pickmore, Francis, 8, 9, 12, 13, 18
Picton, Thomas, 94
Pindaris, 145
Pitt, William, 12
Pollock, George, 224, 225, 226, 227
Pombal, skirmish at, 44-46, 48
Ponsonby, William, 64, 103, 104
Portugal, 22, 26, 33, 37-43, 51, 53, 54, 62, 63, 64, 76, 116
Portuguese Army, 40, 41, 49, 63, 75
Potato Famine, in Ireland, 112
Prince of Orange, 73 *n.*
Prussians, at Waterloo, 92, 93, 95, 102, 104, 108
Punjab, 205, 208
Punkah, 138 *n.*

Quatre Bras, 92, 93, 94, 95, 96, 100
Queen Charlotte, H.M.S., 5
Quetta, 195, 196

Ram, Sita, 189 and *n.,* 195, 196, 198, 201, 218
Ramillies, H.M.S., 4, 9, 10, 12, 13, 15, 16, 17, 18, 19, 20, 28, 33
Reille, Honoré, 65
Reynell, Thomas, 147, 154, 156, 167
Roberts, Abraham, 189
Roberts, Earl, 189
Rohillas, 145
Russel, William, 136
Russia, 184, 186; and threat to Persia and Afghanistan, 177, 180

Sal, Durjan, 144, 145, 146, 152, 157, 158, 159
Salamanca, Battle of, 56-58, 59, 80
Sale, Florentia, 205, 213-21, 225, 226, 227
Sale, Robert, 200, 201, 212, 213, 215, 224, 225
San Sebastián, storming of, 68

32
33
40
51
134 India
135

65 King Joseph's Chamber Pot
170 Lord's Uniform Book